Think Tanks, Foreign Policy and Geo-Politics

Questions about the role and influence of think tanks in matters of foreign policy and geopolitics are both timely and important. The reconfiguration of global power, explosion of social media, shifts away from traditional print and oral-based ways of imparting knowledge, and the dramatic increase in the volume of information and ideas clamoring for the attention of policy-makers are changing the landscape of foreign policy-making and the pathways through which influence is achieved. This book explains the impact of think tanks on the framing of domestic and international conversations on matters of foreign policy and geopolitics. An international group of prominent experts examine these issues in specific countries and also across national and regional borders to better understand how governments and actors in civil society are influenced by the activities of think tanks.

Donald E. Abelson is Professor in the Department of Political science at the University of Western Ontario. He specializes in American politics and US foreign policy. His work focuses primarily on the role of think tanks and their efforts to influence public opinion and public policy and he is a widely published author on Canadian and US think tanks and interest groups.

Stephen Brooks is Professor at the University of Windsor and Director of the Ottawa Internship Program at the University of Michigan.

Xin Hua is Associate Professor and Senior Research Fellow at the Center for EU Studies, Shanghai International Studies University and Senior Research Fellow and Councillor at Shanghai Institute for European Studies.

Think Tanks, Foreign Policy and Geo-Politics
Pathways to Influence

Edited by
Donald E. Abelson,
Stephen Brooks and Xin Hua

LONDON AND NEW YORK

First published 2017
by Routledge
2 Park Square, Milton Park, Abingdon, Oxon OX14 4RN

and by Routledge
711 Third Avenue, New York, NY 10017

Routledge is an imprint of the Taylor & Francis Group, an informa business

© 2017 Donald E. Abelson, Stephen Brooks and Xin Hua selection and editorial material; individual chapters, the contributors

The right of the editors to be identified as the author of the editorial material, and of the authors for their individual chapters, has been asserted in accordance with sections 77 and 78 of the Copyright, Designs and Patents Act 1988.

All rights reserved. No part of this book may be reprinted or reproduced or utilised in any form or by any electronic, mechanical, or other means, now known or hereafter invented, including photocopying and recording, or in any information storage or retrieval system, without permission in writing from the publishers.

Trademark notice: Product or corporate names may be trademarks or registered trademarks, and are used only for identification and explanation without intent to infringe.

British Library Cataloguing-in-Publication Data
A catalogue record for this book is available from the British Library

Library of Congress Cataloging-in-Publication Data
Names: Abelson, Donald E., editor. | Hua, Xin (Political scientist), editor. | Brooks, Stephen, 1956- editor.
Title: Think tanks, foreign policy and geo-politics : pathways to influence / edited by Donald E. Abelson, Xin Hua and Stephen Brooks.
Description: Abingdon, Oxon ; New York, NY : Routledge, 2016.
Identifiers: LCCN 2016013719| ISBN 9781472475855 (hardback) | ISBN 9781315551111 (ebook)
Subjects: LCSH: International relations—Research—Cross-cultural studies. | Research institutes—Cross-cultural studies.
Classification: LCC JZ1234 .T55 2016 | DDC 327—dc23
LC record available at https://lccn.loc.gov/2016013719

ISBN: 978-1-4724-7585-5 (hbk)
ISBN: 978-1-315-55111-1 (ebk)

Typeset in Times New Roman
by Swales & Willis Ltd, Exeter, Devon, UK

Printed and bound by CPI Group (UK) Ltd, Croydon, CR0 4YY

Contents

List of figures vii
List of tables viii
Notes on contributors ix

1 **Struggling to be heard: The crowded and complex world of foreign-policy-oriented think tanks** 1
DONALD E. ABELSON AND STEPHEN BROOKS

2 **Feulner's pendulum: Moving between policy research and political advocacy** 20
DONALD E. ABELSON

3 **Blending advocacy and research: The attributes and brand identities of the foremost human rights advocacy think tanks** 37
STEPHEN BROOKS AND PINAR CIL

4 **The governance turn in EU foreign policy: Are EU think tanks out of the picture?** 63
MARYBEL PEREZ

5 **Think tanks American style** 83
DONALD E. ABELSON

6 **Germany: The think and the tank** 101
JOSEF BRAML

7 **Think tanks and foreign policy in the United Kingdom** 119
MARK GARNETT AND SIMON MABON

8 Chinese think tanks' influence on foreign policy making:
   A case study of the role of CIIS and SIIS in the making of
   China's Europe policy   132
   XIN HUA

9 Still lagging behind? Foreign policy think tanks in Poland:
   origins and contemporary challenges   154
   MONIKA SUS

10 Foreign policies in Spain: The role of think tanks in the
   battle between the central state and Catalonia   166
   OLIVIER URRUTIA

11 And the winner is . . . Why measuring think tank performance
   is inherently problematic: lessons from Canada and beyond 185
   DONALD E. ABELSON

   Index   200

Figures

8.1 The two-dimensional division of the Chinese think tank system 139
8.2 Chinese think tanks' methods to exert policy influence:
a two-dimensional framework 139

Tables

4.1	EU think tanks	67
4.2	Partnerships and financial sources for five EU think tanks working on EU foreign policy	71
4.3	Organisation of foreign policy work and members for five EU think tanks working on EU foreign policy	72
4.4	Number of events and publications for five EU think tanks by EU foreign policy area, 2014–15	75
4.5	Number of speakers at EU foreign policy events for five EU think tanks	77
4.6	EU foreign policy by subject areas	78
8.1	The overall system of Chinese think tanks	137
8.2	The perceptional links and time sequences between CIIS and SIIS and Chinese policy-makers on three major issues related to China's policy towards Europe	142
8.3	The major research projects of CIIS on EU–China relations	143
8.4	Institutionalized high-level China–Europe forums and symposiums operated by CIIS and SIIS	144
8.5	Small-scale bilateral meetings by SIIS during September 2014 to September 2015	145
8.6	The "revolving door" mechanism of CIIS: Official institutions of China's bureaucratic system that provide past work or present concurrent posts to employees of CIIS	146
8.7	The "revolving door" mechanism of SIIS: Official institutions of China's bureaucratic system that provide past work or present concurrent posts to employees of SIIS	148
9.1	Foreign policy think tanks financed by state assets	159
9.2	Non-governmental foreign policy think tanks in Poland	159
10.1	Typology of think tanks specializing in IR	172
10.2	Growth of the foreign policy think tank sector	173
10.3	Structure and activities of foreign policy think tanks	178

Contributors

Donald E. Abelson is Professor of Political Science at the University of Western Ontario, where he has served as director of the Center for American Studies, chair of the political science department, and founding director of the Canada-US Institute. He has published a number of books and articles dealing with the influence of think tanks on public policy and foreign policy and has been called a "foremost authority on think tanks" in Canada and the US. He is a regular commentator on the subject for various media outlets.

Josef Braml joined the German Council on Foreign Relations (DGAP) in 2006 as editor-in-chief of DGAP's Yearbook on International Relations. Prior to that, he was a senior fellow at the German Institute for International and Security Affairs, the project leader at the Aspen Institute Berlin, a consultant at the World Bank, a guest scholar at the Brookings Institution, a congressional fellow of the American Political Science Association and a member of the legislative staff in the US House of Representatives. He earned a PhD in Political Science and a Masters in International Business and Cultural Studies at the University of Passau.

Stephen Brooks is Professor of Political Science at the University of Windsor and Director of the Ottawa Internship Program at the University of Michigan. His research and teaching focus on various aspects of American and Canadian politics.

Pinar Cil is a legal fellow at NATO headquarters in Brussels, focusing on international humanitarian law. She has worked in both governmental and non-governmental sectors, including positions with the Canadian Senate and the International Committee of the Red Cross. Her research interests include the nexus between human rights and international humanitarian law, criminal justice and national security policy. She graduated in 2016 with a joint Juris Doctor/Master of Arts (2016) from the University of Ottawa Faculty of Law and the Norman Paterson School of International Affairs at Carleton University.

Mark Garnett is Senior Lecturer in Politics and International Relations at Lancaster University. He has written numerous articles and books on various aspects of British politics, focusing mainly on the relationship between ideas and practice.

Xin Hua is Associate Professor of Political Science and International Political Economy at the Shanghai International Studies University. He is also a senior research fellow and councillor of the Shanghai Institute for European Studies and a non-resident research professor for the Center for National Strategic Studies, Shanghai Jiaotong University. He regularly provides research reports for several Chinese think tanks and is frequently called upon to offer media commentaries. He has won two academic prizes issued by the Shanghai Federation of Academic Institutions of Social Sciences and received his PhD in international relations from Fudan University.

Simon Mabon is Lecturer in International Relations at Lancaster University and author of *Saudi Arabia and Iran: Power and Rivalry in the Middle East*, *The Origins of ISIS* and *Hezbollah: From Islamic Resistance to Government*, and co-editor of *Terrorism and Political Violence*. He is a research associate with the Foreign Policy Centre and Director of the Richardson Institute.

Marybel Perez is Senior Researcher at the Center for Philanthropy Studies at the University of Basel, Switzerland. Her previous appointments include Adjunct Lecturer at Parsons: The New School in Paris, and ESSCA School of Management and the Catholic University of the West in Angers, France. Perez was a research fellow for Eurosphere at the University of Bergen, Norway, where she obtained her PhD.

Monika Sus is a postdoctoral fellow at the Hertie School of Governance. Before coming to Berlin, she held an assistant professor position at the DAAD-founded Willy Brandt Centre for German and European Studies at the University of Wroclaw in Poland. She has been granted scholarships by several European foundations and has been a visiting fellow at the European University Institute in Florence, the Centre Canadien d'études Allemandes et Européennes at the University of Montreal and the European Union Centre of Excellence at the University in Pittsburgh. She has published widely on European foreign policy, the Eastern Partnership, Europeanization and policy advising.

Olivier Urrutia is Vice-President responsible for partnerships and development at the Paris-based Observatoire des think tanks. Author of many articles and essays on think tanks, he speaks regularly in the French and Spanish media and is a frequent speaker at business, university and public sector forums. He is currently finishing his PhD thesis on think tanks at the University of Barcelona.

1 Struggling to be heard

The crowded and complex world of foreign-policy-oriented think tanks

Donald E. Abelson and Stephen Brooks

Introduction

It was a fairly typical week in mid-May, 2015, and the think tank world in Washington, DC was bustling with activity. At the Brookings Institution, experts were giving talks on "The future of Iraq," "How to defuse the emerging US–China rivalry," "Armenians and the legacies of World War I," "Using data to exercise smart power," "Understanding investment frontiers amid global uncertainty," "Internal displacement in Ukraine" and "Peacekeeping and geo-politics in the 21st century." At the Center for Strategic and International Studies' (CSIS) new $100 million state-of-the-art building on Rhode Island Avenue NW, about a ten-minute walk from Brookings, expert talks and panels dealt with India's nuclear policies, US interests in Eurasia, the state of Afghanistan's security forces, Russia and the Korean Peninsula, and the future of US submarine forces. All of these events were videocast live. Another of the heavyweights in the world of Washington think tanks, the Council on Foreign Relations (CFR; headquartered in New York with a branch office in DC), had fewer events scheduled, but what it lacked in numbers it made up for in the stature of those speaking to CFR audiences. Florida senator Marco Rubio, a candidate for the 2016 Republican presidential nomination, outlined his vision for America's role in the 21st century. Richard Haass, president of the CFR and a former senior diplomat, was the marquee speaker on a panel discussing the crisis in global governance.

There was much more going on that week. At the Woodrow Wilson Center for International Scholars, the Peterson Institute for International Economics, the American Enterprise Institute, the Cato Institute and the Carnegie Endowment for International Peace there were, between them, 14 talks and panels that dealt with foreign policy and geo-political (FP/GP) issues. Dozens of think tank experts appeared before various committees of Congress dealing with matters of foreign policy, including the House committees on Foreign Affairs, Homeland Security and Armed Services, and the Senate committee on Foreign Relations and the Armed Services committee.

The eight think tanks whose events schedules for a single week in May 2015 are described above are widely acknowledged to be among the most influential when it comes to shaping conversations surrounding the content and conduct of US foreign policy. There are, however, dozens more that may credibly claim to be vocal participants in the marketplace of ideas where hundreds of organizations, representing all ideological stripes, and actively engaged in research and advocacy, seek to make their presence felt in the think tank universe. That universe is diverse, large, eclectic, often influential and sometimes controversial. Determining which organizations are influential, and the conditions under which they are able to affect policy change, is often difficult to evaluate.

Washington, DC is still home to the world's largest concentration of think tanks. It is the location of several policy institutes that are thought to wield enormous influence over US foreign policy and world politics. The web of connections that link think tanks to state officials, the media, interest groups and academe assumes a particular form in America, as it does in every country in which think tanks influence the FP/GP conversation. Pathways to influence depend on a number of factors, including the particular institutional characteristics of the state; such features of the think tank marketplace as the number, size, prestige and influence strategies of those organizations competing for the attention of policy-makers; and the personal linkages between think tanks and the state and media elites.

Washington is still the busiest, but the think tank scenes in London, Berlin and Brussels are very active, with dozens of major research institutions and advocacy organizations jostling to be heard. Paris, Madrid and Tokyo also are home to active and influential think tank communities, including organizations whose aim is chiefly to influence foreign policy and ways of thinking about geo-politics. In recent years, there has been an explosion in the number and, according to some commentators, the influence of think tanks in Beijing and Shanghai, such that China is now second only to the US in the number of such organizations. To provide a global perspective, the Think Tanks and Civil Societies Program at the University of Pennsylvania included 6,618 think tanks in its 2014 database, the majority of which have been established since the 1980s. "The drastic increase in think tanks that began in the 1980's," states the program's director, James McGann, "can be largely attributed to greater democratization in formerly closed societies, trade liberalization, and the expansion of both market based economies and globalization." (2007: 2) Although the pace of growth has slowed in recent years, the think tank universe has continued to expand. McGann's think tank database included 5,035 organizations in 2007 compared with 6,618 in 2014. Most of this recent increase is accounted for by growth outside of North American and Western Europe. Although precise numbers do not exist, by all accounts there has been a significant increase in the number of think tanks whose focus is principally FP/GP and transnational issues.

Growth on such an explosive scale begs a number of questions. First, is it a response to increased demand for what think tanks offer? In market theory, an increase in demand for something, in this case information, ideas and policy advice, should lead to growth in the number of suppliers, so long as barriers to entry, including start-up costs, are low. But it is hard to believe that this demand among policy-makers emerged and grew as sharply as the dramatic growth in the number of think tanks between the 1970s and the 1990s, when more than half of all current think tanks were established. If, however, we broaden our understanding of demand to include, among the consumers of what think tanks produce, not only state officials, but others whose goal is to influence policy and ways of thinking about policy, then this growth becomes somewhat less startling. Corporations and industries, labor organizations, NGOs dedicated to a huge range of causes, political parties and social movements have all seen that their interests and values may be advanced through the activities of think tanks. Indeed, many have even assumed some aspects of the form and functions of think tanks, thereby contributing to the expanding think tank universe.

At this point a word on the definition of think tanks is probably in order. Many definitions have been offered and much has been written on why certain ways of conceptualizing and defining think tanks are preferable to others (McGann 2015: 7–29). We adopt a very inclusive definition of the sort that is used in McGann's annual Global Go To Think Tank Index Report. Such a definition includes organizations that are independent of the state; others that are associated with the state in one way or another; think tanks that are the research and advocacy arms of political parties; labor organizations; groups focused on environmental, human rights, climate change and other issues; and those associated with universities. We are a very long way from the world of the early 20th century when the Carnegie Foundation (1910), the Brookings Institution (1916) and the Royal Institute of International Affairs (1920) established the original template for think tanks as non-partisan, independent research centers providing policy advice. It no longer makes very much sense to restrict the definition to "independent." To do so would immediately exclude virtually all of the Chinese think tanks that have emerged in recent decades, on the grounds they lack sufficient independence from the one-party state in that country. Moreover, it would seem to exclude organizations like Human Rights Watch and Amnesty International, whose primary function is advocacy but whose research activities and strategies for influencing the policy conversation and government actions are often identical to those of organizations that conform to a more traditional definition of think tanks.

We define think tanks as organizations that carry out research and analysis of policy issues, whose primary function is to influence the ways those issues are thought about, and that produce policy advice and recommendations. Such a broad definition may be objected to on the grounds that it allows some interest groups and lobbying activities to be included in the universe of think tanks. In fact, however, the evolution of this universe has been such that what once were fairly distinct lines separating interest groups and lobbying from think tanks have become increasingly blurred. Some think tanks are essentially the research-advocacy arms of industries or labor, or even states attempting to influence policy in another country. Corporations have gotten into the act by creating their own think tanks, such as the JP Morgan Chase Institute, created in 2015 (JP Morgan Chase Institute 2015).

The paradox of plenty

Unless demand for what think tanks produce is totally elastic, and the barriers to entry extremely low, one would expect that suppliers will eventually experience diminishing returns, leading some of them to exit the market. This is particularly so when the product is one that is free. While not all of what think tanks provide is free – in fact some of what the best known and most influential think tanks provide is available only to members or donors who have paid considerable money for restricted-access information advice – much of it is free, even in the case of the largest and most prestigious suppliers of policy advice. This produces what Keohane and Nye call the paradox of plenty. "A plenitude of information," they write, "leads to *a poverty of attention*. Attention becomes a scarce resource, and those who can distinguish valuable signals from white noise gain power. Editors, filters, interpreters and cue-givers become more in demand, and this is a source of power. . . . Brand names and the ability to bestow an international seal of approval will become more important." (1998: 89)

In a normal market, a state of hyper-competition between too many sellers would drive many of them out of the market. The fact that so many think tanks have remained in the marketplace and that they are joined each year by new entrants, although at a slower pace than in the 1980s and 1990s, provokes a second question concerning the continued growth in the number of think tanks. We have already stated that one possible explanation is continuous growth in the demand for what think tanks provide, an explanation agreed with by McGann (2015: 13–26) and many others, combined with continued low barriers to entry. If Keohane and Nye are right that "a plenitude of information leads to a poverty of attention," this ought to produce a winnowing out of the providers of policy advice. Steady growth in demand might account for the failure of this winnowing to occur. To be sure, many think tanks have a precarious revenue base and it is not uncommon for some to close up shop. But the evidence is clear: globally, for every think tank that exits the market at least one plus some fraction enters.

It is improbable that demand is elastic enough to explain this rather remarkable and continuing growth. Moreover, Keohane and Nye's "paradox of plenty" suggests that even if demand remains high, non-dominant suppliers in this market should find it increasingly difficult to compete, thereby leading to a reduction in their number. That this has not happened may be explained in part by the highly segmented nature of the think tank market. It is a market divided by language, country, issue specialization, ideological orientation, communications strategies and more. Within a single country, a mere handful of think tanks are likely to dominate, at least according to reputational measures and the frequency with which these think tanks and their experts are cited, interviewed and tweeted. Globally, or at least in those parts of the world that do not practice media and Internet censorship, perhaps a dozen or so think tanks occupy center stage, mentioned more often by the *BBC World Service*, *Al-Jazeera*, *The Economist* and those relatively few newspapers that can legitimately claim to have an international readership.

These dominant think tanks are, of course, those that Keohane and Nye refer to as "brand names." Their influence and credibility is said to derive from the "international seal of approval" placed upon them by those who decide which experts to turn to for a story, what studies and events to cover, and whether a think tank's signature activity – such as an index of some phenomenon, like Transparency

International's annual Corruption Perceptions Index – will be treated as a routine and important part of the annual news cycle. The think tank universe is very lopsided and, indeed, oligopolistic if viewed from the perspective of media attention.

In the realm of think tanks that focus on FP/GP and transnational issues, oligopoly also appears to be the rule. In the US, for example, mentions in the *New York Times* during 2014 for the Brookings Institution and the CFR were several times greater than the number of mentions received by the vast majority of the other American think tanks in the FP/GP category (Brookings, 263; CFR, 177; Heritage, 90; Center for American Progress, 84; CSIS, 83; RAND, 63; Carnegie Endowment, 60; Atlantic Council, 53; Hoover Institution, 45; Wilson Center, 31; Center for a New American Security, 18).[1] In Germany, the Bertelsmann Foundation, the Konrad Adenauer Foundation, the German Institute for International and Security Affairs and the German Development Institute are much more likely than other of the country's think tanks to be cited by German media on matters of foreign and defense policy, geo-politics and transnational issues. Moreover, these leading German think tanks are also much more likely to be cited than Brookings, CSIS and other leading non-German FP/GP think tanks. The situation is very much the same in the UK, where Chatham House and the International Institute for Strategic Studies are far more likely than their national competitors to be mentioned in the media when it comes to FP/GP issues, and also much more likely to be mentioned than non-British think tanks.

These examples point to an important feature of the FP/GP think tank universe. National boundaries matter. The six US-based foreign policy think tanks in the Global Go To Index's top ten for this category received a combined total of 656 mentions in the *New York Times* in 2014, compared to 66 for the four non-American think tanks in this category. The Stockholm International Peace Research Institute, ranked sixth in the world by the same index among foreign policy and international affairs think tanks, received only six mentions in the *New York Times*. The China Institutes of Contemporary International Relations (CICIR), ranked seventh, received none. A preference for analyses of a country's foreign policy produced by experts and institutions that are part of that country is not surprising. But even in the case of what we might call mega think tanks that generate big picture analyses of geo-politics and that employ, or have associated with them, platoons of experts on various countries, regions, conflicts and transnational issues, we observe a preference in a country's media system for think tanks based in that country rather than those abroad.

Part of this may be explained by factors as simple as language and ease of access. L'Institut français des relations internationales, based in Paris, produces reports, holds conferences and conducts its other activities in French. Some of what it does is translated into English, German and Russian, but there is much less content on the its website in these other languages. Its interlocutors – mainly French researchers, journalists, public officials and members of the attentive public – generally will be more at ease in French and expect to be communicated with in the language of Molière. So too in Berlin. The broadcaster *Deutschewelle*, the weekly *Der Spiegel* and the daily newspaper *Die Zeit* turn naturally to experts at the prestigious Stiftung Wissenschaft und Politik or Deutsche Gesellschaft für Auswärtige Politik, not to Washington-based CSIS or London-based Chatham House. It must be said, however, that many of the major non-American and non-British FP/GP think tanks do conduct some of their activities in English and, moreover, they often provide a good deal of English translation at their websites. American and British think tanks do not return the favor.

Ease of access is another factor that reinforces this national preference. In the age of Skype and satellite phones, it might seem that physical proximity ought no longer to matter. But it does, partly because for those who work at think tanks and those on whom they rely to communicate and amplify their ideas, information and advice are not wholly virtual entities. The webinar and real-time videocasts of workshops, briefings and other presentations continue to be rather second-best substitutes for the experience of sharing the same physical space with policy-makers, journalists, experts and advocates. People continue to choose to leave their offices to attend a briefing, speech or other event that could be watched on their iPhone in real time or at their leisure through a think tank's video archive.

Part of the reason for this has to do with culture and personal relationships. Even if the think tank experts at Madrid's Real Instituto Elcano, the journalists for *El País* and *El Mundo*, and Spanish policy-makers did not go to the same universities – although in fact the likelihood that they did is relatively high – they inhabit the same cultural space, which makes them better able to understand one another and the complex web of nuance, allusion, history and narrative that comprises culture. Shared policy interests and cyber communities that cross national borders never entirely erase the affinities and *imaginaire* that make understanding (not necessarily agreement) between those who share a culture more effortless than between those who do not. The psychological literature on trust supports this conclusion. "People trust those with whom they share and recognize a group identity much more than those with whom they do not," writes Dietlind Stolle. "For the shared identity, certain in-group criteria matter, such as behavioral similarity, geographical proximity, frequency of interaction, or common fate." (2002: 401)

Personal relationships constitute an important part of the proximity factor that contributes to the national preference for homegrown FP/GP think tanks. The best known and surely the most effective example of these relationships at work involves the revolving door between think tanks, on the one hand, and the state apparatus and political parties on the other. While chiefly an American phenomenon, which Abelson discusses in Chapter 5, it is not exclusively so. It is quite common in the UK. And Silvia Menegazzi (2015) describes the development of the revolving door in China and what she calls "cross-pollination" between the Communist Party, the military and that country's growing think tank sector.

Although rather obvious, the reason why think tanks typically locate in capital cities is because that is where policy-makers are found. (There are, however, exceptions to this rule. In Canada many of the best known think tanks are located in cities other than Ottawa.) If the transactions between think tank experts, policy-makers, interest groups and members of the media were only about the exchange of ideas and information, then location would not matter as much. In fact, however, it is important to be able to testify before the appropriate legislative committees, meet with policy-makers at their offices or at events sponsored by a think tank and, more generally, establish and maintain personal relations of trust and interdependence. Such relations may develop without face-to-face contact. Nevertheless, research on interpersonal trust corroborates what politicians, lobbyists and advocates have long known: personal contact can matter.

In their 1998 article on what they argue to be the increasing importance of soft power channels of influence on policy, Keohane and Nye write, "The ability to disseminate free information increases the potential for persuasion in world politics. NGOs and states can more readily influence the beliefs of people in other jurisdictions." They add, "Cheap flows of information have enormously expanded the number and depth of transnational channels of contact." (1998: 95) Diane Stone makes a similar argument in describing what she calls transnationalization. "This is occurring," she writes, "alongside higher education internationalisation and the globalisation of research communities helping to create a worldwide 'invisible college'." Stone goes on to argue that,

> Windows of opportunities for knowledge organisations have opened with the forces of regionalisation and globalisation. Without well-defined institutions of authority beyond the nation-state, they become editors of knowledge(s) and arbiters of research quality. In the global agora, the "argumentative field" (Fischer, 2003: 90) is radically different, allowing think tanks to acquire some authority as reputational intermediaries. Think tank transnational activities and analytical work also help constitute the agora. (2013: 62–63)

Stone is right, of course, as are Keohane and Nye. There is no shortage of examples that may be adduced in support of their argument that borders and states matter less today when it comes to the exchange of information and that, as Keohane and Nye put it, "States are more easily penetrated and less like black boxes." (1998: 95)

Geography, however, continues to matter a good deal. Language, cultural affinities and the continued importance of personal relationship ensure that policy-makers will be inclined to turn to and rely on their own national experts, even when the issues are transnational. We would expect this sort of national bias when it comes to domestic and even foreign policy matters. But on such borderless issues as climate change, human trafficking, nuclear arms proliferation and international terrorism the voices of a nation's own think tanks and experts are often the dominant ones, reported in the media and listened to by policy-makers.

Measuring influence

The measurement of influence is seldom straightforward. Determining the impact that factor A has had on outcome B, separate from all the other possible factors that might conceivably have contributed to this outcome, is often difficult enough when studying the natural world. When it comes to the affairs of human beings, the difficulty of measuring influence is almost always greater. We may feel confident in stating, perhaps, that a particular think tank has a reputation for being influential and that its experts and studies are often cited in traditional media and mentioned in social media. This is very far from being able to say just how influential a particular think tank or even think tanks in general have been in the case of a specific issue and outcome, independent of all the other variables that might have been part of the mix.

Despite the fact that virtually everyone acknowledges the difficulties associated with measuring think tank influence, the impulse to do so is irresistible. There are three main reasons for this. First and most obviously, determining influence is essential to the study of politics and *measuring* influence is crucial if such studies are to warrant the label political *science*. Second, think tanks are in competition with one another for prestige, the attention of policy-makers, contributions from donors or other sources of revenue (their revenue models vary significantly), and credibility and respect among those in the community of experts who are engaged in the same fields of research. Third, those who rely on think tank experts, studies, indices and advice – not simply end-users whose policy actions may be influenced by think tank activities, but also members of the media and the attentive public – generally are not indifferent to think tank rankings. When a BBC producer or *New York Times* journalist turns to an expert on Russia who is associated with Brookings or the CSIS, rather than a small boutique think tank that few have heard of, the reasons may be many. But one of them is sure to be that Brookings and CSIS have a reputation, confirmed by the various ranking exercises, for being top-tier think tanks. And thus does reputation reinforce visibility and impact, in turn reinforcing reputation in a sort of inevitable feedback loop.

Reputation is, of course, at the heart of what is certainly the best known annual ranking of think tanks. Since 2006, the Think Tanks and Civil Societies Program at the University of Pennsylvania, under the direction of James G. McGann, has published its Global Go To Think Tank Index Report. The methodology involves a number of steps that may be summarized as follows. Based on nominations from over 6,500 think tanks across the world, as well as over 7,500 journalists, donors and policy-makers, any think tank that receives at least ten nominations, as well as all of those from the previous year's list of top think tanks, are included in a list sent to all of those groups and individuals who had been contacted in the nominations round. In this survey round those contacted are asked to rank the think tanks. The rankings that result from this survey are then reviewed and final selections made by regional and functional panels of experts. Throughout this entire process all participants, at both the nomination and ranking stages, are encouraged to be mindful of 28 specific criteria. They are told, however, that their assessment is not limited to these criteria. Moreover, almost every one of the 28 criteria – indeed, arguably all of them – are reputational. That is, they are based on the participant's subjective assessment of how well think tanks perform, thus placing participants' judgment at the heart of the methodology.

Not surprisingly, this approach has its critics. Before considering their arguments and the alternatives they propose, it is worth acknowledging that reputational measures of influence have a long and respectable history in political science, reaching back to the community power studies in the 1950s and 1960s (see review in Fischer and Sciarini 2015: 61–62). They have been used in the study of public policy and political decision-making for decades. Whatever limitations they may have, reputational measures often provide the best way of ranking cases of a phenomenon or quality that is by its very nature elusive and not easily, if at all, amenable to more precise quantitative measurement.

Nevertheless, such an approach may produce anomalies that cast doubt on the methodology. For example, among the 2014 Global Go To Index's top ten foreign policy and international affairs think tanks, one finds mainly organizations that by any standard belong toward the top of such a list. They include Brookings, Chatham House, the Carnegie Endowment for International Peace, the CFR and other well-known and very prestigious institutes whose reputations extend beyond the countries where they are based. But the CICIR is also in the top ten, ranked seventh in fact, ahead of the RAND Corporation, the International Institute for Strategic Studies and some others. With all due respect to CICIR, whose influence on Chinese policy-makers may indeed be significant, as some researchers believe, it has little profile and influence outside of the very closed world of Chinese foreign policy-making.[2] The same cannot be said of any of the other think tanks in the top ten. The fact that it is ranked so highly can only be explained by a methodology that, to some degree, includes elements of a skewed information market. Nationals of one country may, with the best intentions but perhaps acting with incomplete information, exaggerate the importance of their country's think tanks. Of course, one might say that American, British and German participants in this nomination/survey exercise are as likely as those in China to make these sorts of misjudgments and to show national favouritism. The openness of their societies and media systems, including the lack of media and Internet censorship that is so pervasive in China, make this unlikely.

Critics of the reputational approach to measuring think tank influence go much further than complaints about occasional anomalies of this sort, or of the respective rankings assigned to different think tanks. Enrique Mendizabal, who maintains the blog "On Think Tanks" has referred to the Global Go To Index as a sort of popularity contest based on a biased sample. For reasons that we will explain below, we think that this is unfairly dismissive of what, when all is said and done, may still be the best ranking of think tank influence. *Prospect Magazine* appears to endorse Mendizabal's criticism and offered its own rankings in 2014, based on a quantitative methodology that measures think tank visibility as captured by Google news hits, pages indexed on Google and number of Twitter followers. It produced significantly different rankings from those arrived at by the 2014 Global Go To Index.

Julia Clark and David Roodman of the Center for Global Development (CGD) agree that visibility is preferable to reputation as a measure of think tank performance. They acknowledge that the measurement of influence will always be problematic, so they opt for the public profile of think tanks as perhaps the best that we can hope for in measuring actual think tank performance. By public profile Clark and Roodman mean the success of a think tank in garnering public attention. "We focus on indicators of such attention," they write, "including scholarly citations, media mentions, web traffic, and social network followers. These can be channels of impact in themselves – ideas need to be noticed to be adopted – and can indicate subtler influence behind the scenes, as when reporters quote researchers known to hold the most sway." (2013: 3) In short, their methodology is very much like that used by *Prospect Magazine*, based on measures of think tank visibility. Their indicators of influence include Facebook "likes" and Twitter followers, website traffic, the number of sites that link to a think tank's website, media citations and scholarly citations. Comparison between the rankings that emerge from this one-time CGD study and the Global Go To Index are problematic for a number of reasons, but a couple of points of difference are clear. Such think tanks as the Cato Institute, the Heritage Foundation and the Pew Research Center do much better when the measure of performance is public profile rather than reputation. Others, notably the Carnegie Endowment, the Woodrow Wilson Center and the Peterson Institute for International Economics do not do as well.

All of this, of course, begs the question: what is the best way to measure think tank influence? The metrics relied on for the *Prospect* and CGD rankings are based on the premise that greater visibility is likely to signify greater influence on policy. Some students of think tanks are dubious. "Visibility is far different from influence," writes Andrew Rich, "and [some impacts] might at times be quite different from that which has substantive bearing on policy." (2004: 103) Donald Abelson makes a similar point when he laments the relative lack of attention that has been paid to those who consume what think tanks produce and how they view think tank influence and "the contribution that think tanks have made at different stages of the policymaking process." (2012: 10)

This is a crucially important point that is easily lost sight of in the various efforts to rank think tank influence. That influence may be achieved in various ways and at different points in the policy-making process. Having a large number of followers on Twitter and frequent mentions in the media tell us much about the visibility of a think tank and we might even feel safe in drawing the inference that a larger public profile translates into greater influence on the policy conversation. Beyond this, however, we cannot say very much with confidence. The influence of think tanks on policy-makers may and often does operate in much less visible ways than mentions in the *Guardian* or the *New York Times*. Certainly in a country like China, public profile is not especially useful as a measure of think tank influence.

Even in open societies, however, the influence of think tanks is often experienced in ways that are not particularly visible. For example, Brussels-based Bruegel is regularly ranked among the world's top think tanks in the field of international economics. In addition to its many publications available online, social media presence and occasional public events, Bruegel provides limited-access events and analysis to its public and private members. Indeed, Bruegel's revenue model depends on annual membership fees with no single member permitted to account for more than 5 percent of its yearly budget. Most of the EU nation-states are members, as well as many of the world's largest corporations and European banks. Bruegel's influence on policy-makers and its reputation as one of the world's top think tanks in international economics are based on these more direct and intimate transactions between its experts and leading corporate and public officials and much less on its media footprint.

The Brookings Institution is also acknowledged to be among the world's most influential think tanks. Indeed, the 2014 Global Go To Index ranked it both the top think tank in the world and in the particular field of foreign policy and international affairs. Its media footprint is, compared to most think tanks, enormous. Shaping the policy conversation is an important indirect way through which Brookings achieves influence and maintains its well-deserved reputation. But like many other think tanks Brookings also offers what might be described as enhanced services for donors. For example, those who make an annual donation of at least $100,000 are entitled to a private meeting with Brookings' president, opportunities for private briefings from Brookings scholars, two invitations to "an exclusive reception and dinner with [Brookings' president] and members of the Board of Trustees," and "A customized program of benefits designed in collaboration with the Senior Director of Corporate & Foundation Relations." There is a scale of enhanced services for lesser donors, but the ones most closely tailored to a donor's particular policy interests require an annual donation of at least $50,000.

As in the case of Bruegel's limited-access events and briefings for its contributing members, the more intimate and customized exchanges that Brookings offers to its donors surely are expected by them to provide something beyond that which can be gleaned from listening to a Brookings expert interviewed on the BBC or reading an op-ed that he or she has published in the *New York Times*. These are points of contact between policy-makers – and we include in this category those in the private sector whose decisions have important policy ramifications – and think tanks that are not captured by data on tweets and Google hits.

Pathways to influence

It is widely believed that the influence of FP/GP think tanks is greater in the politics of the US than in other countries. In a 2012 official document produced by Morocco's embassy in Washington, a document intended to explain how that country should proceed in order to enhance its influence with the American government, one finds this key recommendation:

> Think tanks constitute a true power in Washington. They are the real opinion-makers, being staffed by former officials from the White House, the State Department, and the Department of Defense, and who maintain and nurture their privileged relations with an American government on which they have considerable influence. Our actions focus on the most influential think tanks on all sides of the political spectrum (Democratic, Republican or non-partisan) . . . After a year of observation and evaluation, steps toward cooperation and/or partnership with certain of these think tanks are being taken. (Morocco 2012: our translation)

Morocco is not alone, nor was it the first foreign state to appreciate the influence of US think tanks on America's foreign policy and on how that country's policy-makers view other countries and geo-politics more generally. Indeed, foreign contributions to US think tanks have a rather long history. Only recently, however, has some degree of transparency existed, thanks mainly to the work of researchers at the Edmond J. Safra Center for Ethics at Harvard University.[3] Some of these donations, which are almost always tied to a particular research program or project, are truly impressive. For example, Brookings received about $4 million from Norway in 2010–2014, $6 million from the United Arab Emirates in 2010–2012 and $18 million from Qatar in 2011–2013. Morocco, it seems, was late to the game. A 2012 report to the Norwegian Ministry of Foreign Affairs (MFA) spells out with admirable clarity and frankness what the Norwegian government expects to come of its donations to US think tanks:

> The MFA contributes to US institutions because they are leaders in their fields globally; they are global agenda setters that can assist the MFA in developing and promoting a Norwegian foreign policy agenda. They can help the MFA in developing current strategies and foreign and security policy tools. In addition, the US institutions are important to the MFA because they can give the ministry access to experts and events in US foreign policy making.
>
> In Washington, it is difficult for a small country to gain access to powerful politicians, bureaucrats and experts. Funding powerful think tanks is one way to gain such access, and some think tanks in Washington are openly conveying that they can service only those foreign governments that provide funding. Some diplomats interviewed for this report even emphasise that the level of funding a government such as Norway's provides will determine what level of access it gets. For the MFA, the significant contribution to the Brookings Institution is the clearest example of this. Norway is, after Qatar and the UAE, the largest foreign government contributor to Brookings, and Norwegian funding is less restricted than that of the two Arab partner countries. This is of great benefit to Norwegian delegations visiting Washington, and the flexibility of the framework agreement makes it possible to have Norway influence policy on many levels. (Bjørgaas 2012)

If we have focused on Brookings in this discussion of foreign money in the Washington think tank scene, it is partly because unlike most other major think tanks, Brookings at least provides financial information, albeit incomplete, on its donors. Moreover, Brookings is widely thought of as the gold standard when it comes to the quality of its research. Its spokespersons insist that donations, whatever their source, have no impact on the analysis carried out by its experts. Many other A-list think tanks, and lesser ones too, accept foreign money. They seldom reveal more, however, than the names of donors.

All of this raises two issues of special importance for this volume. Is the US unique in the importance of think tanks in relation to American foreign policy and ways of thinking about geo-politics? Over 20 years ago Richard Higgott and Diane

Stone argued that it was. "More so than in any country," they wrote, "the US foreign policy institutes have played an influential role in foreign policy making. This is due to the nature of the [American] political system." (1994: 32–33) Second, is America exceptional in the extent to which foreign money, including money from foreign governments, now constitutes an important component of the revenue model of many think tanks, including some of those acknowledged to be most influential?

A third question of special importance for this volume was also raised by Higgott and Stone's article on the role of foreign policy think tanks in international relations. "Those that are successful," they wrote, "are those that have managed to tap not only the changing international agenda of the 1990s but also the marketing techniques of the era." (1994: 34) Think tanks operate within, and in order to be influential must adapt to the institutional setting of the country in which they operate. They also operate within a media eco-system that is dramatically different today from that which existed when Higgott and Stone made their observation about the importance of marketing techniques. How think tanks have adapted and what marketing and other communications techniques are most likely to provide pathways to influence in the crowded and highly competitive world of FP/GP think tanks is an important focus of this book.

Key findings

In Chapter 2, Donald Abelson elaborates a theme that surfaces throughout this volume, namely the balance between advocacy and research in the activities of think tanks. He uses the metaphor of a pendulum, evocative of significant and self-correcting swings in one direction and then another, to capture the competing forces that are embodied in modern think tanks: the need to be relevant and *to be seen to be relevant* pulls them toward advocacy; awareness that the value of their stock in the marketplace of policy ideas will suffer if the research and analysis on which this advocacy is based is substandard pulls think tanks back toward their original identity as generators of policy-relevant research and advice.

Abelson argues that the swing toward a more aggressive, high-profile advocacy was pioneered by the Washington-based Heritage Foundation. It was soon emulated to varying degrees by other think tanks, including some of the sector's *grandes dames*, such as Brookings. The Heritage Foundation formula shook up the rather staid world of think tanks and, as Abelson argues, revolutionized the role and function of these organizations in the US and abroad.

Advocacy is very definitely the signature activity of the four human rights organizations examined by Brooks and Cil in Chapter 3. Amnesty International, Human Rights Watch, International Crisis Group and Transparency International all began life as advocacy NGOs. This remains their principal identity. Nevertheless, they have become brand names in the world of human rights in no small measure because of their field-based research and the reputations they have earned for credible, first person witness-based analysis. They perennially rank among the world's most influential think tanks, notwithstanding that in each case their self-image remains tied to their origins as human rights NGOs.

Brooks and Cil argue that the activities, visibility and reputations of these four organizations have contributed to the blurring of traditional lines between research, advocacy, journalism and lobbying. Purists might object to their inclusion in the category of think tanks. The point is, however, that their advocacy orientation – and the fact that, in the case of Amnesty International and Human Rights Watch, they may fairly be said to be situated at the heart of global human rights movements – has expanded the parameters of the think tank concept. Just as Edwin Feulner and the Heritage Foundation transformed the advice function of think tanks into a sort of missionary advocacy function, thereby challenging and changing our understanding of think tanks, the human rights organizations examined by Brooks and Cil have broadened the contemporary understanding of what a think tank can look like and how it can harness research in the cause of advocacy.

The last several years, particularly since the Treaty of Lisbon and the creation of the European External Action Service, have seen the emergence of an EU-wide foreign policy. The path has not been without detours and obstacles. But, as Marybel Perez observes in Chapter 4, "intergovernmentalism has given way to governance through EU foreign policy since EU institutions and agencies, and not only states, are involved in policymaking." This development has been paralleled by the growth of think tanks whose principal focus is EU foreign policy.

This think tank scene is different, Perez notes, from that in Washington, DC. Advocacy and marketing techniques intended to increase the visibility of think tanks do not characterize the behavior of these Brussels-based and EU foreign policy focused think tanks. Nor do these think tanks have the sort of impact on the EU foreign policy conversation that think tanks in Washington, London and Berlin have in the countries they are located in. Nevertheless, argues Perez, they play a significant role, particularly in the informal processes of governance. They do so in large part through "events [that] enable the sharing of different points of view and the discussion of alternative scenarios regarding a policy issue." Think tanks whose focus is EU foreign policy help to educate policy-makers on the issues and may, in their modest way, Perez suggests, contribute to the development of consensus on these issues.

The very different world of think tanks and foreign policy in the US is the subject of Chapter 5. If the scene in Brussels is subdued and understated, that in Washington, DC is glitzy and loud. This is the heart of the advocacy model and home to a truly staggering array of think tanks competing for private funding and the ears of policy-makers who are usually eager to hear what at least some of them have to say. The explanation for the unmatched vibrancy of the Washington think tank scene cannot be reduced to a single reason. Foremost among them, Abelson says, "[are] the many opportunities [think tanks] are afforded to participate in the policy-making process."

Abelson suggests that the attempt to measure and rank think tank influence, although interesting and not likely to be abandoned any time soon, is both futile and a distraction from questions that may not lend themselves to quantification, but are more germane to a real understanding of how and when think tanks are influential. "We need to develop," he argues, "a new narrative around think tanks that explains in greater depth what they have contributed, instead of how much *influence* they might have exercised."

The American think tank model is often contrasted to that in Germany, where organizations that fuse research and advocacy have been a less prominent part of the overall think tank scene and where state funding of think tanks has been the norm. In Chapter 6, Josef Braml examines the case of Germany where, he argues, what *The Economist* dubbed a sort of "dull pragmatism" continues to prevail in that country's think tank community. Unlike the US, where think tanks are an important part of an often raucous and confrontational conversation on foreign policy and geo-politics, German think tanks continue to play a role that is less influential and, much of the time, less visible. This is not because of a shortage of think tanks – Germany has roughly 200 of them, dozens of which have foreign policy and geo-politics as either their central or an important focus. It is, argues Braml, due to a combination of factors that include: 1) a broad pragmatic consensus on foreign policy that continues to prevail in Germany; 2) the relatively closed nature of the state, including its foreign policy-making apparatus, to advice from the outside and 3) a state funding system that encourages scientific/academic policy research at the expense of policy-relevant work.

Braml describes the changes that have been taking place in Germany's think tank sector over the past few decades, including the creation of an increasing number of privately funded research institutions and greater efforts on the part of some think tanks to try to influence the policy conversation and framing of issues by getting their analyses and ideas expressed through prestigious media outlets. Only then, he argues, do they have a chance of being taken seriously by policy-making elites. The sort of combative and loud marketplace of ideas that one sees in Washington, DC is not, Braml believes, likely to come to Berlin. He notes that Germany's 20th century history continues to cast a shadow over the country's think tank scene, making many in that sector uncomfortable with the label think *tank* and also with the idea that policy ideas should be tied to ideology. At the same time, he argues that the reconfiguration of global power and the emerging bi-polarity between the US and China is a challenge that Germany's policy elites, and those in the think tank sector, have not yet fully grasped.

The alternative approach to thinking about think tank influence, suggested by Abelson in Chapter 5 and revisited in Chapter 11, is taken seriously by Mark Garnett and Simon Mabon in their analysis of think tanks and foreign policy in the UK. Chapter 7 focuses on the contribution to the British foreign policy conversation of the Institute for International Affairs (Chatham House), the Royal United Services Institute and the International Institute for Strategic Studies. "British think tanks," they write, "have long recognized that their most realistic goal in the areas of foreign policy and defence is to influence 'informed opinion,' rather than hoping for direct decision-making input."

The reasons for this approach are many. Among them is what Garnett and Mabon describe as the prevailing culture of British decision-making when it comes to matters of foreign and defense policy. Unlike other policy areas, including health, education and public finances, where outspoken criticism of government policy and advocacy – as long as they are supported by credible research – is common and not likely to diminish a think tank's relevance in the policy conversation, this style is likely to produce very different results when the issues relate to war and peace. Thus, even in the lead up to the British government's decision to join in the 2003 invasion of Iraq, an issue that might have been expected to generate considerable forthright criticism in opposition to this course, the voices of the major foreign policy think tanks were reserved.

In Chapter 8, Xin Hua examines the case of China, whose think tank scene is much younger than those of the US, the UK and many other western countries. He focuses on two of the most prestigious of China's foreign policy research institutes, the China Institute of International Studies (CIIS) and the Shanghai Institute of International Studies (SIIS) and, in particular, their influence on Chinese policy toward Europe. Westerners may be inclined to dismiss Chinese think tanks as being of little consequence in a country where power is very centralized and criticism of the country's leaders and their policies is not welcomed. Xin Hua shows that such a dismissal is a mistake. While it is true that there is no space for advocacy think tanks in China's authoritarian political system and in a country where civil society is still quite weak and unorganized, this does not mean that there are not ways for think tanks to shape the ideas and policy options considered by state authorities.

Xin Hua shows that the close connections between the CIIS and China's Ministry of Foreign Affairs, and in particular the "revolving door" between the two, provides CIIS with access and credibility in the eyes of China's foreign policy-makers. SIIS has weaker connections to the inner circle of political power in China, but better connections to the country's universities, which, however, occupy a marginal status when it comes to influencing policy. He argues that some features of the Chinese think tank scene are rather similar to those found elsewhere, at the same time as other aspects crucial to understanding the modalities of think tank influence in China are quite different. Xin Hua's analysis serves as a warning about generalizations based on western experiences about when and why think tanks are likely to be influential.

As the refugee crisis spawned by the war in Syria made clear, important divisions exist among EU countries when it comes to their analysis of and preferred responses to geo-political issues. The crisis exposed important differences on matters of national sovereignty and obligations under both international law and the requirements of EU membership, Poland being one of the EU member-states most at odds with Brussels on these issues. In Chapter 9, Monika Sus notes that foreign-policy-oriented think tanks in Poland became more relevant than usual during this crisis, as they also did during the civil protests in Kiev that preceded the civil war in Ukraine and Russia's annexation of Crimea, their ideas receiving wider attention by both the attentive public and policy-makers. As a rule, however, the influence of Poland's foreign-policy-oriented think tanks remains rather marginal. Only a handful of such organizations, Sus argues, can be considered truly relevant in terms of having any sort of real impact on the policy conversation and, potentially, influencing how policy-makers view the issues and what actions they take. The state elite continues to be quite resistant to outside advice and so demand for what think tanks offer is limited.

As in the case of Germany, analyzed in Braml's chapter, there does not exist the sort of revolving door tradition between parties, the state and think tanks that one observes in the US. Nor has the ideological and advocacy model embodied in such American think tanks as the American Enterprise Institute, the Heritage Foundation (both conservative) or the Institute for Policy Studies (progressive) taken hold in Poland. Privately funded think tanks have established an important foothold in Poland, Sus observes, generally funded by money from German or American foundations. "If the Polish think tank sector is to expand and its influence grow," she argues, "a pre-condition would seem to be not only, or perhaps not even principally, greater financial support from the state, but from the business community as in the case in Germany."

Chapter 10 examines the case of Spain, where the long history of tension between centralizing and decentralizing forces and visions is played out in the country's think tank scene. Olivier Urrutia explains that this scene is relatively young and that Spanish think tanks are largely dependent on state financing, making them more like the German model in this respect than the American revenue model. It is also a scene that reproduces in important ways the political rivalry between Madrid and Barcelona and where the activities and analyses of think tanks on matters of foreign policy reflect, to some degree, the competing centralist and autonomist/independence visions.

Urrutia shows that advocacy think tanks in Catalonia often project a strongly nationalist vision through their analyses of foreign policy issues, effectively acting as agents of soft power in support of Barcelona's project of national independence. Even the Barcelona Centre for International Affairs, one of the most prestigious Catalan foreign policy think tanks, which is at least partly dependent on funding from the central state in Madrid, has been accused of complicity in projecting abroad the vision of an independent Catalonia. It co-authored with a Brussels-based think tank a 2015 report that arrived at favorable economic conclusions for Catalonia in the event that it were to become independent. The report was presented to the European Parliament, where the Permanent Representative of the Government of Catalonia to the EU was in attendance. It was very clearly an exercise in public diplomacy on behalf of Barcelona's independence aspirations.

In the final chapter, Donald Abelson focuses on one of the central themes of this book, identified in Chapter 1: how do we know that a think tank is influential? The annual rankings provided by the Global Go To Index have become the "gold standard" for determining this. Those think tanks that do well in the rankings are quick to advertise the fact, issuing tweets, press releases and special communications to those who fund them; in short, investing the rankings with the credibility they have acquired in the eyes of many who want answers to the question of whose ideas matter and are capable of moving the needle of the policy conversation. Abelson joins his voice to those who have expressed deep skepticism about the conclusions that are so often and so quickly drawn from these rankings, arguing that this may be a case where we should be wary of the sort of metrics on which quantitative rankings necessarily rely.

Abelson examines the case of Canada, also citing examples from Sweden, Kenya and Malaysia, to illustrate how rankings and metrics are used by think tanks to boost their reputations for influence, satisfy and attract donors, and reinforce their access to the media and to policy-makers. "Performance indicators," he says, "may allow think tanks to acquire a better sense of how they are doing relative to their competitors and may speak to their level of engagement around particular policy issues, but these and similar data do not provide a clear indication of how much or little policy influence think tanks exercise." Such metrics should be seen, by those who wish to understand when, whether and why a think tank has truly had an impact, as "a point of departure, not a landing, for a much broader discussion about the determinants of public policy." At the same time, the likelihood that any think tank that finishes toward the top of the table in any of the many national, policy field and other categories that are part of the annual Global Go To Think Tank Index Report will not trumpet the fact to the world, Abelson acknowledges, is somewhere between slender and zero.

Notes

1 This is based on the *New York Times* language visualization tool at http://chronicle.nytlabs.com/?keyword=prohibition. It is an imperfect tool that is very sensitive to the exact word or phrase that is searched. Thus, for example, "Wilson Center" will produce a different number than "Woodrow Wilson Center." Nevertheless, it provides interesting approximations of the relative frequency with which words appear over time.
2 The main exception to this generalization involves CSIS–CICIR cooperation since 2010 through the *CSIS–CICIR Cybersecurity* Dialogue.
3 http://ethics.harvard.edu/academia-non-profit/working-papers

References

Abelson, Donald. 2012. "Thinking Out Loud: Think Tanks and Their Quest for Public Exposure." Research Paper 2, Canada-US Institute, University of Western Ontario. Available at http://thecanadausinstitute.uwo.ca/pdf/research_papers/CUSI_Research_Paper_2_Abelson.pdf.

Bjørgaas, Tove. 2012. *From Contributor to Partner: Norway's Role in Foreign Policy Research and Implementation in the United States.* Norwegian Peacebuilding Resource Centre, report produced for the Norwegian Ministry of Foreign Affairs.

Clark, Julia, and David Roodman. 2013. "Measuring Think Tank Performance: An Index of Public Profile." Policy Papers, Centre for Global Development, 28 June. Available at http://www.cgdev.org/sites/default/files/think-tank-index_0_0.pdf.

Fischer, Manuel, and Pascal Sciarini. 2015. "Unpacking Reputational Power: Intended and Unintended Determinants of the Assessment of Actors' Power." *Social Networks* 42: 60–71.

Higgott, Richard, and Diane Stone. 1994."The Limits of Influence: Foreign Policy Think Tanks in Britain and the USA." *Review of International Studies* 20, no. 1 (January): 15–34.

JP Morgan Chase Institute. 2015. "Expert Insights for the Public Good." Available at http://www.jpmorganchase.com/corporate/institute/institute.htm
Keohane, Robert O. and Joseph S. Nye, Jr. 1998. "Power and Interdependence in the Information Age." *Foreign Affairs* (Sept–Oct): 81–95.
McGann, James. 2007. *2007 Survey of Thinks: A Summary Report*. Think Tanks and Civil Societies Program, University of Pennsylvania. Available at http://www.affarinternazionali.it/Documenti/2007_Survey_of_Think-tanks.pdf.
McGann, James. 2015. *2014 Global Go To Think Tank Index Report*. Think Tanks and Civil Societies Program, University of Pennsylvania.
McGann, James, Anna Viden and Jillian Rafferty (eds). 2014. *How Think Tanks Shape Social Development Policies*. Philadelphia: University of Pennsylvania Press.
Mendizabal, Enrique. 2012. "And the Winner is: Brookings . . . But, Once Again, the Loser: Critical Analysis," 20 January. Available at http://onthinktanks.org/2012/01/20/and-the-winner-is-brookings-and-once-again-the-loser-critical-analysis/
Menegazzi, Silvia. 2015. "Chinese Military Think Tanks: 'Chinese Characteristics' and the 'Revolving Door,' " *China Brief* 15, no. 8 (16 April). Available at http://www.refworld.org/docid/5538abf44.html.
Morocco. 2012. "Action de l'Ambassade du Maroc aux Etats-Unis: Bilan et perspectives pour le renforcement de l'action diplomatique." Embassy of Morocco (December). Available at http://www.arso.org/Coleman/Actions_de_lAmbassade_du_Maroc.pdf
Prospect Magazine. 2014. "Think Tank Awards 2014: The Results." *Prospect Magazine*, 17 July. Available at http://www.prospectmagazine.co.uk/politics/think-tank-awards-2014-the-results.
Rich, Andrew. 2004. *Think Tanks, Public Policy, and the Politics of Expertise*. Cambridge: Cambridge University Press.
Stolle, Dietlind. 2002."Trusting Strangers: The Concept of Generalized Trust in Perspective." G. S. Schaal (ed.) *Österreichische Zeitschrift für Politikwissenschaft. Schwerpunktheft* 397–412.
Stone, Diane. 2013. *Knowledge Actors and Transnational Governance: The Private–Public Policy Nexus in the Global Agora*. London: Palgrave Macmillan.

2 Feulner's pendulum
Moving between policy research and political advocacy

Donald E. Abelson

Introduction

Named after French physicist Jean Bernard Léon Foucault, Foucault's pendulum was constructed to demonstrate the earth's rotation. Since its debut in Paris's Panthéon in 1851, replicas of the pendulum have been on display in several museums around the world, including Washington, DC's Smithsonian National Museum of American History. Removed in 1998 to make room for the Star-Spangled Banner Preservation Project, it is unlikely that the famous pendulum will return to the nation's capital. But in Washington, DC there is another pendulum at work – what I metaphorically call Feulner's pendulum – that may help to explain the gravitational forces drawing think tanks closer to the center of America's political universe. Feulner's pendulum does not appear behind protective glass, nor does it require massive bobs, string or wires to demonstrate the evolution and movement of think tanks around different political constellations. In its simplest form, this imagined pendulum highlights how think tanks move freely and perpetually from Point A – Policy Research – to Point B – Political Advocacy – in an effort to influence public opinion and public policy. It reflects a strategy rather than a physical construction and has come to symbolize the vision of a man often credited with transforming American think tanks.

Edwin J. Feulner may not be someone with whom those outside the think tank community are terribly familiar. In Washington policy-making circles, however, he has left a formidable legacy. As president of the Heritage Foundation for 36 years, Feulner was, in many ways, destined to become a pioneer and visionary in the think tank world. Indeed, his strong intellectual curiosity and experience on Capitol Hill, combined with an innate ability to establish an extensive network of personal and professional contacts, all but assured him access to the nation's power brokers. His burning passion for strong conservative principles also endeared him to philanthropic foundations, corporations and individuals only too willing to support his goal of establishing a conservative think tank that could serve as a counter-weight to the more liberal Brookings Institution. Armed with an MBA from the Wharton School of Business, which undoubtedly helped to nurture his entrepreneurial spirit, and a PhD in Political Science from the University of Edinburgh, Feulner understood that competing in the marketplace of ideas required far more than generating rigorous research. Indeed, for the highly educated Feulner, producing solid research was the least policy-makers should expect from think tanks.

In his capacity as a legislative assistant and later chief of staff to Illinois Representative Philip Crane, Feulner was responsible for, among other things, sifting through countless studies and reports pervading the US think tank community. And under the tutelage of Crane, a former history professor at Bradley University, it did not take long for him to discover that to effect policy change, think tanks had to provide policy-makers and other key stakeholders with information that was timely, relevant and accessible. Feulner also realized that think tanks had to aggressively market their policy recommendations to ensure their voices would be heard. To him, it seemed that ideas were like any other commodity being traded on the New York Stock Exchange; they had to be properly showcased to capture the consumer's attention. Otherwise, both the policy recommendations being outlined, and the organizations from where they emanated, would languish in obscurity.

The importance of combining timely and policy relevant research with aggressive marketing was also a lesson Feulner learned from the founders of one of Britain's most distinguished conservative think tanks, the Institute of Economic Affairs (IEA). According to Lee Edwards, Feulner's biographer and a historian of the conservative movement in the US, the aspiring think tank leader was deeply impressed with the IEA and its efforts to promote conservative principles in the UK (2013: 30–31). His fascination and admiration for the IEA, observes Edwards, helped guide Feulner's thinking about creating a similar think tank in Washington, DC.

The purpose of this chapter is not to trace the many intellectual and professional influences which shaped Feulner's political views, nor, for that matter, is it to examine the important role the Heritage Foundation has played as a leading voice in America's conservative community. Both avenues of inquiry have been carefully documented and meticulously explored by others (Edwards 1997, 2013). Rather, my purpose here is to discuss how Feulner's desire to establish a think tank capable of combining rigorous policy research (a by-product of his academic training) with aggressive political advocacy (which spoke to his entrepreneurial spirit) helped revolutionize the role and function of think tanks in the US and throughout the international community. Along with Paul Weyrich, co-founder of Heritage, Feulner helped launch a new generation of think tanks – the so-called advocacy think tank. In the process, he and his colleagues, wittingly or unwittingly, created an institution that embraced a natural and enduring tension between research and advocacy.

According to some scholars, including this author, think tanks in the US have, for many years, placed a higher premium on political advocacy than on policy research (Abelson 1995). However, as Feulner's legacy reminds us, advocating or promoting policy recommendations that are based on questionable research methods provides little more than background noise. The challenge for think tanks committed ostensibly to helping government think its way through complex policy issues is to strike a balance between these competing forces. In the first section of this chapter, a brief analysis of what motivated Feulner and Weyrich to create a public policy think tank that would rely both on experts to analyze a wide range of domestic and foreign policies, and on individuals with knowledge of business and marketing principles to promote policy ideas will be offered. This will serve as a useful segue into a broader discussion of why institutions described as research-oriented are generally seen as more virtuous than those engaged in advocacy. In this section, lengthy consideration will also be given to the confusion that often surrounds discussions about the charitable status of think tanks, and the activities in which they are legally permitted to engage. In the third section, the various factors that may help to explain the growing popularity of advocacy think tanks in the US and abroad will be explored. And finally, some of the challenges think tanks face in moving between research and advocacy will be addressed, along with a solution that several organizations, including the Heritage Foundation have discovered.

An idea whose time had come: The birth of the heritage foundation

When Paul Weyrich, press secretary to Colorado Republican Senator Gordon L. Allott met Edwin Feulner for breakfast on Capitol Hill amidst the controversial debate surrounding the funding of the Supersonic Transport (SST) during the early 1970s, the two could not possibly have imagined how momentous their encounter would be. Before they gulped down their morning coffee, the idea for creating the Heritage Foundation was born. As Edwards observes:

> Weyrich had barely seated himself at breakfast when he waved aloft a monograph from a right-of-center think tank that carefully examined both sides of the SST funding question. It was long, but it embodied the kind of thoughtful research that made it something busy Hill staffers could use to prepare their members for debate. But the study had arrived in Senator Allott's office several days *after* the debate. A perplexed Weyrich contacted the organization's president, a member of his church. "Great study," Weyrich said. "Why didn't we get it sooner?" "We didn't want to try to affect the outcome of the vote," the president responded. "Paul and I decided then and there," recalls Feulner, "that conservatives needed an independent research institute designed to influence the policy debate as it was occurring in Congress – *before* decisions were made." (2013: 66)

After a series of meetings with potential donors and key figures in the American conservative movement, the Heritage Foundation was incorporated as a 501 (c)(3) charitable, tax-exempt research organization in late 1973. And with $250,000 in seed money from Joseph Coors, Heritage opened its doors in early 1974. Although Weyrich and Feulner were convinced that a conservative think tank was necessary to counter the influence of the iconic Brookings Institution, an organization known for policy prescriptions deeply rooted in traditional liberal values, their goal was not to replicate the Brookings model. Indeed, rather than creating a think tank that, in Kent Weaver's words, resembled a "university without students" (1989) where rigorous policy research remained a priority, Weyrich and Feulner aspired to establish a hybrid institution that recognized the benefits and inherent value of engaging both in research and advocacy. Producing weighty tomes on health care, education, the US economy and the challenges facing America on the world stage had been the hallmark of Brookings for years. However, as many political pundits observed half-jokingly, the detailed and complex treatises they produced may have been written for policy-makers, but were read by professors. Unwilling to watch their studies gather dust on bookshelves, the co-founders of Heritage had a different plan in mind for influencing the political climate in the nation's capital. They recognized that research without a proper marketing strategy to promote their ideas would all but guarantee failure. For the two young conservative policy entrepreneurs, it was critically important for Heritage to develop a well-orchestrated campaign to move the US to the right, and in the years leading up to the 1980 presidential election, they put their ideas into action (Abelson 1996: 12–18).

Rather than spend their limited resources on publishing dense studies, Weyrich and Feulner encouraged in-house researchers to write short and pithy policy briefs that addressed key issues being considered in Congress. These reports were hand-delivered to every member of the House and Senate, and, along with op-eds placed in several American and international newspapers, Heritage began to make its mark. Experts from Heritage also regularly testified before legislative committees, provided commentaries to the print and broadcast media, produced and sold audio cassette tapes that recorded lectures from prominent conservatives, and through liaison offices established with both houses of Congress, kept a close watch on emerging policy issues. Several Heritage experts also participated as advisors on the Reagan campaign, providing analyses of various domestic and foreign policy issues. Within a short period of time, "the feisty new kid on the conservative block" (Abelson 1996: 17), as Reagan observed, was acquiring a reputation for producing timely and policy relevant research. But it was the publication of its massive 1981 study *Mandate for Leadership* (Heatherly 1981), one of the few lengthy volumes Heritage compiled during its formative years, that propelled Heritage into the national spotlight. Produced as a blueprint to help the incoming Reagan administration reform government along conservative lines, the study proved a game-changer, not only for Reagan and his transition team but for Heritage.

Weyrich and Feulner's gamble had paid off. By bringing together dozens of experts from across the country to identify the many challenges confronting virtually every major federal government department and agency, and inviting them to outline concrete policy solutions, the two former congressional aides demonstrated that combining research with advocacy could generate handsome dividends. Not only was the Heritage study widely regarded as the bible for the Reagan administration (Abelson 1996: 16), which may account for why it became a bestseller inside the Beltway, but it helped inspire an entire generation of think tanks equally committed to leaving an indelible mark on public policy.

The challenge for Heritage and for other think tanks moving forward was to determine how best to balance research with advocacy.

Policy research vs political advocacy

When it comes to assessing the priorities of think tanks, policy research and political advocacy are often treated as polar opposites. The reality, however, is that they are complementary functions in which all think tanks, in one form or another, engage. The question is what premium or priority do institutions place on each? The answer will ultimately determine how think tanks are portrayed in the mainstream media and to which category they are assigned by scholars intent on developing a typology or classification of public policy institutes.

Given their diverse and eclectic nature, it is not surprising that think tanks are often incorrectly or inaccurately described in and by the media. A case in point is the two organizations referenced above – the Brookings Institution and the Heritage Foundation. With great regularity, the Brookings Institution is referred to as a leading policy research institution or as a world renowned public policy think tank. By contrast, the Heritage Foundation is frequently referred to as an advocacy or advocacy-oriented think tank. The implication of using these descriptors is that the studies and policy recommendations generated by Brookings should be taken more seriously and held in higher regard than those coming from Heritage; after all, as plenty of journalists who follow Washington politics remind us, while the latter is committed to advocating or promoting a particular set of beliefs, the former is primarily concerned with producing scientifically rigorous and neutral policy research. To put it another way, think tanks considered to be predominantly focused on research are thought to deserve greater recognition and respectability than those actively involved in advocacy; research is seen as virtuous, advocacy as sinister.

The distinction drawn between think tanks that engage in research and those known more for advocacy, however, is fundamentally flawed. Indeed, in many ways it presents a false dichotomy. First, there is an abundance of research conducted at universities, think tanks and government facilities that is neither virtuous nor scientifically rigorous. For instance, research conducted in the US and Canada on the relationship between race and intelligence generated heated discussions about whether any of the findings generated by Richard Herrnstein and Charles Murray, authors of *The Bell Curve* (1996), were actually rooted in hard science. And history is replete with examples of less than respectable scholars presenting shoddy work on a wide range of academic questions. To conclude, then, that think tanks devoting the lion's share of their budget to research automatically deserve special recognition and status is, frankly, unwarranted. Moreover, there is also an element of inconsistency in the work of think tanks. At times, the reports of some high-profile institutes are, by most accounts, stellar; at other times, the research appears rushed, with many of the findings left unsubstantiated. And in some isolated cases it has been revealed that think tanks have plagiarized or even falsified reports in an effort to appease donors and other key stakeholders.[1]

Similarly, it is important not to cast aspersions on, or to demean, the work of think tanks known for advocacy. When hospitals ask for more beds, or when public schools sign petitions requesting smaller class sizes to improve the quality of education, their efforts are seen as noble. But when think tanks advocate for a higher military budget, or for school vouchers, their activities in support of these positions is frowned upon or viewed with suspicion. Is it simply that there is a perception that public institutions will naturally act in accordance with the public interest and private institutions will try to subvert it, or is there something else at work? While there is little doubt that think tanks often pursue institutional interests that may compromise the public interest, what concerns scholars who monitor the behavior of these institutions even more is when advocacy appears to spill over into lobbying, a subject to which we will return shortly.

Although it is understandable why this confusion exists, it is important to acknowledge that advocacy is not, in and of itself, a nefarious activity; it is a fundamental feature of democratic life and a legitimate activity in which all NGOs, including think tanks, are involved. What undermines their reputation as repositories of policy expertise is when think tanks, like interest groups and lobbyists, are seen as partisan players in the political arena. In all fairness, Brookings may have a sterling reputation as a top-tier research institute, but it also devotes considerable resources to advocating and promoting a range of policy ideas, many of which strike a responsive chord with key elements of the Democratic Party. But should the fact that Brookings advocates strong policy positions on various domestic and foreign policy issues make them less credible? By contrast, Heritage is often portrayed as the quintessential advocacy think tank, but, for years, has also produced a steady stream of publications which appeal to multiple target audiences. Does this mean that Heritage deserves to appear along with Brookings in Weaver's category of universities without students? As noted, the reality is that both institutions participate in similar activities; the challenge they and other think tanks face is striking a balance between research and advocacy – a balance that affords them the credibility and respectability they require to speak with authority, and the access they need to exercise influence over public opinion and public policy.

In the final section of the chapter, we will address some of the many challenges think tanks face in striking a balance between research and advocacy, assuming of course that this is their intention; however, before this discussion can take place, it is necessary to clarify much of the confusion surrounding these two critically important terms. To do this, we need to understand more fully what is and is not a think tank, and the various functions these institutions are expected to perform. As we will discover in the section below, think tanks may be portrayed as partisan institutions engaged in various lobbying activities, but, legally, they may neither be partisan, nor can they register as lobbyists. Ironically, this has not prevented dozens of think tank staffers at high-profile American think tanks from moonlighting as lobbyists (Williams and Silverstein 2013).

What is and isn't a think tank?

Determining what a think tank is and is not is far more difficult than it appears. To explain what a think tank is, we need to focus on five particular traits or defining characteristics that make them unique. By doing so, we will be able to more effectively distinguish between think tanks and other organizations that compete for visibility and influence in the policy-making community, and will be better equipped to evaluate how think tanks try to balance research with advocacy.

Five ways to identify a think tank

1. Registered charity vs non-profit organization

The majority of think tanks in Canada and in the US qualify as non-profit organizations, a broad category that includes thousands of groups ranging from minor hockey associations to alcohol and drug rehabilitation centres. But in most cases, stand alone (as opposed to university-based) think tanks, such as the Fraser Institute and the C.D. Howe Institute, are also registered as charities under the Income Tax Act.[2] The designation of a charitable organization is reserved for religious institutions, and for organizations committed to education, to the alleviation of poverty, and/or to improving conditions in local communities (by providing animal shelters, libraries, volunteer fire departments, etc.). According to the Canada Revenue Agency (CRA), think tanks are eligible for charitable status because of their commitment to education through policy research. Along with universities, colleges and other educational institutions, think tanks are tax-exempt (as are non-profit organizations that are not registered as charities), and are permitted to issue official donation receipts, a critically important benefit that allows them to attract and retain donor support. Similar benefits are available to think tanks in the US that are registered as charitable organizations under section 501 (c) (3) of the Internal Revenue Code.

2. Non-partisan or non-ideological?

When think tanks apply for charitable status under the detailed guidelines of the CRA, they are well aware that if their application is successful, a legal obligation to remain non-partisan will ensue. This does not mean that, as a registered charity, think tanks must refrain from expressing their views or opinions on policy issues. After all, this is one of the main reasons why think tanks are established – to engage in research and analysis, and to share their findings with multiple audiences. Moreover, adhering to the strictures of non-partisanship does not prevent think tanks from embracing a particular ideological orientation. Even the most casual observers of Canadian politics would have little difficulty distinguishing between the conservative leanings of the Fraser Institute and the more liberal/progressive policy views espoused by the Canadian Centre for Policy Alternatives. To be clear, as charitable, non-partisan institutions, think tanks do not forfeit their democratic right to free expression. Regardless of where they situate themselves along the ideological spectrum, think tanks can and do analyse policy problems through particular political lenses, and rely on various channels to convey their ideas. If experts at think tanks are free to take up and defend positions on any policy issue, and from any political perspective, then what does non-partisanship actually entail? In the CRA's Policy Statement CPS-022,[3] a document that, among other things, outlines what constitutes acceptable and unacceptable political activities for charities, the following declaration is made: "A charity cannot be established with the aim of furthering or opposing the interests of a political party, elected representative, or candidate for public office. Also, a charity cannot be formed to retain, oppose, or change the law, policy, or decision of any level of government in Canada or a foreign country."[4]

As charitable organizations, think tanks are not permitted to publicly support or oppose candidates running for office; however, they are still entitled to allocate "a small amount of resources for political activity." Moreover, while think tanks are prohibited from engaging in partisan political activity, they are allowed to make the public aware of [their] position on an issue provided:

1 [they do] explicitly connect [their] views to any political party or candidate for public office;
2 the issue is connected to its purposes;
3 its views are based on a well-reasoned position;
4 public awareness campaigns do not become the charity's primary activity.[5]

The CRA's list of prohibited and permissible political activities can either be broadly interpreted or narrowly defined – that is the problem. However, what is apparent is that the federal government is trying, albeit not always successfully, to differentiate between partisan involvement and policy engagement. As research institutions, think tanks are expected to generate and disseminate ideas on a range of policy issues to various target audiences, including policy-makers. They can invite elected officials and their staff to conferences, workshops and seminars, provide them with their publications, and even offer solicited and unsolicited policy advice. There is nothing in the CRA guidelines to prevent think tanks from communicating to members of parliament, cabinet or the bureaucracy. They simply cannot support or oppose candidates running for office, contribute funds to political parties, or devote a disproportionate amount of institutional resources to changing a law, policy or decision made by the Canadian government or by a foreign state. Unlike in Germany where a select group of think tanks are funded by the state to serve the research needs of political parties, in Canada efforts have been undertaken ostensibly to establish boundaries between members of political parties and think tanks. While some Canadian political parties might prefer to have stronger ties with particular think tanks, there is not always an incentive for policy institutes to compromise their "independence" by tying their political fortunes to the government or to official opposition, or to other parties represented in parliament.

In the US, even stronger and more precise language has been incorporated in the Internal Revenue Code to restrict the partisan or political activities of think tanks. Unlike the Income Tax Act, which includes rather ambiguous language around acceptable partisan activities for charitable organizations, section 501 (c) (3) of the Internal Revenue Code, points out that all tax-exempt organizations, which include the majority of American think tanks, must adhere to the following:

> All section 501 (c) (3) organizations are absolutely prohibited from directly or indirectly participating in, or intervening in, any political campaign on behalf of (or in opposition to) any candidate for elective public office. Contributions to political campaign funds or public statements of position (verbal or written) made on behalf of the organization in favor of or in opposition to any candidate for public office clearly violate the prohibition against political campaign activity. Violating this prohibition may result in denial or revocation of tax-exempt status and the imposition of certain excise taxes.[6]

It bears repeating that non-partisanship should not be confused with ideological neutrality – the two are not synonymous. All think tanks, regardless of their mission and mandate, produce policy papers that, in some way, reflect a particular ideology or ideological orientation. That some think tanks are more liberal or conservative than others, however, does not cause alarm in policy-making circles in Canada or the US, so long as these institutions respect the limits imposed on partisan activities.

3. Policy research, political advocacy and the marketplace of ideas

As we have discussed throughout the chapter, of all the features or institutional characteristics that enable us to isolate think tanks from the myriad of other NGOs populating the policy-making community, nothing is more salient than the emphasis they place on generating and disseminating applied policy research. Indeed, without a *sustained* commitment to analyzing and dissecting various domestic and/or foreign policies, organizations cannot legitimately claim to be think tanks, nor should they be regarded as such. After all, conducting research is at the very heart of what think tanks do – or is it?

For most think tanks, resolving the many issues surrounding their research programs is only half the battle. What keeps think tank directors up at night is figuring out how best to communicate their research findings to key stakeholders. As the marketplace of ideas becomes increasingly crowded, think tanks have devoted more of their time, energy and resources to thinking about political advocacy. Although they generally view advocacy as an important and necessary component of their work, for some observers (Abelson 2014a), it has evolved into an unhealthy obsession that has undermined the integrity and quality of the research produced by policy institutes.

While there is no doubt that think tanks continue to spend considerable time, energy and money on political advocacy, this does not necessarily mean that they have abdicated their core mission. In fact, it could be argued that by aggressively marketing their research findings, think tanks have simply tried to bring their ideas to life. Advocacy takes different forms, and is played out on different stages, and although often cloaked in mystery, it simply involves promoting a particular vision or set of beliefs to various audiences. As noted, by participating in advocacy-related activities, think tanks are no less noble or virtuous than their competitors who assign a higher priority to research.

4. Ideas and interests

For think tanks to achieve even a modicum of policy influence, their ideas must gain traction. Although they do not claim to speak on behalf of any particular constituency, as interest groups are entrusted to do, think tanks require the support of key stakeholders. In addition to satisfying the concerns of their principal benefactors, think tanks need to consider how the public, policy-makers, journalists, business leaders and other opinion makers will react to their policy prescriptions.

As with political parties that constantly soften or harden their platform to broaden their base of support, think tanks often find themselves massaging their message about various domestic and foreign policies to generate greater visibility and influence. Granted, unlike those seeking public office, think tanks do not have to concern themselves with appeasing voters in a particular district or riding. Still, in order to attract and retain the support of donors, and to establish strong ties to those in positions of power, think tanks must be engaged in the political process. In other words, to achieve the kind of stature and influence they dearly covet, think tanks have to lay a foundation that will allow them to have a prolonged and discernible impact on public policy. Among other things, this requires careful planning, a strategic allocation of resources, a talented stable of experts and a sophisticated and nuanced understanding of the policy-making process. There is no magic formula for achieving a balance between ideas and interests, but there is no doubt that both figure prominently in determining how think tanks position themselves on the political landscape. They are the key ingredients in producing what for them is their raison d'être – to influence public opinion and public policy.

5. Shaping public opinion and public policy

Interest groups, political parties, advocacy coalitions and a host of other non-governmental, governmental and for-profit organizations are committed to shaping public opinion and public policy, but few have the capacity to engage the public and policy-makers as effectively and systematically as think tanks. By bridging the gap between the academic and the policy-making worlds, think tanks, and the experts who populate them, occupy a unique space from which to share and exchange ideas on a host of pressing policy matters. Unlike several of the organizations mentioned above that possess a limited research capacity, think tanks draw upon their expertise and political connections to become entrenched in the policy-making process.

The importance think tanks assign to marketing themselves as research institutions with established expertise in various policy fields cannot be emphasized enough. With expertise comes credibility, or so think tanks claim, a currency they can and have used to earn the trust of the public, policy-makers and other stakeholders. Along with the credibility they have established, it is their capacity to provide timely and relevant advice that is ultimately responsible for allowing think tanks to distinguish themselves from other players in the political arena. While think tanks vary enormously in size, resources, areas of specialization and ideological orientation, they share a common desire to leave an indelible mark on public policy.

What isn't a think tank?

Some of the confusion around what is and is not a think tank stems from the various ways in which these institutions immerse themselves in the policy-making process. Think tanks, like interest groups and lobbyists, rely on both public and private channels to convey ideas to policy-makers and to the public. They organize speakers' series, conferences, seminars and workshops; use social media to keep followers up to date on their most recent projects; give interviews to the print, broadcast and electronic media; encourage their researchers to testify before legislative committees; and circulate newsletters, policy briefs, blogs and other publications that are accessible to diverse audiences. In short, much of what think tanks do resembles the types of activities undertaken by interest groups. Still, there are some notable differences.

First, while policy experts at think tanks conduct research on issues that are often directly relevant to the work of some interest groups, their objective is not to represent the concerns of any particular constituency. Moreover, as noted, unlike interest groups and the political action committees (PACs) and super PACS with whom they interact, think tanks do not publicly support or oppose candidates running for office, or donate funds to political campaigns and/ or to the war chests of political parties. As discussed, in exchange for charitable status, they are prohibited from participating in these and related activities. In addition, think tanks do not become involved in mass demonstrations and protests; circulate petitions; engage in letter writing campaigns that target members of the executive and legislature; monitor and publicize the voting records of legislators; or publicly align themselves with other organized interests, tactics commonly employed by interest groups.

The confusion over what is and isn't a think tank becomes murkier when we introduce lobbyists and lobbying firms into the equation. If scholars agreed that think tanks simply think and lobbyists lobby, there would be little need to engage in further discussion. But the reality is that think tanks do more than think. As part of their ongoing efforts to shape public opinion and public policy, experts from think tanks meet regularly with elected and appointed officials and their staff at all levels and in all branches of government. Staff from think tanks discuss various policy issues with government officials over drinks; invite them to participate in think tank-sponsored conferences, workshops and seminars, including sessions organized to educate incoming members of Congress about pressing domestic and foreign policy concerns; and provide them with the expertise they need to navigate their way through complex policy problems. In exchange for large donations, some American think tanks, including the Atlantic Council, the Center for Global Development, the Brookings Institution and the Heritage Foundation, will also make arrangements for individuals representing foreign governments and private sector interests at home and abroad to meet and interact with top US government officials (Lipton, Williams and Confessore 2014). In these and other ways, think tanks help to facilitate the access of donors to government officials. How is this different from lobbying?

The difference is that, as charitable organizations, think tanks may only devote a limited amount of time and resources to lobbying. Unlike the lobbying performed by professional lobbyists who are paid handsomely to influence policy-makers, lobbying by think tanks constitutes only one of the many functions they perform. Yet, by some accounts, think tanks are beginning to pay far more attention to this lucrative aspect of their work. At the very least, the relationship between think tanks and lobbyists is becoming more incestuous. As pointed out, investigative journalists Brooke Williams and Ken Silverstein (2013) recently revealed that dozens of think tank scholars working at high profile American think tanks also manage their own lobbying firms. While moonlighting as a lobbyist might not be considered illegal, it raises serious ethical and conflict-of-interest issues about the nature and degree of interaction between think tank staffers and policy-makers. Moreover, in a recent exposé, Lipton, Williams and Confessore documented the formal agreements several foreign governments have brokered with prominent Washington-based think tanks to lobby on behalf of their interests (2014). Their investigative research will undoubtedly attract the attention of the IRS, and will once again call into question the priorities of think tanks. It has already attracted the attention of several members of Congress, including Representative Jackie Speier (D-Ca), who, shortly after the report about foreign government funding of think tanks was released, submitted a proposal that would require all think tank scholars testifying before Congress to disclose their sources of funding. The proposal "won immediate bipartisan endorsement" and was passed into law on 5 January 2015 (US House of Representatives 2015).

It is not surprising that policy experts who work at think tanks inside the Beltway are attracted to the world of lobbying. In fact, before taking up residence at one of the many think tanks in or around the nation's capital, some of them will have spent years on Capitol Hill, in the White House and/or in the bureaucracy. Along with this experience, policy experts at think tanks generally possess an intimate knowledge of the inner workings of government, and have strong connections to those in positions of power. With this background, becoming a lobbyist makes perfect sense, and explains why think tank staffers looking to embark on a new career path often find gainful employment with lobbying companies, law firms or government relations firms that assist clients as they maneuver their way through the policy-making process.

Once again, though, it is important to point out that lobbying and government relations firms should not masquerade as think tanks. For example, Hillwatch, Global Public Affairs and Policy Concepts represent a handful of the government relations companies in Canada that offer a wide range of advocacy and communications services to clients, including advising them on how various bills in parliament could affect their financial interests, but they rarely distinguish themselves as leaders in policy research.

Understanding what constitutes and does not constitute a think tank is vital to our discussion surrounding two of the key functions public policy institutes perform – research and advocacy. But as discussed, equally important is acknowledging the differences and similarities between think tanks, interest groups, lobbyists and government relations firms. Although each of these organizations warrant far more consideration, it is important to return to the issue at hand. Thus far, we have touched on the rise of advocacy think tanks, and the challenge policy institutes ostensibly have in achieving a balance between research and advocacy. One of the questions we have yet to address is what accounts for the popularity of advocacy-oriented think tanks in the US and around the globe?

Why are advocacy think tanks so popular?

In light of the meteoric rise of the Heritage Foundation and its perceived influence in Washington policy-making circles, it is not surprising that advocacy think tanks have emerged in large numbers throughout the US and in virtually every country and region of the world. Indeed, Republican Senator Jim DeMint's decision to vacate his senate seat in 2013 to assume the presidency of the Heritage Foundation confirmed what many Washington insiders have long believed – that some think tanks are better positioned and equipped to effect policy change than key government institutions (Abelson 2014b). However, while think tanks throughout the international community have tried to emulate the success of prominent US think tanks, they have come to the realization that few institutes have the resources and political connections Heritage enjoys. They have also come to realize that few other political systems could facilitate the ascendancy of think tanks in the way the US has. Having said that, think tanks in Asia, Africa, the Middle East and in much of Europe continue to look to the US think tank community for guidance on how to generate and disseminate policy ideas.

Think tanks both in the US and beyond its shores generally recognize that the formula adopted by advocacy think tanks works. Even the Brookings Institution, which, for decades, has nurtured a reputation as a research institution known for delivering "quality, independence, and impact," has drawn on Heritage's play book to boost its profile. In recent years, its scholars have become far more sophisticated in interacting with journalists, and have come to appreciate the importance of using social media, blogs, and other forms of communication to reach their intended target audiences.

The emphasis advocacy think tanks place on communicating ideas in a clear, accessible and timely manner also appeals to donors looking to support institutions capable of influencing the political climate. Philanthropic foundations, corporations and individual donors have invested hundreds of millions of dollars in think tanks in the US, Europe and many other regions. And in return, they expect think tanks to promote a set of ideas that will help advance their core interests. As organizations that straddle the academic and policy-making worlds, think tanks have proven to be a wise investment for countless donors. This may explain not only the proliferation of think tanks worldwide, but their low mortality rate. Although some think tanks have re-invented themselves, few have been forced to close their doors. Those that have include the Ottawa-based North South Institute, which had to because it depended far too heavily on government support. This is one of the many reasons why think tanks seek a diverse funding base.

In *Field of Dreams,* the movie adaptation of W. P. Kinsella's novel about the legendary baseball player Shoeless Joe Jackson (Chicago White Sox), Ray Kinsella (played by Kevin Costner) heard a haunting voice that told him "if you build it, he will come." After converting a large portion of his Iowa cornfield into a baseball diamond, they eventually did come. Several famous ballplayers who had long passed found their way to Kinsella's field to play the game that defined their lives. In a similar vein, although perhaps far less magical, Weyrich and Feulner believed that if they built a think tank that filled an important niche, policy-makers, journalists, academics and donors would come, and they did. The co-founders of Heritage had an innate sense that if think tanks presented the right ideas, to the right people, at the right time, they could have a profound impact on public policy.

Weyrich and Feulner discovered the proper ingredients think tanks required to gain notoriety and visibility. But the question of what priority to assign to research and to advocacy has been difficult for them to determine. As in most cases when inventors experiment with different ingredients, it takes time and plenty of luck to arrive at the right formula, and for Heritage it did not happen overnight. Heritage's success, and that of other think tanks that have followed in its wake, depends on a sound strategy and careful execution. But at times, favourable outcomes also depend on trial and error. Successful think tanks understand the importance of adapting to an ever-changing political environment, and, in recent years, Heritage and other think tanks have positioned themselves to take advantage of a political system that has become increasingly polarized. In the concluding section, we will briefly touch on how think tanks known for the priority they assign to advocacy have capitalized on their key strengths.

Conclusion: Balance, what balance? A new generation of think tanks

At the beginning of the chapter, it was noted that one of the challenges think tanks are thought to face as they compete in the marketplace of ideas is finding an appropriate balance between research and advocacy. However, rather than finding a perfect balance between these two competing forces, our metaphor of the pendulum suggests that think tanks seem to move freely from performing one function to the other. Still, what if think tanks do not believe they can accommodate both functions within the same institution, yet still wish to devote significant resources to performing each? In other words, what if think tanks want the freedom to establish a broad-based research program and engage in extensive partisan activity? We know from our previous discussion that the Income Tax Act in Canada and the Internal Revenue Code in the US impose limits on partisan activity, so what can think tanks do?

In recent years, American think tanks have discovered how to insulate themselves, and the political and legislative activities in which they participate, from the IRS. They create sister organizations to execute their advocacy functions. For instance, in 2005, the Center for American Progress established its sister organization, the Center for American Progress Action Fund, to engage in more lobbying. Since then, other think tanks, including the Heritage Foundation, have followed suit. In 2010, Heritage founded Heritage Action for America, also known as Heritage Action, so that it could expand its legislative activities. Considered social welfare organizations under section 501 (c) (4) of the Internal Revenue Code, these non-profit, tax-exempt entities are able to treat lobbying as their primary activity. Among other things, this designation provides them with far more opportunities to participate in legislative matters than those afforded to their 501 (c) (3) counterparts (Troy 2012). Similarly, in Canada, a few institutes have made a conscious decision not to apply for charitable status so they can engage in more partisan activity. They include the Manning Centre for Building Democracy, founded in Calgary in 2005 by Preston Manning, former leader of the Reform Party of Canada, and the Broadbent Institute, established in Ottawa in 2011 by Ed Broadbent, the long-time leader of the federal New Democratic Party.

With the creation of sister organizations devoted almost entirely to advocacy, American, and to a lesser extent, Canadian, think tanks have found a way to have their cake and eat it too.[7] The organizations with whom they are affiliated have the freedom to focus on various research programs while they figure out the most effective ways to engage in advocacy. The trend toward greater advocacy on the part of think tanks in the US and around the globe is unlikely to diminish. Indeed, if anything, the priority assigned to promoting policy recommendations to multiple stakeholders will become even more pronounced. Think tanks have an insatiable appetite for achieving policy influence, and loyal donors are only too willing to keep their plates full.

As a visionary and policy entrepreneur, Edwin Feulner helped revolutionize the world of think tanks, and for over three decades, observed how the Heritage Foundation and countless other public policy institutes developed and executed a strategy that gave life to the ideas they authored. When he stepped down from the presidency of Heritage, the pendulum he put in motion was in full swing. Feulner's desire to see think tanks engage in both research and advocacy has influenced an entire generation of think tanks; however, it is uncertain if in the years to come they will strive to achieve an appropriate balance between the two. In the end, think tanks, like corporations, are committed to maximizing their performance. And while the goal of think tanks is not to enhance their profit margin, they remain determined to acquire and accumulate an even more valuable currency – influence. If they believe they can achieve this by generating path-breaking policy research, think tanks will undoubtedly allocate more resources to this key function. On the other hand, if they are convinced that the policy influence they covet can most effectively be secured through advocacy, think tanks will chart a rather different course. Feulner's pendulum moves aggressively and often seamlessly in both directions.

Notes

1 Private correspondence.
2 The requirements for charitable organizations under the Income Tax Act may be viewed at http://www.cra-arc.gc.ca/.
3 http://www.cra-arc.gc.ca/chrts-gvng/chrts/plcy/cps/cps-022-eng.html#N101D6.
4 Ibid.
5 Ibid.
6 http://www.irs.gov/Charities-&-Non-Profits/Charitable-Organizations/Exemption-Requirements-Section-501(c)(3)-Organizations.
7 Some organizations in Canada such as the Manning Foundation and the Manning Centre for Building Democracy, both created by former Reform leader Preston Manning, have done this by assigning different functions to each body. While the former, a registered charity, carries out research on various public policy issues, the latter engages in extensive partisan activities. The Broadbent Institute, named for former federal NDP leader Ed Broadbent, like the Manning Centre for Building Democracy, made a conscious decision not to register as a charitable organization so it could engage in more overt partisanship.

References

Abelson, Donald E. 1995. "From Policy Research to Political Advocacy: The Changing Role of Think Tanks in American Politics." *Canadian Review of American Studies* 25, no. 1: 93–126.
Abelson, Donald E. 1996. *American Think Tanks and their Role in US Foreign Policy.* London and New York: Macmillan and St Martin's Press.
Abelson, Donald E. 2014a. "National Interest or Self-Interest? Advocacy Think Tanks, 9/11, and the Future of North American Security." In Jonathan Paquin and Patrick James (eds), *Game Changer: The Impact of 9/11 on North American Security.* Vancouver: UBC Press, 175–92.
Abelson, Donald E. 2014b. "Changing Minds, Changing Course: Obama, Think Tanks and American Foreign Policy." In Inderjeet Parmar, Linda B. Miller and Mark Ledwidge (eds), *Obama and the World: New Directions in US Foreign Policy.* 2nd edition. London: Routledge, 107–19.
Edwards, Lee. 1997. *The Power of Ideas: The Heritage Foundation at 25 Years.* Ottawa, Illinois: Jameson Books.
Edwards, Lee. 2013. *Leading the Way: The Story of Ed Feulner and the Heritage Foundation.* New York: Crown Forum.
Heatherly, Charles L. (ed.). 1981. *Mandate for Leadership: Policy Management in a Conservative Administration.* Washington, DC: Heritage Foundation.
Herrnstein, Richard J. and Charles Murray. 1996. *The Bell Curve: Intelligence and Class Structure in American Life.* New York: Simon and Schuster.

Lipton, Eric, Brooke Williams and Nicholas Confessore. 2014. "Foreign Powers Buy Influence at Think Tanks." *New York Times*, 6 September. Available at http://www.nytimes.com/2014/09/07/us/politics/foreign-powers-buy-influence-at-think-tanks.html?_r=0.

Troy, Tevi. 2012. "Devaluing the Think Tank." *National Affairs* 10 (Winter): 75–90.

US House of Representatives. 2015. "House Resolution 5." 114th Congress, 1st Session, 5 January.

Weaver, R. Kent. 1989. "The Changing World of Think Tanks." *PS: Political Science and Politics* 22, no. 2 (September): 563–78.

Williams, Brooke, and Ken Silverstein. 2013. "Meet the Think Tank Scholars Who Are also Beltway Lobbyists." *New Republic*, 10 May.

3 Blending advocacy and research
The attributes and brand identities of the foremost human rights advocacy think tanks

Stephen Brooks and Pinar Cil

Introduction

The term *think tank* seems to have made its first appearance during World War II when it was used to describe a secure location where plans and strategy could be discussed. By the 1960s, the term came to be used in the US to describe non-governmental research organizations whose aim was to generate policy advice. The phenomenon of think tanks, however, pre-dates considerably the emergence of the term. Indeed, some argue that the prototype of the think tank is found in the British Fabian Society, going back to the late 19th century. The Carnegie Endowment for International Peace (1910) and the Brookings Institution (1916), followed by the Royal Institute for International Affairs (1920, now known as Chatham House) and the Council on Foreign Relations (1921), established what was for decades the accepted idea of a think tank. In the words of Diane Stone, a foremost expert on these organizations, think tanks are "relatively autonomous organizations engaged in the research and analysis of contemporary issues independently of government, political parties, and pressure groups." (2001: 15668)

Today there are few who would insist upon such a definition. Much of the explosive growth in the think tank universe during the 1980s and 1990s involved the emergence of organizations whose principle aim was to advance a particular ideological agenda or advocate on behalf of a particular cause or worldview. The idea that think tanks should be independent came to appear increasingly passé. Many of the new think tanks were funded by special interests, thus challenging the purist idea that think tanks should be "relatively autonomous." Some governments created their own think tanks or provided important funding for private ones, ties to the state that the classic definition of think tanks did not accommodate.

Such changes would have been enough to justify a reconsideration of the definition of think tanks. Matters were, however, made even more problematic by the blurring of the lines between research, advocacy, lobbying and journalism. In an increasingly crowded and competitive market, policy idea providers struggle to be relevant and to be able to pay the bills. This has driven many to assume organizational forms and to behave in ways that challenge traditional functional boundaries. Some organized interests have found that assuming attributes of the think tank model increases the credibility of their arguments in the eyes of the public, media and policy-makers. Moreover, the revolutionary changes that have taken place in communications technology over the past couple of decades, especially the rise of social media, have contributed to the blurring of boundaries between what might be called classic think tanks – those that conform to older definitions of the term – and the plethora of hybrid organizations that have joined them.

In this chapter, we will examine four human rights organizations that began life as advocacy groups, but that regularly appear toward the top end of the Global Go To Index of most prominent thinks. They are Amnesty International (AI), Transparency International (TI), International Crisis Group (ICG) and Human Rights Watch (HRW). The 2014 Global Index ranked them 11th, 12th, 21st and 47th, respectively, among the world's top think tanks. Among think tanks with a focus on foreign policy and international affairs, TI was ranked 13th, ICG 23rd and HRW 42nd. In the field of transparency and good governance, all four of these organizations were ranked in the top ten, with TI 1st, AI 2nd, HRW 4th and ICG 10th. Finally, evaluated according to expert perceptions of think tank advocacy campaigns, AI (1st), TI (2nd) and HRW (3rd), were at the top of the table, ICG ranking 9th.

These four organizations are important parts of what Keck and Sikkink call *transnational advocacy networks*. They define these as "networks of activists, distinguishable largely by the centrality of ideas or values in motivating their formation." (1998: 1) Such networks are part of a larger process of the transnationalization of civil society whose pace has accelerated in recent years. The activities of AI, HRW, ICG and TI have been significant drivers of this process. Indeed, more than the impact that any one of them has had on particular policies or conflicts, it is arguable that their most profound influence has been on ideas of state sovereignty, human rights and the processes and architecture of global governance.

AI, HRW, ICG and TI comprise what might be called the "Big Four" of transnational advocacy think tanks. Each organization has become something of a brand in the world of international human rights. We begin with profiles of each organization, including their histories. Their original structures and aims did not conform to the classical idea of thinks tanks, or at least only quite imperfectly. Their strong advocacy origins and missions have been retained, but over time they have acquired attributes that place them solidly within the contemporary understanding of what a think tank is. Indeed, we argue that they have been among the advocacy organizations that have been most influential in shaping current thinking about think tanks and what makes them influential. We also examine the particular activities and attributes of each organization that have contributed to its reputation as one of the world's most prominent think tanks. These activities and attributes, we will see, involve significant blurring of the traditional lines that separated think tanks from lobbyists, journalists and advocacy groups.

Profiles

1. Transparency International

Twentieth-century American jurist William O. Douglas famously coined the phrase, "Sunlight is the best disinfectant." (quoted in Brandeis and Hapgood

2009: 62) Indeed, exposing the cracks of corruption is a necessary precondition to living in a free and just society. However, the very notion of tackling corruption was taboo even in the early 1990s, the era which saw the arrival of Berlin-based NGO, TI. Born out of the impassioned efforts of former "grey suits" (de Sousa 2005: 22) from the World Bank, TI is the leading non-profit NGO devoted to fighting corruption and to promoting transparency and accountability worldwide. Present in over 100 countries, TI's governance structure includes an ever-expanding network of autonomous national chapters (NCs); an international secretariat that supports the NCs and represents TI on the world stage; 30 individual members who provide the secretariat with expertise and support; an international board of directors, which is elected by NC representatives at the annual meetings and an advisory council, which provides the board with recommendations and practical assistance for TI's programs overall.

TI can trace its origins back to its founding member, Peter Eigen. As a World Bank executive in East Africa during the late 1980s, Eigen (2008: 22) witnessed first-hand the destructive nature of corruption in developing economies. He soon realized, however, that political expediency often drove the bank to turn a blind eye on the corrupt practices of member states and their elites. What began as "a minor discomfort with the incentives and modes of operation within the World Bank gradually developed into a significant aggravation." (Eigen 2008: 22) Faced with dismissive responses to addressing corruption, Eigen decided to end his 25-year career at the World Bank and launch an organization of his own, one that would focus on stopping rampant corruption on a global scale. In May 1993, with the support of former colleagues and friends, Eigen spearheaded the young TI in his native Berlin.

Since its inception, TI's guiding principles have rested upon three key tenets: (1) cooperation over confrontation, (2) local presence as a force multiplier and (3) holistic integrity assessments. First, TI does not actively investigate and expose individual cases of corruption. Unlike NGOs such as AI or HRW, TI is not typically in the business of naming and shaming, and instead exercises "quiet diplomacy." (Bonner 1996) As a coalition-builder, TI engages with a variety of actors who have been affected by – or involved in – corruption in order to better understand modern practices. Because corrupt activities tend to be done covertly, TI depends on the cooperation and information of others (Wang and Rosenau 2001: 38). Since TI's primary objective is to raise awareness about corruption, an investigatory function would thus deflect from that stated mission, and discourage governments and corporations from cooperating with TI on implementing reforms. It must be noted that while TI does not assume an investigatory role, it supports whistleblowers, journalists and other civil society members who expose and denounce corruption. For instance, the TI Integrity Awards offer a prime example of TI's recognition of individuals who engage in anticorruption activism. Second, TI seeks to mobilize local "know-how" and community engagement within each of its NCs. For founder Peter Eigen (2008: 26), TI was never intended to act like the Catholic Church or the World Bank, "preaching and dictating from the center." Since the NCs are independently registered, they are able to set their own agendas and governance structures. However, as Luis de Sousa (2005: 21) points out, the typical NC does not operate like a research center or think tank, but rather like a "hub of contacts.... It knows where to get the information and expertise from, but does not develop research capabilities of its own." Moreover, the relationship between the internationally oriented secretariat and the localized NCs can be best described as "symbiotic." (Norad 2010: xiii) While the secretariat's authority derives from the NCs, the NCs in turn "carry more weight in their own countries because they are part of a wider international movement." (Norad 2010: xiii) Third, as part of their holistic approach to assessing the extent and cause of corruption in a given country, TI has adopted the National Integrity System (NIS) concept (Eigen 2008: 26). From governments to civil society groups to the business community, the NIS concept evaluates a variety of institutions for their propensity for corruption in three aspects of society: the rule of law, social development and quality of life.

In order to practice this kind of targeted advocacy, TI employs a number of diagnostic and awareness-raising tools in its anticorruption arsenal. The most noteworthy of these tools is the Corruption Perceptions Index (CPI). While its release in 1995 was unintentional (Eigen 2008: 31) – an intern had leaked a draft index to the German magazine *Der Spiegel* – the CPI immediately put the fledgling TI on the map and has become inseparable from the TI brand. We discuss the CPI is some detail later in this chapter

Although the fight against corruption extends beyond TI, a quick look at TI's literature makes frequent references to "our movement." Yet, is TI a movement on its own? Wang and Rosenau (2001: 39) suggest otherwise, arguing that the organization is more a "network of like-minded elites" than a social movement. Given the hidden nature of corruption, they conclude that it is in fact difficult to assess any real progress on this front. As a result, "it is hard for potential participants to know that they have made a difference... the logic of large-scale collective action breaks down." (Wang and Rosenau 2001: 39) Luis de Sousa (2005: 27) also concurs with this view, stating that TI's "decision to constitute single national units has more to do with its founding fathers' lack of understanding of how a civil society movement ought to look and operate than a product of a carefully thought and designed strategy of membership."

Regardless of criticism, TI's work over the years has contributed to at least three international conventions, namely the landmark UN Convention against Corruption (2003), the OECD Anti-Bribery Convention (1997) and the African Union Convention on Preventing and Combating Corruption (2003). Even TI's former detractors have recognized its merits, most notably the World Bank. In a major policy shift in 1996, then President James Wolfensohn declared war on the "cancer of corruption," acknowledging that it was indeed an economic problem (Eigen 2008: 20). While TI may not be a robust corruption watchdog, its reputation precedes it to be "the most prominent 'corruption fighter' at the global level." (de Sousa 2005: 27)

2. International Crisis Group

What TI is to anticorruption, the ICG is to conflict prevention and its resolution. Established in 1995 as an independent, non-profit NGO, the ICG grew from "a two-person office in London, and a tiny field staff in the Balkans and West Africa" to "the world's leading source of information, analysis and policy advice on preventing and resolving deadly conflict." (Bliesemann de Guevara 2014: 616) Through its headquarters in Brussels, four advocacy offices (New York City, Washington DC, London and Moscow) and 31 field offices worldwide, the ICG employs an experienced mix of analysts, who range from former diplomats to journalists to academics. Based on the seriousness of a situation and the organization's capacity to ensure effective reporting and follow-through, ICG analysts cover up to 70 countries and areas of ongoing or potential conflict.

The ICG was not always a global player. Harking back to the 1990s, during the war in the former Yugoslavia, the ICG was born out of the deliberations of two prominent individuals who lamented the international community's failure in the Balkans and elsewhere. On a chance flight from war-torn Sarajevo, the two men – Morton Abramowitz (then President of the Carnegie Endowment for International Peace) and Mark Malloch Brown (then World Bank Vice President for External Affairs and later Deputy Secretary General of the UN) – discussed the creation of an organization that would, in the words of former US President Bill Clinton, be "the eyes, the ears and the conscience of the global community." (ICG 2008: 3) With the help of American engineer Fred Cuny, philanthropist George Soros and US Senator George Mitchell, among others, the ICG finally came to fruition in 1995.

According to ICG President Emeritus Gareth Evans, the organization's initial focus was on "building a presence in, and energizing an effective policy response to, the ongoing crisis in the Balkans." (Evans 2012) Louise Arbour, then Chief Prosecutor of the International Criminal Tribunal for the Former Yugoslavia (1996–99) and later ICG President (2009–14), also noted the ICG's strong presence in the region, calling it "the first port of call" for anyone working in the Balkans at the time (ICG 2010: 1). Toward the latter half of the 1990s and well into the 21st century, the ICG moved into an era of rapid expansion, "from a strong Balkans and very small African focus to a genuinely global one." (Evans 2012) It moved its headquarters from London to Brussels, partly in a bid to shrug off its Anglo-American roots, but also to extend its fundraising reach. (Evans 2012) The organization also increased in size, growing from just over 20 staff members in 1999 to more than 130 in 2015.

The ICG's *modus operandi* includes three basic elements: (1) field-based research and analysis, (2) practical policy prescriptions and (3) high-level advocacy. First, the ICG provides updated, expert reports on areas where there is concern for an outbreak, recurrence, or escalation of violence (Bliesemann de Guevara 2014: 546). Objective field analyses not only help governments and intergovernmental organizations better understand the nuances of any given conflict or situation, but also reinforce the ICG's credibility among policy-makers. In fact, WikiLeaks cables suggest that ICG reports are widely used in US embassies (Bliesemann de Guevara 2014: 560). Second, ICG analysts provide governments with policy solutions that aim to de-escalate and resolve a particular situation. That is, the ICG translates its analytical field research "into policy prescriptions that are both imaginative and practical – identifying levers and tools that can be used, and the actors, local and international, best placed to use them." (Evans 2012) Finally, the organization complements its research and recommendations with effective, high-level advocacy. By virtue of its elite board of trustees, the ICG is able to engage with decision-makers at the highest level possible. ICG certainly is not the only advocacy group to have very well connected and well known people on its board, but it is fair to say that no group has greater elite representation.

In addition to the over 80 reports and briefing papers published annually, the ICG's Brussels Research Unit produces *CrisisWatch*, a monthly bulletin providing succinct updates on ongoing or potential conflicts around the world. Launched in 2003, *CrisisWatch* has become, in the ICG's own words, one of its "most valued products" (ICG 2010: 30) over the years. Intended as an early warning mechanism, *CrisisWatch* draws on multiple sources to summarize and assess roughly 70 cases worldwide to alert readers to situations where there is indeed a risk of conflict or opportunities for conflict resolution. Its audience includes a diverse set of readers, including politicians, diplomats, policy-makers, humanitarian workers, activists, entrepreneurs and the media, as well as the general public.

It is difficult to categorize ICG. Unlike other human rights organization, ICG is "not adverse to recommending international military intervention to end conflicts." (ICG 2010: 15) On the basis that nearly half of its budget is derived from national governments, Greg Simons (2014: 587) likens the ICG to "a non-profit government research contractor." Gareth Evans argues that of the "thinkers," "talkers" and "doers" in the NGO world, "Crisis Group is best thought of as a rather distinctive combination of all three categories." It perennially ranks high in the University of Pennsylvania's annual McGann assessment of the world's top think tanks, but ICG's predominantly field-based methodology involve forms of research and analysis that are not typical of think tanks. It is also not an advocacy campaign organization along the lines of AI. Lastly, the ICG is not a purely operational organization either; despite its strong field presence, it does not, for example, directly engage in mediation between warring parties. In the end, regardless of how one categorizes the ICG, it has established itself as a foremost go-to organization in the eyes of the media, policy-makers and the attentive public on issues of conflict throughout the world.

3. Human Rights Watch

Risking life and limb for the greater good, members of a special force embark on perilous missions to ensure justice for all. This is not Marvel's Avengers, nor is it The A-Team, but rather The E-Team – members of HRW's Emergencies Division, who investigate human rights violations in conflict-ridden areas around the world. Indeed, not many NGOs can boast of having a Netflix original documentary profiling their top researchers in the field. In fact, however, HRW's activities extend beyond the grit and crusading efforts of the E-Team. Its staff of about 400 persons engage in targeted advocacy and field research worldwide. HRW seeks to promote and defend human rights in accordance with the

Universal Declaration of Human Rights and international law. Since 1993, the New York-based monitoring group has been headed by Kenneth Roth, a former US federal prosecutor who previously worked on the Iran-Contra affair (Watson 2004: 442). Through independent fact-finding missions, HRW monitors governmental compliance with civil, political, cultural, social and economic rights (with greater emphasis on the former two). Furthermore, the organization reminds private enterprises of their social-corporate responsibilities and exposes corporations involved in human rights abuses. In moments of acute crisis, HRW also provides timely updates about the conflicts as they are unfolding (HRW 2015).

HRW has gone by several different names since its inception in 1978. In fact, the organization can trace its roots back to the Cold War era, with the formation of the US Helsinki Watch Committee, at the time known simply as Helsinki Watch (HW) (Slezkine 2014: 346). Originally established as a private American NGO, HW monitored government compliance with parts of the 1975 Helsinki Accords, which sought to minimize Cold War tensions by recognizing the USSR's territorial gains in Europe post-World War II (Watson 2004: 443). Even in the organization's early days, HW adopted a "naming and shaming" methodology where it denounced Soviet bloc governments over their treatment of Eastern bloc dissidents. With an initial $400,000 grant from the Ford Foundation, HW's strong American connection during the Cold War was a challenge to its credibility. However, as Alison Watson notes, the early beginnings of HRW must be viewed "as part of the process of détente and the growing need for the Soviet bloc to have access to Western trade and investment. Human rights concessions, or at least lip service to them, were made in return for access to Western markets." (2004: 443; see also Ignatieff 2002)

Similar to the ICG's expansion trajectory, HRW's focus moved away from Eastern Europe during the first decade of its existence. The 1980s saw the emergence of "The Watch Committees", which included, in addition to the flagship Helsinki Watch (1978), Americas Watch (1981), Asia Watch (1985), Africa Watch (1988) and Middle East Watch (1989). In 1988, the Watch committees officially combined into the umbrella organization, as we know it today – HRW. Watson (2004: 444) argues that HRW's chapter expansion significantly altered the organization's scope on the types of victims it sought to defend. For example, rather than solely focus on the plight of political prisoners, HRW started championing the rights of apolitical prisoners as well, from women and children to refugees and victims of caste discrimination. The organization turned its attention to human rights abuses by non-state actors as well. "In this way, issues such as the laying of land-mines or the use of child soldiers by rebel groups were highlighted." (Watson: 444) Therefore, the organization's rapid expansion resulted in greater rights-based advocacy for vulnerable groups in society – a key research and advocacy focus that endures to this day.

Similar to the other NGOs explored in this chapter, HRW's staff consists of journalists, lawyers, humanitarian activists and academics of diverse backgrounds and nationalities. (Unlike other NGOs, however, HRW's staff tends to be devoid of former politicians and diplomats.) Members of HRW's staff work in divisions organized by geographical area – Africa (Sub-Saharan); the Americas (Latin America and the Caribbean); Asia; Europe and Central Asia; and the Middle East and North Africa. In addition to these geographic desks, HRW runs programs on thematic issues, such as the rights of women, children, refugees and members of the LGBT community; the arms trade; academic and press freedom; religious freedoms; international justice; HIV/AIDS and human rights; and the role of multinational corporations in a human rights context.

As previously mentioned, much of HRW's work surrounds its hallmark fact-finding missions and in-person interviews in conflict zones. Based on these interactions, HRW publishes more than 100 reports and briefings per year, examining the human rights conditions in some 90 countries. Relying on local and international media to galvanize support and effectively broadcast these abuses, HRW relies on this publicity to openly "name and shame" governments. In a way, HRW argues that by using public condemnation as leverage, it is able to "appeal to those in power who often have ties to the very socioeconomic structures that are responsible for the oppression in the first place." (Watson 2004: 446) HRW meets with government officials, the UN, regional groups such as the African Union and the EU, financial institutions, and corporations to press for reforms in human rights policy and practice on a macro level. According to HRW, refugee accounts in its public naming and shaming campaigns "helped shape the response of the international community to recent wars in Kosovo and Chechnya." (Carnegie Council [undated]) Such tactics cannot be successful without credible research and field-based evidence As Robert Blitt (2004: 291) warns, "the mobilization of shame – and consequently leverage politics generally – can be disconnected from the elemental need for verifiable evidence, a crucial prerequisite for any legitimate form of criticism."

4. Amnesty International

Of all the organizations explored in this chapter, AI undoubtedly comes closest to being the embodiment of a movement. For more than 50 years AI has promulgated the notion that ordinary people can demand action and meaningful change. From public rallies to letter-writing campaigns to sending tweets across the Twitterverse, over seven million supporters around the world have joined the "AI movement" in calling for the recognition of international human rights in a number of contexts. AI's mission has primarily revolved around human rights advocacy, specifically exposing violations of physical and mental integrity, freedom of conscience and expression, and freedom from discrimination in all its forms (AI Toronto Organization 2015). Far from being a conventional think tank, AI is an NGO that acts as a global watchdog by denouncing human rights violators. Through lobbying efforts in both the governmental and business realms, AI has sought to pressure various powerbrokers into recognizing their international legal obligations. In 1977 AI was awarded the Nobel Peace Prize, joining the ranks of other notable organizations including the International Committee of the Red Cross.

The history of AI dates back to 1960 when two Portuguese students were arrested for raising a toast to freedom in a Lisbon restaurant. The incident came to the attention of English lawyer Peter Benenson who expressed outrage: "Perhaps because I am particularly attached to liberty, perhaps because I am fond of wine, this news-item produced a righteous indignation in me that transcended normal bounds." (quoted in Buchanan 2002: 575) In 1961 Benenson decided to write an appeal for the students in the British weekend review, *The Observer*. The article, aptly entitled "The Forgotten Prisoners," was reprinted in several newspapers around the world, launching an international call to action for amnesty for the imprisoned students. According to AI, the wave of support among the general public did not simply "give birth to an extraordinary movement," but represented "the start of extraordinary social change." (AI 2015) Moreover, Benenson's article was the first to coin the term "prisoner of conscience," which he defined as "any person who is physically restrained (by imprisonment or otherwise) from expressing (in any form of words or symbols) an opinion which he honestly holds and which does not advocate or condone personal violence." (Benenson 1961) Following the 1963 release by Communist authorities of Ukrainian Archbishop Josyf Slipyi, AI made it a key plank of its mandate to champion the rights of prisoners of conscience worldwide.

Since its initial focus on prisoners and political dissidents, AI has embraced a variety of other global causes. In 1972 the organization launched its campaign against the commission of torture, which eventually contributed to the UN Convention Against Torture in 1984. AI has also been a vocal agent in the movement against the death penalty as well as a key interlocutor in the 2002 establishment of both the International Criminal Court and the global Arms Trade Treaty in 2014. In recent years, AI has moved beyond traditional human rights issues, at times sparking controversy with its policies. For example, in 2015, AI endorsed the decriminalization of the sex trade, prompting criticism from women's rights groups, who held that full decriminalization would legitimize brothel owners and pimps (*The Guardian* 2015b). Another contemporary issue relates to the overwhelming trend of western governments enacting counterterrorism legislation without proper regard for human rights and civil liberties, particularly since 9/11. In Canada, for example, AI was highly critical of the Conservative government's controversial 2015 anti-terrorism legislation, Bill C-51, which substantially increased the powers of the country's intelligence services and law enforcement with what critics charged was little to no oversight or added review mechanisms (Jessica Murphy 2015). AI Canada's call to action against C-51 succeeded, according to some commentators, in influencing public opinion. It was also instrumental in bringing the matter before an international audience and to the attention of the UN Human Rights Committee. In July 2015 the committee issued a report that highlighted what it said was the bill's lack of civilian oversight and noted that such deficiencies would indeed lead to human rights violations (Wählen 2015).

In addition to the organization's growing list of activities and achievements, AI's operational structure has also evolved since the 1960s, shifting from a concentrated

London HQ to regional offices located in more than 70 countries. The international secretariat[1] in London, however, remains an integral organ of the AI movement, carrying out research and reporting, overseeing AI's financial health and ensuring a unitary voice on the global stage. To better monitor human rights abuses in the modern era, AI has also adopted new technological tools, such as a smartphone app that serves as a "personal 'panic button' for activists at daily risk of being arrested or detained." (AI 2015) Finally, in comparison with other NGOs, AI's financial resources are impressive, due largely to its demonstrated ability to fundraise at a grassroots level. Although AI claims that it maintains neutrality in its human rights work and does not accept any government funding, NGO Monitor disputes this claim. It charges that AI has indeed received funds from states and governmental bodies, including the US, the European Commission, the UK Department for International Development, the Netherlands and Norway (NGO Monitor 2015).

Making an impact

1. Transparency International

Although TI was not the first advocacy organization to publish an annual index ranking countries on their human rights performance, its CPI, launched in 1995, very quickly became one of the best known of such indexes. Freedom House was one of the pioneers of such an index; its Freedom in the World rankings of political rights and civil liberties started in 1972. Before the launching of TI's annual index, however, such annual indices were relatively few and for the most part received little global attention. The success of TI's CPI in attracting attention to the scale and human consequences of political and business corruption raised the profile of TI. It immediately became the go-to organization for journalists and policy-makers wanting information and analyses of such issues, which made it much easier for the organization to raise the money necessary to carry out its activities. Any assessment of TI's impact as an advocacy think tank must, we believe, focus mainly on the CPI and how various constituencies and interests react to it.

Imitation, the saying goes, is the sincerest form of flattery. TI's index has been emulated by many organizations, adapted to their particular rights focus. Among these indexes are the Index of Economic Freedom, a collaboration of the Heritage Foundation and the *Wall Street Journal*, published since 1995; the Press Freedom Index, published annually since 2002 by Reporters Without Borders; the Democracy Index, published by the Economist Intelligence Unit since 2006; and the Index of Freedom in the World, a collaboration launched by the Cato Institute, Canada's Fraser Institute and Germany's Liberales Institut in 2012. We do not mean to suggest that in any or all of these cases the only or even principal reason for the creation of an index as a part of an organization's annual activities cycle was the rather immediate and astounding success of TI's index. Indeed, the Economic Freedom Index was launched in the same year as the Corruption Perception Index. Nevertheless, it is probably fair to say that none of these other indices is as identified with the organization that publishes it as is the CPI. It is only a slight exaggeration that it is crucial to the TI brand. Moreover, none of these other human rights indices have generated as much critical reaction as TI's.

That reaction has come from two very different corners. One involves the human rights advocacy community and social science methodologists with an interest in human rights issues. These criticisms – in some cases they are better described as reservations and cautions – began almost as soon as the CPI was released. They boil down to this: the CPI measures the *perception* of corruption and is thus a "proxy for reality." (Andersson and Heywood 2009: 762) Indeed, these criticisms of the CPI are remarkably similar to those often leveled against the Global Go To Index discussed in the first chapter of this book. Expert surveys are prone to charges of sample bias. As Alex Cobham argues, the problem is not that the panels of experts surveyed for the annual CPI do not include people qualified to render an expert judgment on the levels of corruption in the countries about which they are asked. The problem is one of sample bias. Cobham (2013) writes,

> There is a striking commonality in the people whose perceptions are actually assessed. . . . The opinions of an internationally focused elite, typically from a corporate background and perhaps a similar education, may be particularly informative in certain circumstances. . . . But do these sources, when aggregated, produce a broader truth about the public's experience of corruption in a given country?

Other criticisms of the CPI methodology argue that it has embedded in it cultural and specifically western biases (Brown and Cloke 2011); that the focus appears to be on bribe-takers rather than bribe-givers (Andersson and Heywood 2009: 753); and that TI and its CPI are inextricably linked to a neo-liberal agenda of international capitalism, embodied in such institutions as the World Bank and the IMF (Jonathan Murphy 2011). Even the world's elite press has begun to ask questions about the validity of the CPI, *The Economist* (2010) going so far as to refer to it as a "murk meter" and to suggest that TI should either "ditch its score-card, or at least publish it in a less misleading form." Notwithstanding such criticisms, those in the media continue to eagerly await the annual release of the CPI and dutifully report its rankings. Moreover, it remains the case that academic research on corruption and governance routinely cites and takes seriously the CPI assessments.

Indeed, it is precisely because the CPI continues to be considered the gold standard for assessing corruption that the second negative reaction to TI's brand index has arisen. It comes from political and other elites in some of the countries that appear to believe that they have been unfairly judged by the CPI. It may be a compliment to TI rather than a black mark against it that such countries as China, Russia and Kuwait have been heavily critical of their rankings in the CPI. In 2015 Russia's Institute of Law and Comparative Jurisprudence went so far as to create an alternative to what Russian authorities regularly charged were the CPI's inaccurate, subjective and biased assessments (Radio Free Europe/Radio Liberty

2015). That same year the government of Kuwait closed down the country's national chapter of TI, describing it as a "dirty tool of the Muslim Brotherhood" and, more generally, because of its "affiliation with international organizations." (HRW: 2015a)

In response to charges that the CPI has elitist, western biases, TI began to publish another corruption perception index in 2003. Its Global Corruption Barometer (GCB) asks samples of the national populations where TI chapters exist to assess the level of corruption in various institutions in their country, including whether they have ever been asked to pay a bribe. The GCB has its own methodological limitations and receives much less attention internationally than the CPI. Proponents of the GCB argue that its main advantage over the CPI may be that it gives domestic policy-makers a sense of their population's willingness to support reform measures and anti-corruption campaigns (Johnsøn 2012).

For better or for worse – the issue has often surfaced at TI's annual meetings – the CPI is central to TI's identity. The criticisms that have been aimed at the CPI are much less well known than the fact that the corruption perception rankings and country profiles produced by TI are considered the benchmark for any serious conversation on corruption in a country. The fact that TI has come to be seen as the organization to turn to for analysis of corruption throughout the world, and the other ways through which it has been able to have an impact on national and international measures that target corruption, surely must be attributed mainly to the renown that the CPI has brought to it.

These other ways through which TI has managed to affect the conversation on corruption and its consequences and to influence state and transnational actions are important. They have been discussed in significant detail by others, perhaps most dispassionately in a 2010 Norwegian government evaluation of TI (Norad 2010). They include integrity pacts (IPs) between governments or state agencies and bidders for government contracts. These IPs are characterized by undertakings by signatories not to pay or accept bribes or in other ways collude in the bidding process, as well as monitoring systems intended to ensure compliance. TI and many of its national chapters have been involved in the development of many IPs, as well as their implementation and monitoring.

Establishing benchmarks for evaluating corporate and business behavior has been one of TI's chief accomplishments. The organization is universally acknowledged to have played a major role in persuading the United Nations to adopt the 10th principle of the UN Global Compact, which states that "Businesses should work against corruption in all its forms, including extortion and bribery." That statement has been followed by concrete guidelines, developed by TI in cooperation with the UN, recommending how corporations should report on corruption in their corporate operating plans. TI has a long record of working with such international organizations as the International Chamber of Commerce, the IMF, the World Bank, national governments and aid agencies in developing transparency and anti-corruption guidelines. It has also inspired the creation of other anti-corruption organizations, such as Global Witness, Global Integrity, the

Extractive Industries Transparency Initiative and Making Integrity Work, organizations with whom TI has often worked in tandem.

With the exception of the UN's 2004 adoption of the 10th principle against corruption, it is difficult to establish a direct causal link between TI's actions and results. "The degree of attribution that is feasible to find between a TI activity and a change in the situation of corruption in a given context is low," observes the 2010 Norwegian evaluation of TI. "Both the wide variety of factors and the confidentiality of much information prevent such [attribution]." (61) The same may be said, of course, for most think tanks and advocacy groups, most of the time. The fact that TI is regularly judged to be among the world's most influential think tanks is not due to specific results but rather to a widely shared belief that, on matters involving transparency and corruption, TI is the foremost authoritative source for expert analysis and advice.

This reputation was achieved and is maintained in large measure through the CPI, clearly the world's most cited measure of how countries stack up when it comes to corruption. It is also kept alive by more specialized indices, such as the Bribe Payers Index, the business survey that reports on corporation officials' views on the prevalence of corruption and measures that ought to be used to deal with it; programs and the large number of annual and issue specific research reports produced by TI and its national chapters. The quality of this research is high, the topics are usually timely (for example, global corruption and climate change in 2011, education in 2013 and sport in 2016) and it is presented in a manner that makes it attractive to policy practitioners and other stakeholders. These are, of course, attributes of research that are essential if a think tank is to achieve and maintain a reputation for influence. The CPI has been key in establishing the TI brand. This brand would quickly lose luster and credibility with policy-makers and others if the quality of TI's research was seen to be shoddy.

One additional factor needs to be mentioned by way of explaining TI's reputation and influence. Since its inception the organization's advisory board has been a virtual who's who of the international political elite, including Nobel Prize winners and many former heads of state and government. Although board members are not involved in the day-to-day operations of TI, they represent a potentially important resource that may be drawn upon in particular circumstances in order to open channels of communication with decision-makers.

Linkages to the international policy-making elite do not stop with TI's advisory council. As discussed earlier in this chapter, TI's founder, Peter Eigen, was a top official with the World Bank who had close personal connections to the international financial and global governance elite. His successor and TI's current head, Cobus de Swardt, is no less well connected. Like Eigen before him, de Swardt has a sharp entrepreneurial sense when it comes to positioning TI at the forefront of the discussion of corruption. This was seen in his interventions on the issue of corruption in the Federation of International Football Associations (FIFA) in 2015, when de Swardt described FIFA as a "sordid empire of corruption."

50 Stephen Brooks and Pinar Cil

This characterization of FIFA was widely cited in the world press and was accompanied by seven recommendations for immediate reform (TI 2015).

2. International Crisis Group

Each of the four advocacy think tanks examined in this chapter has the status of a "brand" and occupies a particular niche in the market for information and policy advice on human rights and good governance. The ICG brand involves front-line reporting and analysis of conflict in its early stages. Of course many think tanks, including some of the world's most prestigious ones such as Brookings, Chatham House and CSIS, are in the business of analyzing international conflicts and making recommendations for their resolution. What is different about ICG – its "value-added" as some have put it (Denmark 2013) – is its presence in the field, where conflict is taking place. "ICG presents itself as unlike 'armchair' think tanks in DC and other Western capitals by way of its presence in the field," says a former ICG field analyst. "This needs to be emphasized as it leads audiences to attribute much more authority to ICG's reports than to others." (quoted in Bliesemann de Guevara 2015a: 551)

A think tank's outputs should not, of course, be interpreted as the measure of its influence. As Garnett and Mabon point out in their discussion of Chatham House in the UK in Chapter 7, no small part of that organization's influence appears to be achieved through back channel meetings and other activities that do not show up in the pages of the annual report and may not be covered in the press. At the same time, however, some outputs may at least suggest the scope and means of a think tank's influence. In the case of the ICG, the organization's annual output is prodigious. In recent years it has produced roughly 60–90 reports annually, covering 40–50 countries per year and including close to 1,000 policy recommendations. Most of the reports published are translated into other languages, the particular language(s) depending on the regional and cultural focus of the report. A typical ICG report will be 15–25 pages in length, although occasionally longer, and begin with an executive summary and recommendations for action. It will also include a map of the country or region that is the subject of the report. References to academic writings are relatively rare in ICG reports. The sources that are relied on include mainly interviews, local media, primary documents, statistics from various international databases and frontline analysis. All of this is consistent with the ICG brand as an organization that eschews "armchair analysis."

Perhaps more tellingly, in terms of potential influence, ICG officials participate in a large number of advocacy meetings each year, including policy roundtables, testimony before legislative committees and private briefing sessions with the EU, the UN Security Council and other transnational organizations. The 2013 Norwegian government evaluation of the ICG placed the number of such meetings in 2012 at over 5,000 (4). Articles published in the world's press is another tool of influence that the ICG relies upon. The number of such articles has declined somewhat over the past few years, from an average of about 200 per year from 2007 through 2012 to roughly 100 per year since then. Many of these articles are in publications read by the policy-making elite and the attentive public, including the *New York Times*, *Le Monde*, *Foreign Policy* and the *Financial Times*. It is hard to interpret the reasons for this decline, but it may simply be that the organization has shifted some of its communications efforts to blogs, social media, the ICG's YouTube channel and its monthly *CrisisWatch*, which is sent to over 30,000 targeted recipients and well as many more subscribers.

As is also true of TI, the ICG's influence is in large measure achieved through focusing a spotlight on particular cases and framing the story about what is happening and why. And, also true of TI although not so much AI and HRW, the elite linkages that exist between ICG's board of trustees and senior advisors and policy-making elites throughout the West is probably a factor that, in some circumstances at least, lends greater heft to ICG's analysis and recommendations. The importance of these linkages are alluded to by the ICG in its explanation of the three basic elements of its approach to conflict identification and resolution. This explanation acknowledges that having the right arguments, backed up by credible research culled from the frontlines of conflict, is important. It then goes on to state that "having the ability to effectively deploy those arguments, with people of the right credibility and capacity," is also part of the recipe for influence

What the ICG proclaims to be a strength, and what is undeniably one of the reasons why, by all accounts, it has had exceptional access to international decision-makers, is seen by others as an important part of what is wrong with the organization. For it is a fact that for all the praise that the ICG has received over the years, it has its detractors. They are the same critics who charge TI with being a tool for the advancement of a "liberal governance agenda" that is supported by the IMF, the World Bank, the US, the EU and members of the "transnational capitalist class" (Robinson 2014) who gather annually at Davos.

At first blush that may appear to be an odd charge. The ICG has often been very critical of the wealthy world's apparent indifference to human catastrophes unfolding in various parts of the world. Moreover, it has regularly criticized the US, the EU and other western governments for what it has believed to be their failure to take the proper steps in a conflict or crisis situation.

In the eyes of some, however, such criticisms have been too infrequent and are far overshadowed by the ICG's role as a legitimizer of western liberal values and institutions (the premise being that this is necessarily a regrettable thing or, at least, culturally insensitive and a modern form of colonialism). Berit Bliesemann de Guevara argues that there is a "tension between the ICG's self-narrative as a corrective to Western governments and politics (hence its emphasis on independence and non-partisanship), while at the same time it is deeply entrenched in Western/ international policy circles through its staff members' formal and informal professional networks and its Board of Trustees." (2015b: 629) Not surprisingly, according to Greg Simons (2014: 593), "the organisation tends to reinforce or agree with the policy proposed by leading (western) countries. . . . This suggests that ICG reporting could be a means to 'legitimise' certain government policies in armed conflict zones, which is helped by the ICG's brand as an 'independent' NGO." This conclusion is shared by Sonja Grigat (2014: 576), who argues that "the ICG contributes to (re-)producing the global discourse on liberal peace and liberal governance." "ICG reporting fulfils a function that transcends the immediate contribution to preventing and resolving violent conflicts," she writes, adding that "ICG publications essentially aim to discursively discipline their audience through practices and procedures characteristic of liberal governance in this specific form of social action and corresponding mind-sets, thus perpetuating liberalism as the global 'regime of power'." (2014: 565) Roland Kostić (2014: 647) goes even further, accusing the ICG of being a willing accomplice in the production of a narrative in the Balkans that served the interests of the Clinton administration: "Though not visible to an ordinary observer, the ICG's work in the early 2000s in Bosnia-Herzegovina was seemingly part of a broader knowledge production [network] united by a common effort to promote the position of the US Department of State."

The fact that the ICG or any other advocacy think tank enjoys a reputation for reliable and insightful analysis and advice among the world's policy elite is, by this reasoning, sufficient proof that it is somehow complicit in an ideological enterprise that seeks to reproduce the dominance of the transnational capitalist class. We agree with what is the least contentious part of the critics' analysis: the influence and reputation of the ICG rest largely on its unmatched ability to construct a narrative about situations of conflict or human crisis. The ICG's credibility and influence certainly are not hurt by its star-studded roster of trustees and senior advisors, so many of whom are by anyone's definition prominent members of the global political and economic elites. Indeed, they may even be boosted from time to time by these elite linkages. But without the organization's frontline presence and demonstrated ability to communicate its analyses and recommendations to people whose understanding of the issue may make a difference, this star power would not be enough to maintain the ICG brand.

3. Human Rights Watch

> As for the universe of think tanks – those peculiar places of research, policy-shaping and advocacy that are neither bureaucracy nor university – it too is shifting. No self-respecting think tank now lacks a blog, YouTube channel or twitter feed. (Medcalf 2015)

All four of the advocacy think tanks that we are examining in this chapter have sophisticated web presences and make extensive use of social media. HRW and AI have gone furthest in their adoption of non-traditional communications methods, contributing to the reconceptualization of what a think tank looks like and how it achieves influence. Australian diplomat Rory Medcalf's observation that "No self-respecting think tank now lacks a blog, YouTube channel or twitter feed" just scratches the surface of the innovations that have driven this change.

Even before the widespread use of the Internet by individuals and organizations, HRW was adapting its communications strategies to changing technology.

The annual HRW Film Festival (HRWFF) was launched in 1988 in New York. It expanded in 1996 to include screenings in London and today includes major cities in North America and Europe throughout the year. In her review of films from the 2009 HRWFF, Safia Swimelar notes that "HRW believed then [1988] and now that film was one of the best mediums to educate and activate people on human rights issues." (1069) Secretary of State Hillary Clinton attended a showing of an HRWFF film in 2009, and the presence of celebrity activists, helping to generate attention for the festival and HRW, is not uncommon. The visual framing and communication of human rights issues also takes place through HRW's YouTube channel and the videos and photos posted on its website. The YouTube videos usually generate about 3,000–7,000 views, although many do much better and some, such as the 4 February 2014 video showing gay men being beaten in Russia, have gone viral. One year after its release this particular video had well over four million views.

HRW has also been at the leading edge of what is sometimes called advocacy journalism. In 2014 it entered into an arrangement to supply content to the politically progressive online news feed organization Upworthy. Upworthy is supported by the Bill and Melinda Gates Foundation and includes Pro Publica and Climate Nexus as non-paying content contributors, but also paying contributors such as the American Civil Liberties Union. *Slate* contributor Dan Gillmor (2014) refers to the advocacy journalists at HRW and some other think tanks, including the Cato Institute, as "almost journalists." They are, he says, engaged in "coverage with a clearly stated worldview – and often leading the way for traditional journalists." Traditionalists might lament the injection of a worldview into the reporting enterprise, but the quality of HRW's journalism, as in the series of articles it published in 2015 on the plight of the Yezidis in Iraq, is very high (HRW 2015b). Moreover, the decline of the international news bureaux of the traditional media, a phenomenon that has been underway for at least three decades, has created the opportunity and perhaps even the need for this sort of advocacy journalism. Glenda Cooper (2009) recounts the story of the award-winning photographer-journalist Marcus Bleasdale, who claims to have contacted 20 newspapers and magazines in 2003, offering to cover the conflict in Darfur, without success. "Yet I made one call to Human Rights Watch, sorted a day rate, expenses and five days later I was in the field."

Social media tools have become important means of communication for most think tanks and are among the metrics used in some rankings of the influence of think tanks (Clark and Roodman 2013). The degree to which think tank staff embrace Twitter, Facebook and other social media, and how these platforms are integrated into an organization's overall communications strategy, vary significantly. At HRW they have been taken very seriously. The role of HRW's senior online editor, Jim Murphy, is described as follows: "Murphy has sought to amplify the reach of the global human rights organization via new technologies and social media. He's been at the helm of the organization's Twitter feed, guiding it toward one million followers, and has conducted numerous Twitter trainings as more than 150 staff members tweet their respective beats." (HRW 2015c) Murphy says that HRW systematically monitors the interactions between the organization's tweeters and their audiences, including policy-makers and journalists, using the tracking program SocialFlow (Beth's Blog 2015).

In 2008 HRW attempted to develop more systematic measures of its impact on policy. Its 2009 report found "a strong attachment to interpreting visibility – especially our presence in major US media outlets – as a measure of success per se, even if that visibility did not produce the real success we were seeking, namely a positive change in respect for human rights." (Gorvin 2009: 481) In the absence of measurable evidence of direct impact on policy – evidence that is unavoidably elusive and almost impossible to report in other than a narrative form – the organization's social media presence and other measures of visibility, such as mentions in elite media and requests for interviews, serve as benchmarks for influence. Several of HRW's staff are among the most followed tweeters in their respective policy domains, including the organization's executive director, Kenneth Roth, and Jo Becker, the advocacy director on child rights (Twiplomacy; *The Guardian* 2015a).

It is clear that the advocacy side of HRW is strong and that the organization has been and continues to be effective in communicating its analyses and recommendations for action. The research side of HRW is a more contentious affair. Perhaps in acknowledgment of this, HRW devotes a very long section at its website to the matter of how it goes about conducting research in order to ensure the accuracy of its analyses. As is also true of the ICG and AI, HRW stresses that its approach relies on field-based research. In the "About Our Research" section of the HRW website, readers are told that "conduct[ing] field investigations, interviewing victims and witnesses to put the human story front and center of our reporting and advocacy," and reliance on "local civil society activists, lawyers, and journalists" and "trusted contacts in the local activist community," as well as "contacts with state and government officials" are central to the organization's research methodology. Great emphasis is placed on the interviewing techniques and sensitivities of the organization's field investigators, as well as on photography, video and satellite imaging that may be used in order to establish the facts of what happened in a specific place at a particular time. HRW typically publishes several reports per month, in most cases from 30 to 90 pages in length. Many of them include a photo gallery or accompanying video. The reports tend to be written in the detailed style characteristic of a legal document, and indeed the victim- and witness-based reports of HRW are often used in legal proceedings and investigations by international organizations, including the International Court of Justice and the United Nations. The organization's research is widely cited and relied upon by activists and academics working on human rights issues.

There are, however, critics of HRW's research. Indeed, the most common criticism leveled against the organization is that its research is systematically biased. This charge comes chiefly from two very different points on the political spectrum. One set of critics argues that HRW has shown a blatant bias against Israel in its coverage of Middle Eastern affairs, particularly conflicts between Israel and the Palestinians. The other set of criticisms comes from those activists and intellectuals for whom the US is the leading threat to world peace and justice and the world's main human rights offender. In the eyes of these critics, HRW is complicit in the maintenance of American global hegemony.

The anti-Israel controversy came to a head in 2009 when HRW's founder and former chairman, Robert Bernstein, wrote an open letter in the *New York Times*. In it he charged the organization with systematically ignoring or understating the human rights violations and aggressions of Israel's enemies and of being obsessed with criticisms of Israel at the expense of coverage of human rights violations in closed societies, including the predominantly Muslim societies surrounding Israel. Similar charges have been made by other critics (Abrams 2011, 2015) At about the same time as HRW's founder made these charges of anti-Israel bias, claims were made that HRW's senior Middle East official had been fundraising in Saudi Arabia, telling donors that her organization confronts the "pro-Israel lobby." (Goldberg 2009) All of this relates to a larger and longstanding claim from some quarters to the effect that HRW, AI and some other human rights groups are systematically and intractably anti-Israel and anti-US. There are really two questions here. First, is this claim true? Second, if it is true, what explains this bias?

We will leave aside the evidence that has been offered by NGO Monitor and other organizations that might plausibly be thought to have their own biases when it comes to this matter. In 2009 two Canadian professors, James Ron and Howard Ramos, published the results of a review that they had begun six years earlier. Based on HRW and AI documents covering the periods 1980–2000 and 1991–2000 (two data sets covering these overlapping periods were used for methodological reasons), Ron and Ramos found that of the top ten countries covered by these organizations, the US (1st) and Israel (9th) were the only non-authoritarian countries on HRW's list. They were also on AI's list of top ten mentions, 1st and 2nd, respectively. The UK was the only other non-authoritarian country on the AI list.

Whether the inclusion of the US and Israel on such lists is warranted and why other countries, known to be egregious human rights abusers, might have not have made such lists we leave to readers to determine. Ron and Ramos suggest interesting possible answers in their 2009 study, based in part on interviews with officials at HRW and AI. We would say, however, that more frequent critical mentions of the US and Israel by human rights organizations is neither surprising to someone who is familiar with the community of human rights activists, academics and international human rights lawyers, nor something that is likely to hurt the reputation of a human rights advocacy think tank in the eyes of most members of this community. It is simply a fact that the US and Israel are viewed quite negatively on issues of human rights by many, if not even most, members of this transnational advocacy network. Ron and Ramos suggest that in providing what some might think to be disproportionate coverage of the US and Israel and less coverage to some authoritarian regimes who might be thought to be greater offenders against human rights, organizations like HRW and AI are responding to demand. "The watchdogs can and do seek to stimulate demand for information on the forgotten crises," argue Ron and Ramos, "but this is an expensive and high risk endeavor, not to be done lightly or too frequently. It's easier to sell people what they already want than to try to create new demand, and businesses that do too much of the latter will quickly run into trouble."

A second criticism of HRW and AI – we saw in the sections on TI and the ICG that this is also a criticism that has been made of them – is that they are complicit in the maintenance of American hegemony. Far from being fair in their criticisms of the US when it comes to human rights abuses, HRW and AI are not critical enough. In light of the data in the Ron and Ramos study, this may seem a rather astounding and even absurd contention. Although it is not the mainstream view among members of the human rights transnational community, it is one that is held by many in this community, including some rather prominent intellectuals and activists.

4. Amnesty International

If the annual Global Go To Index included a "hippest think tank" category, AI would surely win it. Between 1986 and 1998 the organization's human rights concerts, featuring the likes of Sting, Bruce Springsteen, U2 and Tracy Chapman, enabled the organization to make its existence known to younger people and to imprint its brand on popular culture. At its 50th annual general meeting in New York in March 2015, celebrities were prominently featured in the program, including singer-songwriter Annie Lennox; Laura Poitras, the director of *Citizenfour*, the Academy Award-winning documentary about Edward Snowden; Piper Kerman, the writer of the memoir, *Orange is the New Black: My Year in a Women's Prison*, which was the basis for the hugely successful television series; and Jesse Williams, one of the stars of *Grey's Anatomy*. Its long list of "celebrity supporters" spans the generations to include such well-known figures as John Cleese, Al Pacino and Joan Baez, along with those better known to younger supporters of the human rights movement, including Adele, Jennifer Lopez and Jon Stewart. AI is widely acknowledged to be one of the most recognized non-profit organizations in the world and is arguably the best known "brand" among human rights NGOs.

AI describes itself as a global movement, a claim that seems warranted by the fact that it has over two million supporters across the world who receive its regular email updates. Responsiveness to that community of supporters in order to "empower people worldwide to take injustice personally"[2] is a central feature of AI's identity. At the same time, however, AI has come to embrace the label "think tank," although some parts of the organization have worried that the "advocacy" part of "advocacy think tank" might suffer because of this. Nevertheless, under "What We Do" at AI's website, the organization emphasizes that its advocacy and campaigning start with research. "Human rights change starts with the facts. Our experts do accurate, cross-checked research into human rights violations by governments and others worldwide." At its "Careers" webpage, AI proudly and prominently acknowledges its high ranking by the Global Go To Index.

AI's research takes a few main forms. Much of it is tied to specific campaigns for the liberation of a prisoner, the righting of a particular wrong, or a more general issue, involving what are usually very short, 1–2 page bulletins that provide a narrative based on firsthand, eye witness and local accounts, ending with a request that the reader sign an online petition, send a tweet, or send a letter to a state official to show solidarity with the person or group that is the subject of the campaign. AI will sometimes release more than a dozen of these research bulletins in a day. The organization also produces longer reports as submissions to legislative bodies and international agencies. But perhaps the best known of AI's research documents is its annual report. It includes overviews of the human rights situation in all of the world's main regions, followed by 1–5 page entries on particular countries that focus on what AI believes to be the most egregious instances of human rights violations and the circumstances that contribute to them. The hallmark of all this research, in whatever form it takes, are the voices of people in the field where the human rights abuses are taking place. According to Ann Marie Clark (2001: 17), this style of research began early: "by 1965 AI was receiving about half of its information about potential prisoner adoptions from independent contacts with international organizations, opposition groups, families and friends of prisoners, and sometimes prisoners themselves."

As is also true of HRW, AI and its research are routinely cited in the media most likely to be followed by the attentive public interested in human rights issues. Matthew Powers (2015) notes that the combined references to AI and HRW in the *New York Times* in 1980 was 80, a number that had increased to 495 in 2013. The same pattern occurred over this period of time in the case of *The Guardian*: combined citations grew from 95 in 1980 to 332 in 2013 (Powers 2015: 190). AI and HRW research is also routinely cited by academics working in the field of human rights. Powers (2015: 191–93) notes that both AI and HRW developed more robust and credible research capabilities as part of a strategy for increasing their legitimacy vis-à-vis political and media elites.

Not everyone, however, is impressed with AI's research. The most common charge brought against it is not that it is shoddy or inaccurate – although some groups such as NGO Monitor regularly make this claim – but that it focuses inordinately on such countries as the US and the UK and not enough on many authoritarian countries known to be egregious human rights violators. This, we saw, is a claim that some make about HRW and its research. As Ron and Ramos (2009) show, there is little doubt that the research of these two organizations is skewed in ways that one might not have expected. The usual explanation is ideological bias on the part of those who determine the research agenda of these organizations and write their reports. A rather different explanation is offered by Hendrix and Wong (2014: 33):

> Because [international NGOS] have limited resources, they face tradeoffs in reporting on different countries and cases of human rights abuse. When selecting a case for advocacy, INGOs must weigh the severity of violation with perceptions about whether advocacy effort is likely to affect 1) political outcomes and 2) the organization itself. These two factors will affect many if not all INGO decisions, as INGOs both want to effect political change and survive as organizations.

Organizational imperatives rather than ideology are stressed by Hendrix and Wong. A similar explanation is offered by *The Economist* (2007): "Amnesty may to some extent be the captive of its need to keep a mass membership enthused with new and compelling causes, even at the cost of narrowing its appeal to those with unfashionably positive views about America or global capitalism." AI's country chapters report their finances separately. This makes it difficult to state with certainty what percentage of AI's overall funding comes from which countries. It is clear, however, that individual contributors in the US and UK account for a disproportionate share of total AI revenues, followed by contributors in other western democracies. The idea that donors from these countries might be, on the whole, more interested in hearing about human rights abuses in their societies than in Sri Lanka, Zimbabwe, or North Korea, combined with the fact that it is easier and safer to investigate and acquire information on the state of human rights in open societies than in those that are not, seems plausible.

Conclusions

In Chapter 2 Donald Abelson writes, "When it comes to assessing the priorities of think tanks, policy research and political advocacy are often treated as polar opposites. The reality, however, is that they are complementary functions in which all think tanks, in one form or another, engage." The balance between advocacy and research and the modalities through which think tanks attempt to influence policy varies between organizations. We are today a very long way from the classical model of think tanks pioneered in the early 20th century by the Brookings Institution, the Carnegie Endowment for International Peace, the Brookings Institution and the Royal Institute for International Affairs. The four human rights organizations that we have examined in this chapter very clearly place the emphasis on advocacy to a degree and in ways that were unimaginable within the parameters of the classical model.

At the same time, however, credible, timely, expert research remains crucial to the brand status that each of these organizations has achieved. Occasional charges of ideological bias or accusations of shoddy research that are sometimes leveled against one or another of these organizations are not different from the criticisms and charges occasionally made against many other prominent think tanks. Even the venerable Brookings Institution has had to defend itself against charges that the manner in which its revenue model has developed in recent years may influence the research that it does and the analyses and recommendations that it produces.

Influencing policy directly or indirectly by moving the needle of elite or public opinion on an issue is always the proximate goal of think tanks. We would suggest, however, that international human rights organizations have long had another less immediate, but no less important goal. It has been to shift the way in which opinion leaders, lawmakers and attentive publics think about state sovereignty versus the universality of human rights. The greatest success achieved by AI, HRW, ICG and TI has involved their contribution to the idea that state sovereignty should not be allowed to shield countries from the application of universal standards of human rights. There is, of course, no way to measure this influence. Nevertheless, the AI, HRW, ICG and TI brands are synonymous with this universal ethos and derive much of their status from the manner in which they have combined research and advocacy in the promotion of this wider goal.

Notes

1 The International Secretariat is organized into two legal entities, in compliance with UK law. These are Amnesty International Limited and Amnesty International Charity Limited.
2 https://www.amnesty.org/en/wire-magazine/

References

Abrams, Elliott. 2011. "Human Rights Organizations Off the Deep End." Pressure Points [blog], Council on Foreign Relations, 12 October. Available at http://blogs.cfr.org/abrams/2011/10/12/human-rights-organizations-off-the-deep-end/.
Abrams, Elliott. 2015. "Human Rights Watch and the Destruction of Rafah." Pressure Points [blog], Council on Foreign Relations, 20 January. Available at http://blogs.cfr.org/abrams/2015/01/20/human-rights-watch-and-the-destruction-of-rafah/.
AI (Amnesty International). 2015a. "Who We Are." Available at https://www.amnesty.org/en/who-we-are/ (accessed 5 September 2015).
AI (Amnesty International). 2015b. "Financial Information." Available at http://www.amnesty.ca/about-us/financial-information.
AI (Amnesty International). 2015c. "Structure and People." Available at https://www.amnesty.org/en/about-us/how-were-run/structure-and-people/.
AI (Amnesty International) Toronto Organization. 2015. "About Amnesty International." Available at http://www.aito.ca/node/27 (accessed 1 September 2015).
Andersson, Staffan, and Paul Heywood. 2009. "The Politics of Perception: Use and Abuse of Transparency International's Approach to Measuring Corruption." *Political Studies* 57, no. 4 (December): 746–67.
Benenson, Peter. 1961. "The Forgotten Prisoners." *The Observer*, 28 May. Available at http://www.theguardian.com/uk/1961/may/28/fromthearchive.theguardian (accessed 4 September 2015).
Bernstein, Robert. 2009. "Rights Watchdog, Lost in the Mideast." *New York Times*, 20 October (accessed online).
Beth's Blog. 2015. "Case Study: How Human Rights Watch Leverages Employee Personal Brands on Twitter," 24 March. Available at http://www.bethkanter.org/hrw-employee-champions/.
Bliesemann de Guevara, Berit. 2014a. "Studying the International Crisis Group." *Third World Quarterly* 35, no. 4: 545–62.
Bliesemann de Guevara, Berit. 2014b. "On Methodology and Myths: Exploring the International Crisis Group's Organisational Culture." *Third World Quarterly* 35, no. 4, 616–33.
Blitt, Robert Charles. 2004. "Who Will Watch the Watchdogs? Human Rights Non-governmental Organizations and the Case for Regulation." *Buffalo Human Rights Law Review* 10: 261–398.
Bonner, Raymond. 1996. "The Worldly Business of Bribes: Quite (sic) Battle is Joined." *New York Times*, 8 July. Available at http://www.nytimes.com/1996/07/08/world/the-worldly-business-of-bribes-quite-battle-is-joined.html.

Boyle, Francis. 2002. Interviewed by Dennis Bernstein. *Interview: Amnesty on Jenin* (13 June 13).
Brandeis, Louis D., and Norman Hapgood. 2009. *Other People's Money and How the Bankers Use It*. New York: Cosimo, Inc.
Brown, Ed, and Jonathan Cloke. 2011. "Critical Perspectives on Corruption: An Overview." *Critical Perspectives on International Business* 7, no. 2: 116–24.
Buchanan, Tom. 2002. " 'The Truth Will Set You Free': The Making of Amnesty International." *Journal of Contemporary History* 37, no. 4 (October): 575–97.
Carnegie Council. (undated). "Human Rights Watch – Innovators." Policy Innovations. Available at http://www.policyinnovations.org/innovators/organizations/data/00869.
Clark, Ann Marie. 1995. "Non-Governmental Organizations and their Influence on International Society." *Journal of International Affairs* 48, no. 2 (Winter): 507–25.
Clark, Ann Marie. 2001. *Diplomacy of Conscience*. Princeton, NJ: Princeton University Press.
Clark, Julia, and David Roodman. 2013. "Measuring Think Tank Performance: An Index of Public Profile." Policy Papers, Centre for Global Development, 28 June. Available at http://www.cgdev.org/sites/default/files/think-tank-index_0_0.pdf.
Cobham, Alex. 2013. "Corrupting Perceptions: Why Transparency International's Flagship Corruption Index Falls Short," 22 July. Available at http://foreignpolicy.com/2013/07/22/corrupting-perceptions/.
Cooper, Glenda. 2009. "When Lines between NGO and News Organizations Blur." Neiman Foundation, Harvard University, 21 December. Available at http://www.niemanlab.org/2009/12/glenda-cooper-when-lines-between-ngo-and-news-organization-blur/.
de Sousa, Luis. 2005. "Transparency International in Search of a Constituency: The Franchising of the Global Anticorruption Movement." Available at http://www.ancorage-net.org/content/documents/pdp05-14.pdf.
Denmark. 2013. Ministry of Foreign Affairs, Department for Stabilization and Security, 3 May. Available at http://um.dk/en/~/media/UM/English-site/Documents/Danida/About-Danida/Danida%20transparency/Documents/Grant%20committee/2013/Int%20doc/03%20ICG.pdf
Duffield, Lee. 2007. "Media and Global Conflict: An International Crisis Group Case Study." *Pacific Journalism Review* 13, no. 2: 113–38.
The Economist. 2007a. "Amnesty International: Many Rights, Some Wrong," 22 March. Available at http://www.economist.com/node/8888792 (accessed 4 September 2015).
The Economist. 2007b. "The World's Biggest Human-Rights Organisation Stretches Its Brand," 22 March. Available at http://www.economist.com/node/8888792.
The Economist. 2010. "Murk Meter: The Best-Known Corruption Index May Have Run Its Course," 28 October (accessed online).
Eigen, Peter. 2008. "Removing a Roadblock to Development Transparency International Mobilizes Coalitions Against Corruption." *Innovations* 3, no. 2: 19–33.
Evans, Gareth. 2012. "The International Crisis Group: The Role of a Global NGO in Preventing and Resolving Deadly Conflict." 17 May. Available at http://www.gevans.org/speeches/speech471.html (accessed 1 September 2015).
Gillmor, Dan. 2014. "In Praise of the Almost-Journalists." *Slate*, 28 March. Available at http://www.slate.com/articles/technology/future_tense/2014/03/human_rights_watch_and_other_advocacy_groups_doing_great_journalism.html
Goldberg, Jeffrey. 2009. "Fundraising Corruption at Human Rights Watch." *The Atlantic*, 15 July. Available at http://www.theatlantic.com/international/archive/2009/07/fundraising-corruption-at-human-rights-watch/21345/
Gorvin, Ian. 2009. "Producing the Evidence that Human Rights Advocacy Works: First Steps towards Systematized Evaluation at Human Rights Watch." *Journal of Human Rights Practice* 1, no. 3: 477–87.

Grigat, Sonja. 2014. "Educating into Liberal Peace: The International Crisis Group's Contribution to an Emerging Global Governmentality." *Third World Quarterly* 35, no. 4: 563–80.

The Guardian. 2015a. "Twitter list: Nine Top Tweeters on Business and Child Rights," 12 May. Available at http://www.theguardian.com/sustainable-business/2015/may/12/twitter-list-nine-top-tweeters-on-business-and-child-rights?CMP=share_btn_tw

The Guardian. 2015b. "The Guardian View on Amnesty International's Call to Decriminalise Sex Work: Divisive and Distracting," 2 August. Available at http://www.theguardian.com/commentisfree/2015/aug/02/guardian-view-amnesty-international-call-to-legalise-sex-work-divisive-and-distracting (accessed 30 August 2015).

Hendrix, Cullen, and Wendy H. Wong. 2014. "Knowing Your Audience: How the Structure of International Relations and Organizational Choices Affect Amnesty International's Advocacy." Review of International Organizations 9, no. 1: 29–58.

HRW (Human Rights Watch). 2015a. "Kuwait: Authorities Dissolve Transparency Society," 21 June. Available at https://www.hrw.org/news/2015/06/21/kuwait-authorities-dissolve-transparency-society

HRW (Human Rights Watch). 2015b. "Iraq: ISIS Escapees Describe Systematic Rape," 14 April. Available at https://www.hrw.org/news/2015/04/14/iraq-isis-escapees-describe-systematic-rape

HRW (Human Rights Watch). 2015c. Available at https://www.hrw.org/about/people/jim-murphy

HRW (Human Rights Watch). 2015. "World Report 2015."

HRW (Human Rights Watch). 2015. "About." Available at https://www.hrw.org/about (accessed 28 August 2015).

HRW (Human Rights Watch). 2015. "History." Available at https://www.hrw.org/history (accessed 28 August 2015).

Ignatief, Michael. 2002. "Human Rights, Sovereignty and Intervention." In Nicolas Owen (ed), *Human Rights, Human Wrongs*. Oxford University Press, 52–87.

ICG (International Crisis Group). (undated). Available at http://www.crisisgroup.org/en/support/why-support-crisisgroup.aspx

ICG (International Crisis Group). 2008. "Annual Report: Review of 2007 and Plans for 2008."

ICG (International Crisis Group). 2010. "Fifteen Years on the Frontline."

ICG (International Crisis Group). 2015. "About Crisis Group." Available at http://www.crisisgroup.org/en/about.aspx (accessed 1 September 2015).Johnsøn, Jesper. 2012. "When, Why and How to Use the Global Corruption Barometer." *U4 Brief* 5, Chr. Michelsen Institute, Bergen. Available at http://www.cmi.no/publications/publication/?4505=why-when-and-how-to-use-the-global-corruption.

Keck, Margaret, and Kathryn Sikkink. 1998. *Activists beyond Borders: Advocacy Networks in International Politics*, Ithaca, NY: Cornell University Press.

Korey, William. 1998. *NGOs and the Universal Declaration of Human Rights: "A Curious Grapevine."* New York: St Martin's Press.

Kostić, Roland. 2014. "Transnational Think-Tanks: Foot Soldiers in the Battlefield of Ideas? Examining the Role of the ICG in Bosnia and Herzegovina, 2000–01," *Third World Quarterly* 35, no. 4: 634–51.

Medcalf, Rory. 2015. "Think Tanks and Foreign Services that Shun Social Media are Being Left Behind." *American Review*. Available at http://americanreviewmag.com/opinions/The-diplomatic-tweet.

Murphy, Jessica. 2015. "Canadian Activists Turn to UN with Challenge to Controversial Anti-Terror Bill." *The Guardian*, 6 July. Available at http://www.theguardian.com/world/2015/jul/06/canada-anti-terror-bill-united-nations-amnesty-international (accessed 28 August 2015).

Murphy, Jonathan. 2011. "Capitalism and Transparency." *Critical Perspectives on International Business* 7, no. 2: 125–41.
NGO Monitor. 2015. "Amnesty International (AI)." 9 August. Available at http://www.ngo-monitor.org/article/amnesty_international (accessed 30 August 2015).
Norad [Norwegian Agency for Development Cooperation]. 2010. "Evaluation of Transparency International." Report 8. Available at http://www.oecd.org/derec/norway/47447924.pdf.
O'Leary, Donal. 2006. "The Role of Transparency International in Fighting Corruption in Infrastructure." Available at http://siteresources.worldbank.org/INTDECABCTOK 2006/Resources/OLeary.pdf.
Powers, Matthew. 2015. "NGOs as Journalistic Entities: The Possibilities, Promises and Limits of Boundary Crossing." In Matt Carlson and Seth Lewis (eds), *Boundaries of Journalism: Professionalism, Practices and Participation*. New York: Routledge, 184–98.
Radio Free Europe/Radio Liberty. 2015. "Russian Government Unveils New 'Eurasian' Corruption-Monitoring Index," 12 August. Available at http://www.rferl.org/content/corruption-russian-monitoring-eurasia/26972282.html.
Robinson, William. 2014. *Global Capitalism and the Crisis of Humanity*, Cambridge, UK: Cambridge University Press.
Ron, James, and Howard Ramos. 2009. "Why are the United States and Israel at the Top of Human Rights Hit Lists?" *Foreign Policy*, 3 November. Available at http://foreignpolicy.com/2009/11/03/why-are-the-united-states-and-israel-at-the-top-of-human-rights-hit-lists/.
Shipsey, Bill. 2011. "The 'Toast to Freedom' that Led to Amnesty International," 22 September. Available at http://www.huffingtonpost.com/bill-shipsey/the-toast-to-freedom-that_b_976849.html (accessed 5 September 2015).
Simons, Greg. 2014. "The International Crisis Group and the Manufacturing and Communicating of Crises." *Third World Quarterly* 35, no. 4: 581–97.
Slezkine, Peter. 2014. "From Helsinki to Human Rights Watch: How an American Cold War Monitoring Group Became an International Human Rights Institution." *Humanity Journal*, 16 December. Available at http://humanityjournal.org/issue-5-3/from-helsinki-to-human-rights-watch-how-an-american-cold-war-monitoring-group-became-an-international-human-rights-institution/.
Stone, Diane. 2001. "Think Tanks." In Neil J. Smelser and Paul B. Baltes (eds), *International Encyclopedia of the Social & Behavioral Sciences*. Oxford, UK: Pergamon, 15668–71.
TI (Transparency International). 2015. "Seven Steps FIFA Must Take Now that Blatter Has Stepped Down." Transparency International, 2 June. Available at http://www.transparency.org/news/pressrelease/seven_steps_fifa_must_take_now_that_blatter_has_stepped_down.
Twiplomacy. 2015. "How Do International Organizations Tweet in 2015?" Twiplomacy blog. Available at http://twiplomacy.com/blog/how-do-international-organisations-tweet-2015/#section-3.
Wählen, Claire. 2015. "United Nations Human Rights Committee Calls for Changes to C51." iPolitics, 23 July. Available at http://ipolitics.ca/2015/07/23/united-nations-human-rights-committee-calls-for-changes-to-c-51/ (accessed 28 August 2015).
Wang, Hongying, and James N. Rosenau. 2001. "Transparency International and Corruption as an Issue of Global Governance." *Global Governance* 7: 25–49.
Watson, Alison M.S. 2004. "Human Rights Watch." *New Political Economy* 9, no. 3 (September): 441–53.

4 The governance turn in EU foreign policy
Are EU think tanks out of the picture?

Marybel Perez

Introduction

The studies collected in this book have one important element in common: the foreign policy of sovereign states. In this chapter, however, the challenge is to analyse the foreign policy-making of a supranational entity, a phenomenon that a few decades ago would have seemed to contradict realist views of international relations (Krotz and Maher 2011). The idea that states might relinquish their exclusive right to decide key elements of their relations with other states – such as security and defence – seems to go against nature. In fact, as Diedrichs (2011) points out, there have been several attempts in Europe to cooperate on these areas of foreign policy, but they have failed.

Nevertheless, the launch in 1970 of the European Political Cooperation, an informal framework for consultation between EU countries, planted the seeds of what in 1987 became the Common Foreign and Security Policy (CFSP), with its formal inclusion in the Single European Act.[1] As a result, EU members now work with a supranational structure through which they coordinate part of their foreign policy. While states retain significant control, EU foreign policy now encompasses a wide variety of subjects and is designed, implemented and executed by different agencies and institutions at the EU and national levels. Moreover, similar to other policy areas, EU foreign policy has become increasingly complex and various forms of governance[2] have emerged (Diedrichs 2011).

One outcome is that intergovernmentalism has given way to governance through EU foreign policy since EU institutions and agencies, and not only states, are involved in policy-making. Moreover, governance takes on a different dimension when policy-makers rely on informal governance – that is, when policy-makers discuss policy issues through uncodified rules and in informal arenas that have an impact on formal decision-making (e.g. Christiansen and Neuhold 2012; Kleine 2013). The governance picture becomes still more complex when different policy actors such as corporations, NGOs, think tanks and foreign governments search for mechanisms to influence policy-makers at the national and EU levels, especially through informal governance. Arguably, it is in these processes of governance (Stone 2014), and particularly informal governance, that think tanks can play a significant role.

For this reason, the purpose of this chapter is to examine EU think tanks' contribution to EU foreign policy. Are EU think tanks concerned with EU foreign policy? What are their objectives and what strategies do they pursue? The examination of EU think tanks' contribution to EU foreign policy-making not only helps us understand the think tank phenomenon at the international level but also helps us better understand the nature of EU foreign policy-making.

This chapter is divided into five sections. Following a brief introduction of the policy areas and organisation of EU foreign policy, the second section presents a view of EU foreign policy governance and the implications for think tank activity. The third section briefly introduces the EU think tanks and explains their general position in EU policy-making. The fourth section summarises the work of EU think tanks in EU foreign policy, based on a survey of think tanks' activities in 2014–15. The chapter concludes with a short section discussing the contribution of EU think tanks to EU foreign policy.

1. What is foreign policy in the EU?

In order to understand the participation of EU think tanks in foreign policy-making, it is necessary first to consider the particularities of the EU's foreign policy. These particularities determine the degree of think tanks' involvement, the strategies employed and the subject focus chosen.

Different aspects of EU foreign policy have been prioritised differently over time and as a result can be separated into two main clusters. The first has progressively included humanitarian aid and civil protection (H&CP), development and cooperation, enlargement, and trade. The second, which has been slowly and relatively recently incorporated into EU foreign policy, comprises the CFSP; this includes the Common Security and Defence Policy (CSDP).

These policy areas have enjoyed particular attention at different moments in EU history. For instance, trade policy was a major issue from the beginning of the EU, while enlargement policy enjoyed considerable attention during the 1990s and early 2000s as a result of the significant addition of EU members and enlargement's effects on the EU's structure. Accordingly, it is expected that EU think tanks concentrate their resources on the currently salient subjects in EU politics. The technical character of the subject is another aspect to consider (Broscheid and Coen 2007; Rasmussen, Carroll and Lowery 2014). EU think tanks are best equipped to work as information brokers of politicised subjects (Perez 2014a); consequently it is expected that they will be more frequently involved in areas such as democracy and the rule of law than in trade issues.

Institutionally, these two clusters of foreign policy areas have evolved at different speeds and have been carried out by different sets of institutions. Actions under the CFSP and CSDP are defined by the European Council, implemented by the Council of the EU, and coordinated and executed by the High Representative of the Union for Foreign Affairs and Security Policy (until 2019 Federica Mogherini)[3] with the support of the European External Action Service (EEAS) – the EU's diplomatic corps. Unanimity of the European Council and the Council of the EU is the decision-making rule for the great majority of issues – particularly those falling within the CSDP – which indicates tight control by states in these two areas of foreign policy. This structure of the CFSP and CSDP is the result of reforms of the Maastricht, Amsterdam and Lisbon treaties, particularly the latter. Meanwhile, humanitarian aid and civil protection, development and cooperation, enlargement, and trade are foreign policy areas that fall within EU responsibilities and as a result are less controlled by member states. This means that, in most cases, decision-making follows the ordinary legislative procedure and the legislation is implemented by the European Commission (with its respective departments: ECHO, DEVCO, ELARG and Trade), supporting agencies such as the Emergency Response Coordination Centre, and member countries.

These different institutional settings determine the interest group environment in terms of the types of group that gain most attention and the channels of access available. As a result, the interest group environment in Brussels will be lively in policy areas regulated by EU institutions, while it will be negligible on policy areas controlled by the states – so in this case interest groups will concentrate on the national level. In other words, as was stated in the introduction of this book, think tanks' spheres of influence are to an extent limited by the specificities of the political system in which they operate. However, these boundaries are sometimes crossed and foreign affairs think tanks from member countries establish think tank networks and partnerships to operate in Brussels (see below). Accordingly, it would be expected that EU think tanks expend fewer resources on CFSP and CSDP areas. Nevertheless, as will be explained in the following section, policy-making in the CFSP and CSDP is more complex than the legislation describes, providing opportunities to various different interest groups – including think tanks – to be involved in these areas.

2. Beyond intergovernmentalism in EU foreign policy

As member states have given EU institutions more responsibility in the regulation of policy issues and as EU institutions have transformed the policy-making process to include a wide array of policy actors, the EU polity has been characterised by increased governance. At the same time that the EU has gained more legislative power (Eising 2008), interest groups in Brussels have mushroomed. This applies particularly for one subset of EU foreign policy areas: humanitarian aid and civil protection, development and cooperation, enlargement, and trade. But, as was described above, decision-making in the CFSP and CSDP is characterised by a high degree of intergovernmentalism.

Nevertheless, some researchers argue that the institutionalisation of the CFSP and CSDP at the EU level has opened a window for governance. As Carta (2013) explains, the policy-making process of the CFSP and CSDP is in reality complex. In order to develop the CFSP and CSDP a number of agencies operating in Brussels have been created and, as a result, a number of intergovernmental and EU agencies such as the Foreign Affairs Council, the Political and Security Committee and the EEAS cooperate, amongst themselves and with the main institutions and member state governments. As they evolve, these agencies are acquiring a certain degree of autonomy from member states (Sjursen 2011): EU institutions, for instance, seem to increasingly influence CSDP policy-making (Dijkstra 2013). In this process, consensus-building tends to replace hard-bargaining (Juncos and Pomorska 2011) and this tendency increases the reliance on informal governance. Moreover, Carta (2013) shows that at the policy formulation stage, actors from the two foreign policy clusters merge and "different decision-making styles alternate". In fact, some subject areas of the CFSP overlap with humanitarian aid and civil protection, development and cooperation, enlargement, and trade policies. Nevertheless, this move towards more governance and even informal governance in the CFSP and CSDP does not entail an open governance process in which interest groups participate.

However, Joachim and Dembinski (2011) have documented the participation of NGOs in the development and implementation of EU foreign policy, particularly the European Code of Conduct on Arms Exports. They point out that civil society organisations concerned with foreign and security issues – including the think tanks International Security Information Service, Europe (ISIS-Europe) and the International Crisis Group (ICG)[4] – began to appear in Brussels at the beginning of the 1990s when the CFSP and CSDP started to be formalised in the Maastricht Treaty. They argue that the participation of NGOs in this policy area has progressively expanded as a result of the institutionalisation of foreign policy at the EU level and the decrease in barriers to access. Greater institutionalisation and fewer barriers to access are the product of increased interdependences between policy-makers, the participation of institutions that naturally seek interest groups' advice – notably the Commission and the Parliament – and the need for legitimacy conferred by civil society.

Thus, if EU and national agencies in Brussels are gaining autonomy in foreign policy, if informality is practised and if policy-makers are open to external influences, then the growth of interest groups in the CFSP and CSDP fields will be driven by factors similar to those in other policy areas (Eising 2008; Joachim and Dembinski 2011). As will be explained in the following section, these factors have also defined the role of think tanks in EU politics although in a different way than is true of most interest groups (Perez 2014a, 2014b).

3. Researching EU think tanks' engagement in EU foreign policy

The EU think tanks comprise 25 organisations located in Brussels and characterised by an EU-transnational origin, an interest in EU subjects and the intention to contribute to EU policy-making. They are shown in Table 4.1. However, there are a number of national and global think tanks operating in Brussels that may also have an interest in EU foreign policy issues (see appendix in Perez 2014a). Moreover, the Commission has created two agencies that provide specific support: the European Political Strategy Centre,[5] which has a team working on foreign policy, and the EU Institute for Security Studies (EUISS), which operates in Paris.

Table 4.1 EU think tanks

Think tank name	EU foreign policy included in mission statement	Date founded	Transparency Register 28/02/2015
The Trans-European Policy Studies Association (TEPSA)	✓	1974	03/01/14
Centre for European Policy Studies (CEPS)	✓	1983	16/09/11
Observatoire Social Européen		1984	
European Institute for Asia Studies (EIAS)		1989	07/03/13
Confrontations Europe		1992	05/10/11
Migration Policy Group		1995	
European Research Institute For Mediterranean and Euro-Arab Cooperation	✓	1996	12/12/12
European Policy Centre (EPC)	✓	1997	22/01/09
Madariaga – College of Europe Foundation	✓	1998	
Friends of Europe (FoE)	✓	1999	23/09/11
Pour la Solidarité		2002	20/12/12
European Corporate Governance Institute		2002	
European Ideas Network		2002	
European Policy Institutes Network (EPIN)		2002	
The Lisbon Council for Economic Competitiveness		2003	05/10/08
Bruegel		2004	27/09/11
European Centre for International Political Economy		2006	06/12/14
European Liberal Forum		2007	
Wilfried Martens Centre for European Studies	✓	2007	19/02/15
Centre Maurits Coppieters	✓	2007	15/02/11
Institute of European Democrats		2008	
Foundation for European Progressive Studies	✓	2008	27/02/12
Eurodemocracy	✓	2009	
New Direction	✓	2010	
Eurasian Council on Foreign Affairs		2014	

In contrast to most contexts, in the EU think tanks are a relatively new phenomenon which has grown and adapted as the EU system has expanded (Sherrington 2000; Ulrich 2004). Even newer is the subject of foreign policy in EU think tanks. While foreign affairs think tanks have a long tradition in the US and UK (Abelson 2014a) and a simple internet search reveals a significant number of foreign affairs think tanks in every region of the world, the lack of the "foreign affairs" label in the names of the EU think tanks listed is striking.

In general, think tanks are seen as organisations that contribute to the creation of information, development of arguments and improvement of organisational capacity. But EU think tanks rarely engage in policy advice, only a small number invest resources in the research which is most often associated with research programmes funded by the Commission (Perez 2014a), and for the most part they are uninterested in mass media attention (Perez forthcoming). Nevertheless, EU think tanks play a role in the development of networks and the reproduction of EU ideas (Perez 2014b, 2015). As a result, the study of visibility or engagement in the different stages of official policy-making only occasionally leads to an understanding of EU think tanks' participation in politics.

The challenge is even greater when the particularities of EU foreign policy-making are included in the equation. As explained above, if think tanks engage in foreign policy-making it is through governance processes; we must therefore look at spaces where the collaboration between states, EU institutions and private actors is established in the foreign policy-making process. EU think tanks are characterised by a preference for informal policy-making spaces (Perez 2014b). Consequently, the examination of EU think tanks' participation in EU foreign policy-making is a difficult task.

Being the first study of the subject, the task of this chapter should be straightforward: to map the scope and character of EU think tanks' work in the EU foreign policy area. To this end, it is necessary in the first place to identify the degree of commitment to the EU foreign policy agenda and the specific policy areas in which EU think tanks are interested. Then, if – as is customary – think tanks are seeking to contribute to the development of networks, the actors involved in their activities need to be identified. Therefore, the speakers at events and in partnerships created to organise events and write reports are scrutinised, as well as the types of think tank members. Members are seen as the actors demanding information, while partners and speakers make up the network creating and reproducing information. In terms of impact, it is assumed that when think tanks are highly interested they will invest considerable resources in strategies and innovation to increase policy impact.

The purpose here is not to discuss think tanks' visibility as an indicator of influence. As has already been shown, and pointed out in the introduction of this book, visibility is a misleading measure of influence. Moreover, visibility in mass media is not one of the main concerns of EU think tanks (Perez 2014a and forthcoming). Following the premises of informal governance (Christiansen and Neuhold 2012; Kleine 2013), think tanks have to be able to alter the process and outcome of formal decision-making to have an impact on policy-making. Thus, the indicators of impact are more related to how power is enforced through think tank networks and relationships than how visible they are, particularly at the international level.

The results are presented in the following section. They come from the examination of information collected from think tanks' websites, annual reports and events and research reports collected in July 2015 for the period January 2014–June 2015. The think tanks studied work on a large number of issues, but for the purpose of our analysis I have focused on the EU policy areas described in the first section of this chapter and sub-topics related to them.

4. EU foreign policy think tanks

EU think tanks working on EU foreign policy are organisationally distinct from foreign policy institutes in the US and Europe (Abelson 2014b; Higgott and Stone 1994). Although a significant number of generalist or specialist foreign policy think tanks exist in the US and Europe, there are no foreign policy think tanks in the EU. Those that devote part of their work to foreign policy are generalist EU think tanks – that is, organisations that focus on a wide range of EU policy areas, from agriculture to sport.

Table 4.1 shows that more than a third of EU think tanks include in their mission statement the intention to contribute to EU foreign policy. Nevertheless, a deeper examination shows that only five think tanks invest resources systematically to develop their foreign policy agenda (see Table 4.2). It is worth noting that the major EU think tank networks of national think tanks working on international relations (EPIN and TEPSA) invest negligible resources in EU foreign policy. This suggests that these networks work as a link for the discussion of EU internal politics and are not major sources of foreign policy information. In fact, it was observed that the think tank members of these networks frequently participated in the events of the EUISS and the EU think tanks examined below.

Organisational traits

The five think tanks working systematically on EU foreign policy are among the ten oldest EU think tanks, established between 1983 and 1999 (see Table 4.2). Despite their non-partisan approach, these think tanks have more in common with the new partisan institutes described by Higgott and Stone (1994) than with the old guard think tanks in terms of size, interest in targeting a variety of audiences, and emphasis on timely problem-solving information.

In order to expand their organisational capacity, these think tanks usually work in partnership with different institutions (see Table 4.2). Friends of Europe (FoE) and Madariaga–College of Europe Foundation seem to create partnerships to increase their expertise around specific subjects and programmes. FoE's Development Policy Forum is conducted in partnership with the German Federal Enterprise for International Cooperation, the French Agency for Development, the Japan International Cooperation Agency, the United Nations and the World Bank. In accordance with its EU–China Programme, Madariaga's list of partners includes eight institutions and organisations focused on Asian and Chinese issues such as the Mission of the People's Republic of China to the European Union and the Chinese Academy of Social Sciences. In contrast, the European Policy Centre (EPC) has established long-term partnerships with six think tanks in different European countries, including the Hellenic Foundation for European and Foreign Policy and the Finnish Institute of International Affairs, may be seen as a sign it wishes to increase its network capacity and its expertise.

In terms of funding, these think tanks seem to follow a similar path to that of their US counterparts, which have a variety of financial sources. As Table 4.2 shows, think tank budgets tend to be characterised by diversification and limited EU participation – with the exception of research and project grants at the Centre for European Policy Studies (CEPS) and EPC. Nevertheless, it is worth noting the importance of funding from corporations, professional and business associations and diplomatic representations. This constituted more than half of FoE's 2014 budget and between one-fifth and one-third of CEPS and EPC budgets. In these last two cases the contribution comes in the form of membership (see Table 4.3), which in both think tanks gives members exclusive or privileged access to events and publications. In its annual report, the EPC lists a total of 361 members, of which two-thirds are corporations, professional and business associations and diplomatic representations (EPC 2013). The CEPS has a very large number of corporate members, particularly considering that what are labelled as institutional members include a variety of policy actors such as academic and research institutes, international organisations, professional associations and, most numerous of all (40 in total), diplomatic representations (CEPS 2014).

The EU foreign policy agenda

In their review of the evolution of foreign policy in the US, Higgott and Stone (1994) highlight think tanks' adaptation of their agendas to new subjects. They show how diplomacy and strategy gave way to democratisation, globalisation and the environment. EU think tanks are slightly similar. Their agendas orbit more around subjects that overlap the CFSP and the other cluster of foreign policy areas; however, this is not surprising given the intergovernmental character of the CSDP and part of the CFSP.

The EU foreign policy agenda is integrated in different ways in the various think tanks (see Table 4.3). While EPC and CEPS have general sections on foreign policy that seek to cover a wide range of policy areas, FoE and Madariaga have created special programmes and sections dedicated to particular subjects. Madariaga, for instance, has the EU–China Programme, which broadly "aims at enhancing mutual understanding".[6] In FoE, in addition to the Development Policy Forum that runs parallel to the Africa Programme, the Global Europe section devoted to EU foreign policy contains the Development Policy Forum that runs parallel to the Asia Programme. As a result, the EPC and CEPS seem to emphasise their capacity to tackle a wide range of subjects, while FoE and Madariaga emphasise their specialist know-how.

Table 4.2 Partnerships and financial sources for five EU think tanks working on EU foreign policy

Think tank name	CEPS	EIAS	EPC	Madariaga	FoE
Partnerships (websites and annual reports)	NA	NA	Core partners: the King Baudouin Foundation	Other partners: demos Europa Centre for European Strategy; Deutsche Gesellschaft für Auswärtige Politik German Council on Foreign Relations; Hellenic Foundation for European & Foreign Policy; Finish Institute of International Affairs; European Think Tank for Global Action; Institute for International Political Studies*	Core partners: Alumni Association of the College of Europe; Charles Stewart Mott Foundation; College of Europe; Leuven Centre for Global Governance Studies; Mission of the People's Republic of China to the European Union	Partners range from EU and non-EU governments to international bodies; from EU institutions to NGOs; and from "big business" to trade associations. Leading media organisations, other think tanks, universities and schools from across Europe and beyond+
Finance (annual reports)	45% EU research contracts and tenders awarded; 19% from membership fees; 18% from private organisations and 5% from foundations; 7% of CEPS' events and balance from new projects	NA	25% grants from European foundations, mainly from strategic partners, the King Baudouin Foundation and the Compagnia di San Paolo. 5% EU; 31% membership fees 39% contributions to EPC's programmes	Mott Foundation 10%; College of Europe 30%; Chinese Mission to the EU 20%; Peace Tour Foundation 40%	European and international institutions (8.9%); diplomatic missions, national, regional and local authorities (26.2%); corporate sector (companies and trade associations) (28.3%); private non-corporate (foundations and NGOs) (14.9%); contributions from members (21,8%) (website)

* Source: www.epc.eu/about.php
+ Source: www.friendsofeurope.org/financing/

Table 4.3 Organisation of foreign policy work and members for five EU think tanks working on EU foreign policy

Think tank name	CEPS	EIAS	EPC	Madariaga	FoE
Organisation of EU foreign policy work (websites)	Section: Europe in the world (with sub-sections: neighbourhood, diplomacy, security, trade)	NA	Section: enlargement (with sub sections: Turkey, Western Balkans)	NA	Global Europe (with sub-sections: Asia forum and development policy forum)
Members (annual reports)	corporate (112); institutional (91)	NA	platinum (4); corporate (59); professional and business associations (74); diplomatic (87); foundations (25); governmental (3); inter-governmental organisations (18); platforms of NGOs (2); NGOs (43); regional bodies and local authorities (37); religious organisations (5); academic (3); other (1)	Section EU foreign policy (with sub-sections: Eastern Europe and Russia, EEAS, EU–Asia, EU–China, Europe in the world, South Caucasus, North Africa and the Middle East)	NA

In terms of EU foreign policy subjects, EU think tanks are primarily focused on CFSP; in terms of geographical focus, Eastern neighbours and Asia – particularly China – capture most of their attention. Despite their intention to cover a wide range of subjects, during 2014 and the first half of 2015 the CEPS and EPC concentrated the largest part of their foreign policy work on the Eastern neighbourhood policy. However, part of the interest in Eastern Europe was due to the crisis in Ukraine. The negotiations of the Transatlantic Trade and Investment Partnership (TTIP) were also an issue in the 2014 EU agendas of the CEPS and EPC. In fact, all think tanks devoted some effort to tackling current issues, particularly the TTIP and the crisis in Ukraine. Enlargement policies occupy second place in the CEPS and EPC foreign policy agendas.

FoE and Madariaga are also significantly focused on the CFSP, although for different reasons. The EU–China Programme dominated Madriaga's foreign policy agenda in 2014–15, covering issues of cooperation, rule of law and the environment. Finally, FoE has the most varied policy focus. While their Asia Programme focuses on CFSP issues of cooperation and the rule of law, the Development Policy Forum covers issues of poverty and sustainable development within development and cooperation policy. FoE is the only think tank carrying out specific and plentiful work on the CSDP. This is the result of the absorption of the think tank Security and Defence Agenda (SDA), which operated between roughly 2002 and 2014. SDA's transformation together with the demise of ISIS-Europe may be taken as a sign of low demand for security and defence analysis by EU think tanks. But the scant interest in humanitarian aid and civil protection policy is also striking.

Strategies

As Abelson has explained, think tanks use a great variety of strategies to make their present felt in different environments. As many studies have recounted, media exposure is a mechanism for think tanks to contribute to public opinion formation and increase visibility. But, as has been discussed elsewhere (Perez forthcoming), the lack of mass EU media and a fragmented public sphere has left EU think tanks with little interest in this strategy.

Media attention can be a form of indirect influence, but think tanks seeking direct influence in politics frequently develop an advisory capacity. Nevertheless, EU think tanks tend to do little advisory work (Perez 2014a) and this also seems to be the case with the think tanks examined here. The CEPS, EPC and FoE have all signed the EU Transparency Register, which means that at some point they have supplied policy analysis to the Commission or Parliament. However, there was no evidence of these think tanks doing advisory work on EU foreign policy issues for these institutions. Nevertheless, some channels for informal communication with EU policy-makers may be open. Marietje Schaake, who has contributed to FoE's activities, is a trustee of FoE and a member of the European Parliament. Pierre Defraigne, contributor to most of the Madariaga papers written on EU foreign policy and executive director of Madariaga, has a history working for the Commission in different areas of foreign policy that dates back to the 1970s. The close relations between politicians and experts, reinforced by the revolving door phenomenon (experts becoming politicians becoming experts), has proved a key strategy enabling think tanks to influence politics (Abelson 2014b). However, the importance of this phenomenon in the EU still needs to be assessed.

Another way of influencing policy-makers is through research. In the EU one particular means of policy influence is research through framework programmes granted by the EU Commission (Perez 2014b). Examination of their budgets showed that a sizeable share of CEPS and EPC budgets came from EU grants. Nevertheless, no research project in the area of foreign policy that was funded by EU institutions was found.

Judging by their strategies, the five think tanks in EU foreign policy seem to oscillate between roles as educators, knowledge brokers and, sometimes, expert brokers. They can be considered educators because most of their work involves providing timely policy analysis in the form of summaries, briefings, essays and commentaries and organising events in which different policy actors participate (see Table 4.4).[7] The CEPS foreign policy agenda is mostly carried out through publications. These publications are "CEPS commentary" and "policy briefs" written by its own staff with the purpose of introducing a subject, summarising the latest advances or providing a specific perspective. Meanwhile, the EPC has used its organisational capacity to organise a remarkable number of events in 2014–15 at which an apparently wide range of policy actors have been given the opportunity to speak.[8]

In addition, Madariaga has a knowledge broker trait. Most of its work in the foreign policy domain involves the organisation of events at which the main speakers are from academic and research institutes. Academic and research institutes are usual partners of EU think tanks. They frequently attend think tank events and collaborate with them on policy research and framework programmes. Nevertheless, the emphasis on having academics as speakers is a particular strategy of Madariaga.

FoE can be considered an expert broker. Through both events and publications, FoE seems to put its emphasis on expert knowledge. The largest part of FoE's policy analysis is made up of "guest contributions". These two-page pieces provide an expert perspective on one or other of the foreign policy areas on which FoE works. However, the basis of the expertise is not academic – at least not all the time – but practical. For example, there is a piece on development written by Donald Kaberuka, president of the African Development Bank Group, and another on security written by Holger Becker from Microfluidic ChipShop GmbH. And FoE appears to organise its conferences around the same expert principle, inviting the most diverse and evenly representative types of speakers. By bringing together experts from different environments FoE seems to have developed a kind of stakeholder approach, which is sometimes sought by EU institutions.

Table 4.4 Number of events and publications for five EU think tanks by EU foreign policy area, 2014–15

Think tank name	Events							Total number of events	Publications					Total number of publications
	Policy Area								Policy Area					
	CFSP	CSDP	H&CP	ENL	TRADE	DEV			CFSP	CSDP	H&CP	ENL	TRADE	
CEPS	2	4	0	4	2	1		12	25	10	0	11	20	68
EIAS	4	1	2	0	3	1		11	3	0	0	0	2	6
EPC	17	8	1	11	11	0		48	21	7	0	4	4	36
FoE	9	12	0	2	5	4		30	12	5	0	0	0	29
Madariaga	11	5	0	1	4	0		23	5	0	0	0	3	8
Total	43	30	3	18	25	6		124	66	22	0	15	29	147

CEPS, EPC, FoE and Madariaga events count on the significant presence of academics and research institutes, EU institutions – notably the Commission, EEAS and Parliament – and governments (Table 4.5). Taking the EUISS as a reference for think tank foreign policy work, this would seem to be the usual community orbiting around foreign policy issues. A quick glance at the events organised by the EUISS during 2014 and up to June 2015 reveals that the most regular participants are EU institutions, with members of the EEAS, diplomatic services and governments in first place and foreign policy think tanks and professional and business associations in second place. It is interesting, though, to note how little exchange there was between EU think tanks and the EUISS: EU think tanks were rarely seen among the think tanks participating in EUISS events[9] and EUISS members were identified at only a few EU think tank events.

Despite these modest strategies, there are signs that these think tanks are interested in improving their foreign policy agenda and playing a more active role. Specifically, two actions should be considered as attempts by think tanks to improve their analytical capacity and innovate and gain some visibility in the foreign policy field. The first is the "Brussels think tank dialogue". This is an open event organised by ten think tanks located in Brussels – including the CEPS, EPC, FoE and Madariaga – that has taken place once a year since 2011. At this event, members of these think tanks and other policy actors come together for a day to discuss current issues in EU politics. Since its inception this event has included on its agenda a discussion of foreign policy issues. The second is the Security Jam, initially organised by SDA in 2010 and 2012 and relaunched by FoE in 2014. This event consists of an online discussion in which interested people offer advice on global security. As FoE recounts, in the 2014 Jam, 2,300 participants from 129 countries gave their opinion on the issue.[10] Subsequently, FoE elaborated a report that included ten main recommendations.

5. Conclusion

EU think tanks' foreign policy agenda is modest, focused mainly on politicised aspects of the CFSP and those areas that are most relevant for the EU, namely Eastern Europe and China. EU think tanks working on EU foreign policy do not display the "marketing techniques" of foreign affairs think tanks in the US or the UK referred to in the introduction of this book. Rather than investing in research and advocacy they focus on educating policy actors in EU foreign policy subjects through policy analysis and debate. Although the EU system, and particularly the EU foreign policy field, hardly operates as a marketplace as in the US, EU think tanks are investing in subjects that those interested in EU foreign policy – including EU institutions – seek to debate. But it can be questioned whether the use of various "marketing techniques" secures think tanks' influence. As in the US, EU think tanks have captured the attention of a wide range of policy actors, despite their limited marketing techniques. This is seen in the EU think tanks' revenue model, which includes member states and foreign

Table 4.5 Number of speakers at EU foreign policy events for five EU think tanks*

Think tank name	EC	EP	EEAS	EUISS	Other	Diplomatic	Governmental institutions	International governmental organisations	Academic and research institutes	Corporate
CEPS	6	2	2	0	0	3	11	2	28	9
EIAS	6	4	3	0	1	8	0	5	9	0
EPC (Only 13 events)	2	0	2	1	0	2	5	0	3	1
FoE	9	8	7	0	3	11	22	20	19	7
Madariaga	6	1	4	2	3	2	2	0	46	4
Total	**29**	**15**	**18**	**3**	**7**	**26**	**40**	**27**	**105**	**21**

EU total: 72

*This table only shows the most salient speakers at the events. Other types of speakers identified in a few events are regional and local governments, professional and business associations, foundations, NGOs, and journalists.

Table 4.6 EU foreign policy by subject areas

CFSP	CSDP	H&CP	Enlargement	Trade	Development
Preserve peace and strengthen international security	Conflict prevention	Food and nutrition	New Membership	Trade liberalisation	Sustainable development
Promote international cooperation	Crisis management	Shelter			Eradication of poverty
Develop and consolidate democracy, the rule of law and respect for human rights and fundamental freedoms.		Healthcare and medical support			
Diplomacy and partnership in education, the environment, security and defence, crime and human rights		Water and sanitation			
		Protection, coordination and support; disaster preparedness; transport			

Source: EC 2014 and www.europe.eu

governments, corporations, foundations and EU institutions. Nevertheless, given the lack of advocacy among EU think tanks, the influence of these actors on EU think tanks' agendas may not be as significant as in the US.

Consequently, the relevance of EU think tanks in foreign policy is difficult to assess. There are relatively few EU think tanks working in the field. However, those concerned with EU foreign policy are some of the longest established think tanks in Brussels. Their focus on foreign policy is limited considering the scope of their agendas and their strategies seem to pursue a modest educating objective. Nevertheless, these think tanks have a steady level of activity that attracts a fair number of policy actors, notably from EU institutions (particularly those concerned with EU foreign policy like the EEAS), governments, diplomatic services and international institutions. To expand their informational and organisational capacity in foreign policy, these think tanks rely on academics and fellow research institutes in different European countries.

The question is, what does EU think tank behaviour tell us about EU foreign policy governance? It would seem that in Brussels instances of informal governance are mostly found in politicised areas of foreign policy where EU institutions are interested in outsider input. The fact that EU think tanks concentrate on politicised topics and that the main EU institutions concerned with the work of EU think tanks are the Commission, the Parliament and the EEAS indicates that think tanks are mainly contributing to policy areas dominated by ordinary legislative procedure. Moreover, a number of elements suggest that think tanks remain at the periphery of official governance – i.e. that governance processes are not open to a variety of policy actors. One element is the lack of advocacy in this policy area. Another element is the lack of EU investment in the development of policy actor expertise. Think tanks have received grants from EU institutions in relation to a number of policy issues for the purpose of developing research and giving policy advice, but none of them fall in the foreign policy area.

Another question is: what is the role of EU think tanks' events in EU policy-making? From the perspective of informal governance, in order to be considered "governance" think tanks' events need to somehow alter the process and outcome of formal decision-making, otherwise they are simply a practice (i.e. a custom that has no impact on policy-making). However, EU events regularly bring together a number of important policy actors, including EU institutions. In principle, think tanks' events enable the sharing of different points of view and the discussion of alternative scenarios regarding a policy issue. This implies that EU think tanks may reduce uncertainty and contribute to the development of policy consensus. As a result, they have the potential to influence the process of agenda setting, but unless it is possible to identify how a debate becomes policy, a think tank event can only be considered a practice. In order to understand think tank influence on EU foreign policy, it is necessary to identify the conditions that make think tanks part of informal governance processes and explain how they may contribute to the crystallisation of policy makers' thinking about policy options.

Notes

1 See http://eur-lex.europa.eu/legal-content/EN/TXT/?uri=URISERV:a19000
2 For discussions of the concept, see e.g. Bache, George and Bulmer 2011; Kohler-Koch and Rittberger 2006.
3 This is actually a hybrid position – High Representative of the Union for Foreign Affairs and Security Policy/Vice-President of the Commission – associated with both the Council of the European Union and the European Commission (see more on the evolution of this post in Rüger 2011).
4 These think tanks are not included in this research. ISIS-Europe ceased activities in January 2015 and the ICG is not considered a EU think tank for the purposes of this research (see section 3).
5 During the Barroso administration this was called the Bureau of European Policy Advisers.
6 See: www.madariaga.org/programmes/eu-china-programme.
7 The examination of events looked for the presence of EU institutions' representatives (Commission, Parliament, EEAS and other), diplomatic and governmental representatives, international institutions, academic and research institutes (including think tanks), corporations and professional and business associations, foundations and NGOs and journalists.
8 EPC does not provide detailed information on the speakers or attendants to their events. However, in their events' reports they sometimes list the names of the speakers. Our assessment is the result of an examination of 13 events where the speakers were listed.
9 In the 30 activities examined, FoE and the EPC attended a few times while the European Institute of Asian Studies and Wilfried Martens Centre for European Studies attended only one activity.
10 See: www.friendsofeurope.org/security-europe/security-jam-2014-top-10-recommendations/.

References

Abelson, Donald. 2014a. "Old World, New World: The Evolution and Influence of Foreign Affairs Think-Tanks." *International Affairs* 90: 125–42. doi:10.1111/1468-2346.12099.
Abelson, Donald. 2014b. "Changing Minds, Changing Course: Obama, Think Tanks and American Foreign Policy." In Inderjeet Parmar, Linda Miller, and Mark Ledwidge (eds), *Obama and the World: New Directions in US Foreign Policy*. Abingdon: Routledge, 107–19.
Bache, Ian, Stephen George, and Simon Bulmer. 2011. *Politics in the European Union*. 3rd ed. Oxford: Oxford University Press.
Broscheid, Andreas, and David Coen. 2007. "Lobbying Activity and For a Creation in the EU: Empirically Exploring the Nature of the Policy Good." *Journal of European Public Policy* 14, no. 3: 37–41. doi:10.1080/13501760701243749.
Carta, Catherina. 2013. "The EEEAS and EU Executive Actors within the Foreign Policy-Cycle." In Mario Telò and Frederik Ponjaert (eds), *The EU's Foreign Policy. What Kind of Power and Diplomatic Action?* Farnham: Ashgate, 87–103.
CEPS (Centre for European Policy Studies). 2014. *Highlights 2014–15*. Brussels.
Christiansen, Thomas, and Christine Neuhold. 2012. "Introduction." In Thomas Christiansen and Christine Neuhold (eds), *International Handbook on Informal Governance*. Northampton: Edward Elgar.

Diedrichs, Udo. 2011. "Modes of Governance in the EU's Common Foreign and Security Policy." In Udo Diedrichs, Wulf Reiners and Wolfgang Wessels (eds), *The Dynamics of Change in EU Governance*. Cheltenham: Edward Elgar, 149–79.

Dijkstra, Hylke. 2013. *Policy-Making in EU Security and Defense. An Institutional Perspective*. Basingstoke: Palgrave Macmillan.

EC (European Commission). 2014. *The European Union Explained: Trade*. Luxembourg: Publications Office of the European Union. doi:10.2775/58022.

Eising, Rainer. 2008. "Interest Groups in EU Policy-Making." *Living Reviews in European Governance* 3 (4): 1–32. http://www.livingreviews.org/lreg-2008-4.

EPC (European Policy Centre). 2013. *2013: A Year in Review. The State of Cape Town Central City Report*. Brussels. Available at www.capetowncid.co.za.

Higgott, Richard, and Diane Stone. 1994. "The Limits of Influence: Foreign Policy Think Tanks in Britain and the USA." *Review of International Studies* 20, no. 1: 15. doi:10.1017/S0260210500117760.

Joachim, Jutta, and Matthias Dembinski. 2011. "A Contradiction in Terms? NGOs, Democracy, and European Foreign and Security Policy." *Journal of European Public Policy* 18 (February 2015): 1151–68. doi:10.1080/13501763.2011.615204.

Juncos, Ana E., and Karolina Pomorska. 2011. "Invisible and Unaccountable? National Representatives and Council Officials in EU Foreign Policy." *Journal of European Public Policy* 18 (February 2015): 1096–114. doi:10.1080/13501763.2011.615197.

Kleine, Mareike. 2013. *Informal Governance in the European Union. How Governments Make International Organizations Work*. Ithaca, NY: Cornell University Press.

Kohler-Koch, Beate, and Berthold Rittberger. 2006. "The 'Governance Turn' in EU Studies." *Journal of Common Market Studies* 44, no. 1: 27–49.

Krotz, Ulrich, and Richard Maher. 2011. "International Relations Theory and the Rise of European Foreign and Security Policy." *World Politics* 63: 548–79. doi:10.1017/S0043887111000141.

Perez, Marybel. Forthcoming. "The Contribution of Think Tanks to the European Public Sphere." In Hakan Sicakkan (ed), *European Integration, Diversity and the Making of a European Public Sphere*. Cheltenham, UK: Edward Elgar.

Perez, Marybel. 2014a. "Does EU Policymaking Allow for Skilful Networkers But Limited Knowledge Managers? The Think Tanks' Tale." *International Journal of Politics, Culture, and Society* 27: 323–42. doi:10.1007/s10767-013-9172-5.

Perez, Marybel. 2014b. "EU Think Tank Fora as Transaction Cost Reducers : A Study of Informal Interest Intermediation in the EU." *Journal of Contemporary European Research* 10, no. 2: 146–65.

Perez, Marybel. 2015. "What Kind of Public Sphere Shapes the European Educational Research Space?" In Martin Lawn and Normand Romuald (eds), *Shaping of European Education. Interdisciplinary Approaches*. Abingdon: Routledge, 151–69.

Rasmussen, Anne, Brendan J. Carroll and David Lowery. 2014. "Representatives of the Public? Public Opinion and Interest Group Activity." *European Journal of Political Research* 53, no. 2: 250–68. doi:10.1111/1475-6765.12036.

Rüger, Carolin. 2011. "A Position under Construction: Future Prospects of the High Representative after the Treaty of Lisbon." In Gisela Müller-Brandeck-Bocquet and Carolin Rüger (eds), *The High Representative for the EU Foreign and Security Policy – Review and Prospects*. Baden: Nomos, 201–33.

Sherrington, Philippa. 2000. "Shaping the Policy Agenda: Think Tank Activity in the European Union." *Global Society* 14, no. 2: 173–89. doi:10.1080/13600820050008430.

Sjursen, Helene. 2011. "Not so Intergovernmental after All? On Democracy and Integration in European Foreign and Security Policy." *Journal of European Public Policy* 18 (January 2015): 1078–95. doi:10.1080/13501763.2011.615194.

Stone, Diane. 2014. *Non-Governmental Public Action: Knowledge Actors and Transnational Governance.* Basingstoke: Palgrave Macmillan.

Ulrich, Heidi. 2004. "European Union Think Tanks: Generating Ideas, Analysis and Debate." In Diane Stone and Andrew Denham (eds), *Think Tank Traditions. Policy Research and the Politics of Ideas*. Manchester: PUBLISHER, 49–68.

5 Think tanks American style

Donald E. Abelson

Introduction

For the eighth consecutive year, the Global Go To Think Tank Index Report confirmed what scholars of think tanks have known for years – that the US boasts the largest and, presumably, most diverse population of public policy institutes on the globe (McGann 2015). With 1,830 think tanks spread across its 50 states, the country has more institutes conducting research on domestic and foreign policy than there are in all of Europe (McGann 2015: 53). According to the report's extensive database, there are more think tanks based in Washington, DC (396) – where the largest concentration of think tanks in the US can be found – than in the UK (287), Germany (194), and Canada (99) (McGann 2015: 53, 57). While the sheer number of American think tanks is impressive, those who monitor their growth and evolution have become even more consumed by the extent to which some of these institutions have become entrenched in the policy-making process. Indeed, as a select group of think tanks have made their presence felt during key debates over American foreign and defence policy, scholars have begun to pay closer attention to the various ways policy institutes, in cooperation with key stakeholders, are able to help shape public opinion and public policy. Although claims regarding the widespread influence of think tanks are often exaggerated and unfounded, there is a perception in the media and in some policy circles that these organizations occupy an important space at the intersection of the academic and policy-making worlds. And as the stature and visibility of think tanks on the American political landscape has grown, so too has scholarly interest in a subject once considered of marginal interest to those who study domestic and foreign policy.

The purpose of this chapter is not to provide a sweeping history of American think tanks, nor, for that matter, is it to assess the state of literature in the field. Rather, my aim is to reflect on why scholars, journalists and political pundits have become far more invested in chronicling the activities of American think tanks, and why their impressions of these institutions have changed so dramatically in recent years. Once revered as organizations committed to the advancement of knowledge, think tanks such as the Heritage Foundation, the Center for Strategic and International Studies (CSIS) and the CATO Institute, to name a few, are now more often portrayed as institutions intent on furthering their institutional interests at the expense of the national interest. Although this characterization may not be entirely accurate or fair, there is little doubt that think tanks of all ideological stripes remain committed to shaping the political climate of the nation. There is also little doubt that in recent decades think tanks, both inside and beyond the Washington, DC beltway, have developed a pronounced swagger in approaching policy issues. They are more advocacy-oriented, politically and media savvy, and increasingly adept at promoting and marketing policy recommendations. Think tanks also exude a confidence, born from past policy successes, that with the right stakeholders in place, and with secure access to decision-makers at the highest levels of government, they can leave an indelible mark on public policy. But it is not only think tanks in the US that have convinced themselves that they are well suited and equipped to effect policy change. In virtually every corner of the globe, from Shanghai to Warsaw, organizations engaged in research and analysis have, in one way or another, tried to emulate the American think tank experience.

Although think tanks should not be treated as a uniquely American phenomenon, in the US they do possess a certain style – a more assertive advocacy orientation – that institutes from other countries find appealing. Think tanks in some countries, including a handful in Canada, can only dream of the financial and staff resources available at America's elite think tanks. But what attracts foreign think tanks to their American counterparts even more is their ability to establish strong and lasting ties to policy-makers and other stakeholders, a subject that we will examine in this chapter. In short, what makes American think tanks unique, and what affords them a certain style, is not the multimillion dollar budgets and hundreds of staff that only a small fraction of US institutes enjoy. Rather, *it is the many opportunities they are afforded to participate in the policy-making process that set them apart.*

To sharpen the parameters of this inquiry, two central themes, particularly important and relevant to how think tanks in the US are studied and evaluated, will be explored. The first, which informs the prevailing narrative around the think tank phenomenon in the US, is what sociologist Thomas Medvetz (2012: 112) aptly calls the transformational thesis. Simply put, proponents of this thesis, of which I am one, contend that since the latter half of the twentieth century, think tanks have undergone a conversion or reorientation from organizations known for conducting rigorous policy research to institutions that place a higher premium on political advocacy. By shifting their priorities, so the argument goes, think tanks have come to more closely resemble interest groups, political action committees, lobbyists and other bodies committed to policy change. Although Medvetz takes issue with some of the underlying assumptions of the transformational thesis, he too is concerned that as think tanks enjoy even greater success as policy advocates the voices of social scientists conducting research at universities will be further marginalised, the implications of which will be discussed.

The second theme relates to the impression shared by many political commentators in Europe and in North America that think tanks in Washington, DC have assumed too much power and influence. With close and enduring ties to key policy-makers on Capitol Hill, in the White House and throughout the bureaucracy, think tanks are perceived as powerful organizations with influential friends who occupy prominent positions in the policy-making establishment. This access to power is not lost on investigative journalist Brooke Williams and her colleagues, who have uncovered the incestuous relationship between top-tier think tanks, lobbyists, major corporations, and foreign governments (Williams and Silverstein 2013; Lipton, Williams and Confessore, 2014). This impression is reinforced even further when two other factors are considered: the critically important role the media play in enhancing the public visibility of think tanks; and the considerable financial backing high profile think tanks such as the Heritage Foundation, the American Enterprise Institute, Brookings, CSIS, the Center for American Progress, and several of their competitors receive from philanthropic foundations (Bellant 1991; Stefancic and Delgado 1996; Parmar 2012). In light of the considerable access think tanks have to some of the nation's most important power brokers, it is not surprising that these institutions are perceived as ambitious and influential players in a high stakes political game. Nonetheless, as this chapter will demonstrate, these perceptions do not necessarily mirror reality. While it is in the interest of think tanks to create the impression they wield tremendous influence, the scholars who study them must determine the most appropriate ways to evaluate their impact.

By investigating these two interrelated and overlapping themes, a much clearer picture will emerge as to why American think tanks have shifted their priorities in recent years, and why this reorientation appeals to think tanks beyond America's shores. The chapter's first section provides a brief history of think tanks in the US, and identifies the various factors that have contributed to their development. Following this, a short discussion of the many strategies upon which they rely to convey their ideas to multiple stakeholders will be offered. Finally, I will turn my attention to the question of think tank influence. Rather than trying to measure how much or little influence think tanks wield, which often amounts to little more than an exercise in futility, I suggest scholars focus more on the value think tanks bring to policy discussions. This might help to shed light on the more pressing questions of how, and under what circumstances, think tanks can make a positive contribution to advancing the interests of the US.

Reflections on the evolution of American think tanks

Andrew Carnegie, the Scottish-American steel tycoon, Robert Brookings, a St Louis businessman, Herbert Hoover, a mining engineer who would later become the 31st president of the US, and other leading philanthropists and visionaries of the Progressive era (1880–1920) were well aware of the formidable challenges confronting the US in the decades prior to, and in the aftermath, of World War I. They understood, as did many of their contemporaries in the public and private sector, the need for social, economic and political reform, the importance of creating a government that was more efficient and accountable, and the vital contribution "experts" could make in improving the life of the nation. Among other things, they believed that for America to move forward the intellectual resources of the country had to be harnessed and managed in creative and innovative ways.

Their appreciation for how social science expertise could help address many of the ills plaguing the US was undoubtedly inspired by the ground-breaking role settlement houses played at the end of the nineteenth century.[1] Known more for helping immigrants adapt to life in America, settlement houses also served as a laboratory for scholars to study the working conditions of the poor. These institutions accomplished this by inviting sociologists and other university faculty with knowledge of social welfare issues to live and work in the settlement houses. As Jane Addams, co-founder of Chicago's Hull House (1889) observed, the purpose of social science was not only to investigate, but to advocate (Addams 1910; Ross 1992). As Addams and many of her disciples acknowledged, scholars during the so-called Progressive era believed in using their scientific expertise to address tangible social problems (Ibid). This philosophy was not lost on Carnegie, Brookings, Hoover and other influential figures with whom Addams interacted. By the early decades of the twentieth century, each of these men played a crucial role in establishing organizations, which later became commonly referred to as think tanks, to identify the many problems underlying American domestic and foreign policy (Smith 1991a; Ricci 1993; Abelson 1996).

The first wave, 1900–45

The early decades of the twentieth century proved a formidable period for think tank development in the US. Although several prominent universities existed at the time, a coterie of philanthropists, including those named above, and a handful of policy-makers, armed with vision and determination, believed that what were needed were institutions whose primary focus was not teaching, but research and analysis. Guided by the belief that modern science could be used to solve social, economic, and political problems, a philosophy that was widely embraced during the Progressive era (Smith 1991a), they set out to establish privately funded research institutes dedicated ostensibly to serving the public interest (Parmar 2012). With generous funding from Robert Brookings, Andrew Carnegie, Herbert Hoover, John D. Rockefeller, Sr. and Margaret Olivia Sage, among others, several of America's most venerable institutions were founded. These included the Russell Sage Foundation (1907), the Carnegie Endowment for International Peace (1910), the Conference Board (1916), the Institute for Government Research (1916; it merged with the Institute of Economics and the Robert Brookings Graduate School of Economics and Government to form the Brookings Institution in 1927), the Hoover Institution on War, Revolution and Peace (1919), the National Bureau of Economic Research (1920), and the Council on Foreign Relations (1921) (Smith 1991a; Abelson 1996). Although these and other think tanks were created under different and often unusual circumstances, they shared a commitment to debating and investigating a wide range of domestic and foreign policy issues in the hope of improving governmental decision-making. With the support of dozens of scholars recruited primarily from the social sciences, think tanks created during this era claimed to place a premium on producing objective and neutral policy research. However, as previous studies have revealed, their goals were not always entirely altruistic, nor were those of their generous benefactors (Parmar 2012).

While many of the studies produced by these institutes adhere to the highest scholarly standard, the institutes themselves can rarely be regarded as value-neutral research bodies. The Brookings Institution is a case in point. One of America's oldest and most iconic think tanks, Brookings has cultivated a reputation as an independent institute committed to providing objective research and analysis. This commitment was reaffirmed by Brookings President Strobe Talbott following the publication of a *New York Times* article on 6 September 2014 which documented the millions of dollars in funding donated by foreign governments to several high-profile US think tanks. The article, co-written by investigative journalist Brooke Williams, a fellow at Harvard University's Edmond J. Safra Center for Ethics, claimed that in return for the sizeable donations the governments of Qatar and Norway expected the Brookings Institution to lobby on their behalf (Lipton, Williams and Confessore 2014). In a formal statement issued the morning after the publication of the *New York Times* article, Talbott wasted little time addressing these serious allegations. He stated:

> Brookings has over 200 scholars and more than 700 funders for hundreds of research projects. Our scholars determine our research and policy recommendations, not our contributors. We accept funding from foreign governments with the understanding that they are supporting our independent research.
> (Talbott 2014)

What distinguishes Brookings and other early twentieth-century policy institutes from more contemporary think tanks is not their reluctance to become involved in the political arena – after all, Brookings has become far more advocacy-oriented in recent years – but the emphasis they continue to place on engaging in medium- and long-term research. In short, unlike the Heritage Foundation and its many disciples who focus on what is commonly known as "quick response policy research," – publications that can be produced quickly for elected officials – many first-generation think tanks focus on issues policy-makers may want to consider for years to come.

The second wave, 1946–70

By the end of World War II, a new wave of think tanks was emerging in the US, largely in response to growing international and domestic pressures confronting American policy-makers. Acknowledging the invaluable contribution that defence scientists had made during the war, the Truman administration considered the enormous benefits that could be derived by continuing to fund private and university-based research and development centres. By tapping into the expertise of engineers, physicists, biologists, statisticians, and social scientists, policy-makers hoped to meet the many new challenges that they inherited as the

US assumed its role as a hegemonic power in the atomic age. It was in this environment that the idea for creating the most prominent government contractor, the RAND Corporation (RAND is an acronym for research and development), was born (1948). In addition to making many important contributions to American defence policy, RAND was a prototype for other government contractors, including the Hudson Institute, founded by Herman Kahn, and the domestic-policy-oriented Urban Institute, whose creation was strongly endorsed by President Lyndon Johnson (Abella 2008; Kaplan 1985).

In the post–World War II era, policy-makers in Washington, like several philanthropists during the early part of the twentieth century, recognized the important role think tanks could play in several crucial policy areas. They also recognized the potential benefits of drawing on the expertise of independent research institutes that had the luxury of engaging in medium- and long-term strategic research instead of relying on government officials who were often drowned in daily paper work. Particularly in the broad field of national security and foreign policy studies, it was crucial for the government to be able to rely on think tanks that had assembled some of the best analysts in the country and who, unlike policy-makers and bureaucrats in Washington, were less likely to be influenced by partisan interests; however, this was not always possible, as the political leanings of some of America's leading scientists often influenced their policy recommendations. Much has been written about the political views of J. Robert Oppenheimer, director of the Manhattan Project, who would later assume the directorship of the Institute for Advanced Study at Princeton. Along similar lines, studies have documented the politics of Herman Kahn and Edward Teller, father of the hydrogen bomb. Both scientists enjoyed long careers at some of America's leading think tanks.

The US had entered an era in which its actions abroad would have a profound impact on the world in which it had assumed the role of a global power. What it required was sound, informative policy advice, and, for much of it, it turned to RAND and the Hudson Institute. But just as the federal government relied on these and other think tanks for advice on defence, foreign policy and security issues, President Johnson looked to the Urban Institute to suggest ways to alleviate the many economic, social, and political problems contributing to urban unrest throughout the turbulent decade of the 1960s. For Johnson, the war waging inside the US deserved as much, if not more, attention as conflicts taking place beyond America's borders. The onset of the Cold War and the war on poverty placed new demands on the US government and provided greater opportunities for think tanks to make their presence felt. Like the generation of think tanks before them, government contractors began to fill a void in the policy-research community.

The postwar period in the US also witnessed the emergence of several other think tanks, including the CSIS and the Institute for Policy Studies (IPS), which were not established as government contractors but, nonetheless, quickly became immersed in Washington's policy-making community. Founded in 1962 and home to such luminaries as Zbigniew Brzezinski, national security adviser to President

Carter, Admiral William Crowe, former chairman of the Joint Chiefs of Staff, and James Schlesinger, former secretary of defense, CSIS often works closely with incoming administrations to outline foreign and defence policy issues. In many respects CSIS functions both as a research institution and as an advocacy think tank, and according to a team of investigative journalists and scholars is a favourite among foreign governments looking for more leverage and influence on Capitol Hill (Lipton, Williams and Confessore 2014; Smith 1993). The IPS, co-founded by Marcus Raskin and Richard Barnett in 1963, is another Washington-based think tank known for its interest in American foreign policy; however, unlike the more mainstream CSIS, the IPS has developed a reputation as Washington's think tank of the left for its Marxist/radical approach to US foreign policy. Few would dispute its status as an ideologically driven advocacy think tank (Powell 1988).

The third wave, 1971–89

In the US in the mid-1970s and 1980s, a new breed of policy institute – the advocacy think tank – was beginning to attract considerable exposure. What distinguished advocacy think tanks from the earlier types of think tanks already established in the US was not their desire to study public policy issues, but their profound determination to market their ideas to various target audiences. Rather than reflecting on important policy issues from the comfort of their book-lined offices, advocacy think tanks embraced an entrepreneurial spirit by immersing themselves in the political arena. Ideas in hand, they began to think strategically about how to most effectively influence policy-makers, the public, and the media. Dipping into the American Enterprise Institute's (1943) play book, the Heritage Foundation, founded in 1973, (Edwards 1997, 2013) was at the forefront of this new wave, elevating political advocacy to new heights. Specializing in quick-response policy research, Heritage, before the dawn of the internet, stressed the importance of providing members of Congress and the executive with hand-delivered 1–2 page briefing notes on key domestic and foreign policy issues. Encouraged by the critical role Heritage played during the Reagan transition of 1980, dozens of think tanks combining elements of scholarship with aggressive marketing techniques began to take root throughout this period. These included the Rockford Institute (1976), which enjoyed close ties to Reform presidential candidate Pat Buchanan, the libertarian Cato Institute (1977), and the Economic Policy Institute (1986).

The think tank population in the US grew considerably during the 1970s and 1980s as both policy-makers and policy entrepreneurs began not only to identify the need for independent policy advice, but to discover how effective think tanks could be in influencing public opinion and public policy. The growth of conservative advocacy institutions, in particular, was largely driven by generous benefactors who believed that with sufficient funding think tanks could have a significant impact in shaping the political dialogue. Think tanks continued to spring up across the US in the 1990s and into the 2000s, and, in many cases, are making their presence felt. While many recent think tanks share much in common with earlier generations of policy institutes, there are, as the most recent wave of think tank development reveals, some notable differences.

The fourth wave, 1990–2015

Over the past 25 years, different varieties of think tanks have emerged, some resembling a hybrid of previous generations, contributing to an increasingly diverse population. Although they may not constitute a new wave, vanity or legacy-based think tanks, which can be found both in the US and Canada, deserve some recognition. In the US, legacy-based think tanks such as the (Jimmy) Carter Center (1982) at Emory University and the (Richard) Nixon Center for Peace and Freedom (1994), renamed the Center for the National Interest in 2011, have developed a wide range of research programs to help advance the legacies of their founders. By contrast, vanity think tanks, usually established by sitting, aspiring, or retiring office holders, are more concerned with framing ideas and issues that will help lend intellectual credibility to their political platforms, a function no longer performed adequately by mainstream political parties.

Vanity think tanks are also established, some have claimed, to circumvent spending limits imposed on presidential candidates by federal campaign finance laws (Abelson 2009). Examples include: former Senator Bob Dole's (R-Kansas) short-lived institute, Better America; the Progress and Freedom Foundation (1993), an organization with close links to former Speaker of the House and republican presidential candidate Newt Gingrich; United We Stand, established by Texas billionaire Ross Perot; and Empower America, founded in 1993 by an impressive band of neo-conservatives, including the late Jeane Kirkpatrick, William Bennett, and former republican vice-presidential candidate Jack Kemp, who passed away in 2009. In July 2004, Empower America joined forces with Citizens for a Sound Economy to form FreedomWorks, a Washington, DC-based conservative and libertarian lobby group which, to its credit, does see itself "primarily as a think tank."

The proliferation of think tanks in the US showed few signs of slowing down as we entered the new millennium. In the US, a handful of newcomers, including the Center for a New American Security (2007), a think tank with close ties to the Obama administration, were making an impression (Abelson 2014). And there is little evidence to suggest that the emergence of think tanks will come to a halt. But why do think tanks continue to take root in the US? What is it about this country that provides think tanks with such fertile soil to grow and expand? It is to this question that we now turn.

The perfect storm: Why think tanks thrive in the US

For think tanks to communicate ideas effectively, they require access to decision-makers and to other key stakeholders (Abelson 2006, 2009). The highly decentralized and fragmented nature of the American political system offers innumerable channels through which to interact with elected and appointed officials in every branch and at every level of government. When this very porous system is combined with a weak party system that does not require members to tow the party line, and a federal bureaucracy that undergoes considerable turnover every time administrations change, think tanks can target hundreds of policy-makers. Newly elected members of Congress lacking policy expertise, seasoned White House officials in need of advice, and thousands of bureaucrats looking to tap into extensive policy networks can benefit from strengthening their ties to think tanks. Think tanks also understand that policy-makers in Washington generally have little trust in government. Indeed, the general distrust many policy-makers have of government institutions is one of the reasons why they are only too willing to turn to the external policy research community for advice.

The so-called "revolving door" phenomenon in the US is also useful in explaining why think tanks have gained such notoriety inside the Beltway. This phenomenon, which is observed generally in the weeks and months following the installation of a new presidential administration, refers to the exodus of scholars from think tanks into government and the steady flow of dozens of battle hardened policy-makers to think tanks. Scholars from think tanks, looking to make their mark in politics, often decide to vacate the comfort and serenity of their book-lined offices to participate directly in policy-making. Indeed, in some cases, think tanks serve as governments in exile, waiting for the right time to emerge on the political stage. This was certainly the case for scholars at the more liberal/centrist Brookings Institution during the administrations of George W. Bush. When his two terms in office came to an end, several Brookings scholars made their way into the Obama administration along with a handful of policy experts from the Center for American Progress and the Center for a New American Security. Once their taste for Washington politics has been satiated, or their careers have come to an abrupt end, policy-makers often return to think tanks to decompress and to write their memoirs. They are often joined by other mid and high-level policy-makers who decide to cash in on their status as political insiders to secure a lucrative post at a prominent think tank. For many seasoned policy-makers, including Condoleeza Rice, former US Secretary of State and National Security Advisor, think tanks become their retirement homes. Rice currently holds an endowed chair at the Hoover Institution, located on the picturesque campus of Stanford University.

A favourable tax regime further explains why the US offers such a hospitable environment for think tanks. Registered as charities under the Internal Revenue Code, think tanks have benefited enormously from the contributions of several philanthropic foundations and corporations (Parmar 2012; Bellant 1991). In return for their gift, donors receive a generous tax deduction. But even more importantly, donors who make sizeable contributions are often able to shape the research agenda of think tanks in ways that satisfy their interests. Moreover, donors can be rewarded with access to powerful policy-makers (Hamburger and Gold 2014; Abelson 1996).

Think tanks have also benefited from a strong culture of policy entrepreneurship in America. Several of the most visible think tanks in the US, including the

Heritage Foundation, the CATO Institute and the Center for American Progress were established by policy entrepreneurs willing and able to secure the funds required to help advance and promote their vision of the country. Unlike in other advanced industrial nations such as Canada, where several think tanks owe their existence to government initiatives and to generous public coffers, the majority of think tanks in the US are financed by the private sector (Abelson 2009).

When the various factors highlighted above are taken into account, it is not surprising the US has produced so many think tanks. Not only do there appear to be sufficient funds available to underwrite the cost of establishing more of these institutions, but there is a growing demand on the part of policy-makers, journalists, business leaders and other opinion makers for the various products and services think tanks provide. Ironically, while the currency of think tanks might have decreased because of the lack of serious policy research they produce, an observation made recently by Hudson Institute scholar Tevi Troy (2012), the market value of think tanks may be increasing. In other words, since think tanks such as the American Enterprise Institute (Rubin 2014) Heritage (Edwards 2013) and Brookings (Abelson 2014) are able to cater to the varied needs of stakeholders – from providing succinct and pithy policy briefs to validating a presidential candidate's policy prescriptions – their relevance and standing in the Washington political community appear to be on the rise (Troy 2012). From framing policy discussions around the war on terror, to pushing back attempts to reform health care in the US, think tanks, and the sister organizations they have created to engage in more public advocacy (Abelson 2014), are making their voices heard. If their stature and visibility is growing, and there is ample evidence to suggest it is, it is even more important to consider if the reorientation of think tanks from repositories of policy expertise to agents of advocacy has enhanced or undermined their status in the policy-making process.

The more things change . . .

When scholars on both sides of the Atlantic observe the behaviour of more advocacy-oriented think tanks in the US, the UK and throughout much of Europe, it is difficult for them not to become nostalgic about early twentieth-century policy research institutions. Reflecting on think tanks of this period, social and cultural historian James A. Smith (1991a), political scientist David Ricci (1993), and several others conjure up images of experts working tirelessly at their desks to identify the underlying causes of economic, social and political unrest. Given the avowedly ideological leanings of many of today's think tanks, it is understandable why these and other admirers of Britain's Fabian Society and Chatham House, home of the Royal Institute of International Affairs, and of the Brookings Institution during its formative years are concerned about the direction think tanks have taken in recent decades. For those longing for the re-emergence of more traditional policy research institutes, it is both troubling and worrisome that think tanks such as the Heritage Foundation (Edwards 1997, 2013), the Adam Smith Institute (Pirie 2012) and countless others have, in effect, become lobbyists for various political causes. Indeed, as Williams and Silverstein (2013) point out, while employed at think tanks, several scholars have gone one step further in this direction by establishing lobbying firms to advance the interests of clients on Capitol Hill. In short, rather than helping government think its way through complex policy problems, a goal articulated by institutions during the Progressive era, critics (Stefancic and Delgado 1996) contend that contemporary think tanks have embarked on a dangerous and far less virtuous path. But have they?

In retracing the history of think tanks, it is tempting to portray Progressive-era think tanks as high-minded and virtuous, and advocacy think tanks as opportunistic and sinister. But to label advocacy think tanks (which often promote progressive policies) as nefarious and self-serving would be inaccurate and misleading. At the turn of the twentieth century, think tanks such as the Russell Sage Foundation (1907) and the Carnegie Endowment for International Peace (1910) may very well have made a concerted effort to inject both social science and a social conscience into discussions around various public policy issues. Nonetheless, it would be naïve to suggest that their goals were entirely altruistic. They did not turn a blind eye to how their research could influence policy debates in ways that they deemed important both for their institution and for their country.

Exercising influence need not have negative repercussions. Heralded as the quintessential think tank because of its commitment to policy research, the Brookings Institution, for example, took great pride in advising members of Congress to draft the Budget and Accounting Act of 1921 (Critchlow 1985; Smith 1991a). This legislation resulted in the creation of institutions and practices that are still used to oversee and implement the federal budget. Similarly, in the same year, the New York-based Council on Foreign Relations was established as an exclusive club for intellectuals and statesmen to discuss America's role in the world (Parmar 2004). Some of the earliest think tanks refrained from interfering directly in deliberations on Capitol Hill and in the White House; however, from the time these institutions took root in America, they were well aware of how their ideas could shape and influence the politics of the day.

Think tanks created during the Progressive era understood the power of ideas. After all, this is why Carnegie, Brookings, Hoover and other philanthropists invested in these institutions. They were established to help inform, educate, advocate and, yes, at times, to indoctrinate. What allowed them to succeed was their ability to make their views known. Progressive-era think tanks might have assigned a far higher priority to generating rigorous policy research than do many advocacy think tanks of the late twentieth and early twenty-first century, but they should not be seen as altruistic guardians of the public interest. Institutions, regardless of whether they are classified as think tanks, interest groups or lobbyists, are motivated by similar goals – to shape and influence public opinion and public policy in ways that satisfy their core interests. Where they differ is with respect to how they define their priorities, the resources they allocate to research and marketing, and the strategies they employ to achieve their desired objectives.

Early twentieth-century think tanks, as well as those created over the past 40 years, perform similar roles and functions. Yet, regardless of when they were incorporated, what sustains them is their ability to engage in policy research and public advocacy. It is not the role of think tanks that has changed. What has changed is the higher premium think tanks place on advocacy and marketing over policy research, a trend that was popularized by the Heritage Foundation in the early 1970s. Indeed, no other think tank in the US or, for that matter, around the globe, has had a greater impact in changing the complexion and orientation of think tanks than Heritage (Edwards 2013). It was the Heritage Foundation that stressed the importance of providing policy-makers with timely and policy-relevant research; and it was Heritage that influenced generations of think tanks to combine policy research with aggressive marketing. The rise of the Heritage Foundation and hundreds of other advocacy think tanks continues to generate concerns in scholarly circles, but the decision of think tanks to become more invested in advocacy than in research, a subject that is explored in more detail in Chapter 2, was predictable, particularly in a political system that values political expediency over the creation and dissemination of knowledge. In fact, think tanks such as the Heritage Foundation that can provide policy-makers and other key stakeholders with the ammunition they need to achieve their political goals are handsomely rewarded. By satisfying the wishes of their core constituents, think tanks may, at the very least, become even more entrenched in the policy-making process.

Recognizing the importance of conveying their ideas to multiple target audiences, think tanks have become adept at making their presence felt. They rely on a range of governmental and non-governmental channels to make their views known. These range from taking part in interviews on political talk shows and network newscasts to testifying before congressional committees, and serving as advisors on presidential campaigns and transition teams. As the marketplace of ideas has become increasingly congested, think tanks have devoted even more time and resources to extending their reach (Abelson 2006).

The strategies of American think tanks

Determining what constitutes a think tank has and continues to elude most scholars in the field, but identifying the various ways these kind of organizations interact with decision-makers and other influential stakeholders is hardly a mystery. During the Progressive era, think tanks communicated their findings primarily by producing and disseminating reports, and by holding conferences and meetings with policy-makers, business leaders, academics and journalists. In recent years, several studies have documented the extensive ties that were established between prominent think tanks such as Brookings, the Council on Foreign Relations and RAND (Smith 1991b; Parmar 2004; Abella 2008) and the leading political and business leaders with whom they discussed and debated a range of issues.

By the late 1960s and early 1970s, think tanks began to think more strategically about how to capture the attention of policy-makers and the public. And, as noted, no organization would prove to have more of an impact in shaping how think tanks would communicate in the future than the Washington, DC-based Heritage Foundation. Established in 1973 by former congressional aides Edwin Feulner and Paul Weyrich, the Heritage Foundation not only changed the complexion of the think tank community, but introduced new and revolutionary techniques for think tanks to enhance their visibility (Edwards 1997, 2013). For Feulner and Weyrich, think tanks could become far more relevant in the policy-making process if they better understood the needs of policy-makers. Rather than replicating what the Brookings Institution and other more traditional think tanks had done for years, Heritage introduced a model based on what they called "quick response policy research." Simply put, instead of only producing book-length studies that policy-makers rarely had the time or inclination to read, Heritage researchers were instructed to write and disseminate briefs on timely and relevant policy issues. The briefs were typically 4–6 pages in length, offered recommendations on how the US could address specific domestic and foreign policy challenges, and, in the pre-internet age, were hand delivered to every member of Congress. In addition, Heritage produced several other types of publications that catered to different target audiences.

By the time Ronald Reagan assumed the presidency in January 1981, Heritage had become one of the leading think tanks in the country, thanks in part to the publication of *Mandate for Leadership* (Heatherly 1981), a weighty tome that served as a blueprint for the incoming administration. Heritage's meteoric rise was also due in no small measure to its commitment to marketing ideas aggressively, the hallmark of advocacy think tanks. For Feulner, a graduate of the Wharton School of Business who held onto the presidency of Heritage for over three decades, ideas were no different than commodities being traded on the New York Stock Exchange. During his lengthy tenure, he often noted that ideas could only gain traction if they were properly marketed to and endorsed by large segments of the population. As important as it was to Feulner and to Weyrich to strengthen their ties to key business, media and political figures, they never lost sight of the importance of connecting with the American people. In its early years, a large percentage of Heritage's budget was derived from thousands of small donations.

Heritage's approach to marketing its ideas to multiple stakeholders has been adopted by hundreds of other think tanks both inside the Beltway and across the US. Not surprisingly, those institutions that have bought into the Heritage model rely on similar channels to enhance their visibility. Scholars from think tanks appear regularly as "talking heads" on television and radio programs; testify before legislative committees; organize seminars, workshops and conferences for policy-makers, journalists, congressional staffers and academics; establish close ties to appointed officials throughout the bureaucracy; distribute publications electronically; maintain blogs on their websites; use social media, including Twitter and Facebook to communicate to younger audiences; deliver lectures at various universities; and occasionally take a leave of absence to work on congressional and presidential campaigns.

The strategies employed by think tanks are carefully coordinated for maximum results. But unlike for-profit organizations, their success or failure is not measured by quarterly losses or gains. It is determined by how much of an impact they have had in influencing public policy. Directors of think tanks employ several metrics, such as media exposure and the frequency with which their scholars testify before congressional committees, to gauge their standing in the policy-making community. Unfortunately, these and other indicators have proven to be unreliable measures of policy influence. While think tanks have a vested interest in convincing stakeholders that their organizations wield tremendous influence, the scholars who study them have yet to agree on how to evaluate their performance. In the final section, our attention will turn to how we might be able to more accurately assess the impact or influence of think tanks.

Think tanks by the numbers

It was not long ago when think tank directors, and university administrators for that matter, celebrated the publication of a study that enhanced the prestige of their institution. The quality of the book or article written by one of their scholars, and the positive reviews it generated, was what mattered most. However, in recent years, as the competition for funding has intensified, the priorities of those entrusted to oversee research programs at think tanks and institutions of higher learning have changed dramatically. Think tanks and universities have adopted the language of corporations, and, in doing so, devote much of their time to discussing metrics and performance indicators. In the era of corporatization, numbers matter. For think tanks, this means identifying the various ways their achievements can be evaluated relative to their competitors. Although they may disagree on which indicators or measurements are most significant, there are few numbers they can afford to disregard.

In an effort to lure potential donors, and to appease those who have already contributed generously, think tanks track how often their institution has been cited by the print and broadcast media; the number of interviews experts have given; how many followers they have on Twitter and Facebook; and the number of times their colleagues have been asked to testify before congressional hearings. They also keep a close watch on the number of publications that have been downloaded from their website; the number of visits to their website; the number of followers they have on Twitter and Facebook; and how many of their staff have served in various government posts (Abelson 2006). If that is not enough, some think tanks monitor the number of times they have been referred to in the Congressional Record and in other government and academic indices. And, of course, they are vigilant when it comes to determining how well they have done in fundraising.

Many of these so-called indicators of policy influence such as media exposure make their way into the annual reports of think tanks, and are showcased in the most positive light. For think tanks, these numbers are intended to convince stakeholders that with more funding they could become even more influential players in the political arena. Unfortunately, in their efforts to paint a glowing portrait of their accomplishments, directors of think tanks fail to point out the vast difference between public visibility and policy relevance. While there is no doubt that some of the indicators referenced above may help scholars determine how much visibility think tanks enjoy, they are of little use when it comes to assessing how much of an impact these institutions have in influencing policy outcomes. Recording the number of publications downloaded from a think tank's website, or how often the media refer to policy institutes does not provide valuable insight into who or what influenced the actions of Congress or the White House.

To make better sense of the complex world of policy-making, and the role think tanks play in it, scholars must rely on far more than numbers; they require context. Through interviews and surveys with key participants in the policy-making process, and by accessing relevant archives, it is possible to shed far more light on the conditions under which think tanks are able to achieve influence. But to do this requires the construction of case studies that provide a detailed account of how ideas advanced by various think tanks made their way through the policy-making process. Still, isolating the impact that think tanks have had at different stages of the policy cycle remains a formidable undertaking. As Martin Anderson, a senior fellow at the Hoover Institution observed, "Every successful idea has a hundred mothers and fathers. Every bad idea is an orphan." (Abelson 2010)

Determining how much or little influence think tanks wield is inherently difficult, a conclusion reached several years ago by Leslie Gelb, former President of the Council on Foreign Relations. In reflecting on this issue, he remarked on how it is virtually impossible to measure the influence of think tanks on Congress, the executive branch and on the media as it tends to be "highly episodic, arbitrary, and difficult to predict." (Abelson 2006: 167) Yet, notwithstanding the methodological obstacles that must be overcome to properly assess the impact of think tanks on public opinion and public policy, directors of think tanks remain convinced that their institutes wield enormous influence. When funding dollars are at stake, think tanks have an incentive to measure their performance. However, the preoccupation think tanks have with metrics need not become an obsession for the scholars who study them. In fact, as think tanks continue to proliferate in the US and around the globe, historians, political scientists and sociologists will need to think more critically about how to evaluate the contribution these organizations make to policy development.

Conclusion: New thinking about think tanks

As interest in the role of think tanks in the US and in other countries continues to grow, it is important to take stock of what we know and don't know about these eclectic and diverse organizations. While much has been written about the evolution of think tanks, and the various strategies on which they rely to influence policy change, we know far less about their impact on specific policy outcomes. There has been ample speculation about how a small group of think tanks convinced President George W. Bush to wage war on Iraq (Abelson 2006), and even more discussion in the media about the prevalence of think tank scholars in the Obama administration. But, despite being a popular topic for discussion in the media, scholars still know very little about how to evaluate the impact of think tanks. Part of the problem is that those who study think tanks need to ask different questions. Rather than fixating on how much or little influence think tanks wield, we should try to determine what value or contribution institutes make to important policy discussions. How have they enriched our understanding of complex policy issues? Were their ideas useful? How so? And if their ideas were deemed irrelevant, why was this the case? Did the political climate in Washington facilitate or undermine the ability of certain think tanks to participate in policy debates? In other words, we need to develop a new narrative around think tanks that explores in greater depth what they have contributed, instead of how much *influence* they might have exercised.

The orientation of think tanks has indeed changed dramatically since the days of Carnegie, Brookings and Hoover. As this chapter has illustrated, these institutions now devote far more attention to advocacy than to policy research, and this is unlikely to change. It is unlikely to change because, despite increased competition for funding, think tanks have grown in numbers and in popularity. Indeed, over the past three decades, hundreds of think tanks have taken root throughout the industrialized and developing world. While they vary enormously in terms of size and scope, what they share is an admiration for what American think tanks such as Brookings and Heritage have achieved. Although those nostalgic for Progressive-era policy institutes may mourn the rise of advocacy think tanks, their apparent success will, in all likelihood, ensure their longevity. The founders of early twentieth-century think tanks might not have imagined a time when these organizations would become such an integral feature of the political landscape, and might have taken issue with some of the tactics they employ to enhance their visibility. They might also have been disappointed with think tanks that do not place a premium on generating rigorous policy research. However, they would have celebrated the extent to which these organizations have been able to encourage and stimulate discussion about important policy issues.

It is understandable why think tanks are appealing to policy-makers and to other stakeholders who expect and desire little more than a basic knowledge of US domestic and foreign policy. It is also very troubling. As Thomas Medvetz (2012: 225) observes in his recent book, the success and popularity of think tanks has made it increasingly difficult for social scientists at universities to have their voices heard. Policy-makers want policy briefs, not lectures, from the professoriate. The unlimited value social science research could bring to the US motivated Carnegie, Brookings and Hoover to establish think tanks at the turn of the turn of the twentieth century. Ironically, within a matter of decades, the discipline they valued most has been marginalized by the very institutions they created. They had the right idea – it is how think tanks have executed their strategy that has caused some concern.

References

Abella, A. 2008. *Soldiers of Reason: The Rand Corporation and the Rise of the American Empire.* Orlando, FL: Harcourt, Inc.
Abelson, Donald E. 1996. *American Think Tanks and their Role in US Foreign Policy.* New York and London: Macmillan and St. Martin's Press.
Abelson, Donald E. 2006. *A Capitol Idea: Think Tanks and US Foreign Policy.* Kingston and Montreal: McGill-Queen's University Press.
Abelson, Donald E. 2009. *Do Think Tanks Matter? Assessing the Impact of Public Policy Institutes.* 2nd edition. Kingston and Montreal: McGill-Queen's University Press.
Abelson, Donald E. 2010. "Think Tanks – Definition, Their Influence and US Foreign Policy." Interview with Leonhardt van Efferink, *Exploring Geopolitics.* Available at www.exploringgeopolitics.org/Interview_Abelson_Donald_Think_Tanks_Definition.
Abelson, Donald E. 2014. "Changing Minds, Changing Course: Obama, Think Tanks and American Foreign Policy." In Inderjeet Parmar, Linda B. Miller, and Mark Ledwidge (eds), *Obama and the World: New Directions in US Foreign Policy.* 2nd edition. London: Routledge, 107–19.
Addams, Jane. 1910. *Twenty Years at Hull House.* New York: Macmillan.
Bellant, R. 1991. *The Coors Connection: How Coors Family Philanthropy Undermines Democratic Pluralism.* Cambridge, MA: South End Press.
Critchlow, D.T. 1985. *The Brookings Institution, 1916–52: Expertise and the Public Interest in a Democratic Society.* Dekalb, Illinois: Northern Illinois University Press.
Edwards, L. 1997. *The Power of Ideas: The Heritage Foundation at 25 Years.* Ottawa, Illinois: Jameson Books.
Edwards, L. 2013. *Leading the Way: The Story of Ed Feulner and the Heritage Foundation.* New York: Crown Forum.
Hamburger, Tom, and Matea Gold. 2014. "Google, Once Disdainful of Lobbying, Now a Master of Washington Influence." *Washington Post*, 12 April.
Heatherly, C.L. (ed). 1981. Mandate for Leadership: policy management in a conservative administration. Washington, DC: Heritage Foundation.
Lipton, Eric, Brooke Williams and Nicholas Confessore. 2014. "Foreign Powers Buy Influence at Think Tanks." *New York Times*, 6 September.
McGann, J.G. 2013. *2012 Global Go To Think Tank Index Report.* Philadelphia: University of Pennsylvania, Think Tanks and Civil Societies Program.
McGann, J.G. 2015. *2014 Global Go To Think Tank Index Report.* Philadelphia: University of Pennsylvania, Think Tanks and Civil Societies Program.
McGann, J.G., and R.K. Weaver (eds). 2000. *Think Tanks & Civil Societies: Catalysts for Ideas and Action.* New Brunswick, New Jersey: Transaction Publishers.
Medvetz, T. 2012. *Think Tanks in America.* Chicago: University of Chicago Press.
Parmar, I. 2004. *Think Tanks and Power in Foreign Policy.* Basingstoke: Palgrave Macmillan.
Parmar, I. 2012. *Foundations of the American Century: The Ford, Carnegie, & Rockefeller Foundations in the Rise of American Power.* New York: Columbia University Press.
Pirie, M. 2012. *Think Tank: The Story of the Adam Smith Institute.* London: Biteback Publishing.
Powell, S. Steven. 1988. *Covert Cadre: Inside the Institute for Policy Studies.* Ottawa, Il; Green Hill Publishers.
Ricci, D.M. 1993. *The Transformation of American Politics: The New Washington and the Rise of Think-Tanks.* New Haven: Yale University Press.

Ross, Dorothy. 1992. *The Origins of American Social Science*. New York: Cambridge University Press.
Rubin, Jennifer. 2014. "Why the American Enterprise Institute Chief Is so Popular." *Washington Post*, 2 April.
Smith, J.A. 1991a. *The Idea Brokers: Think Tanks and the Rise of the New Policy Elite*. New York: The Free Press.
Smith, J.A.. 1991b. *Brookings at Seventy-Five*. Washington, DC: The Brookings Institution.
Smith, J.A.. 1993. *Strategic Calling: The Center for Strategic and International Studies 1962–92*. Washington, DC: Center for Strategic and International Studies.
Stefancic, J., and R. Delgado. 1996. *No Mercy: How Conservative Think Tanks and Foundations Changed America's Social Agenda*. Philadelphia: Temple University Press.
Talbott, Strobe. 2014. "A Message from Strobe Talbott, President of the Brookings Institution." *Brookings Institution News Release*, 7 September.
Troy, T. 2012. "Devaluing the Think Tank." *National Affairs*, 10. Available at http://www.nationalaffairs.com/publications/detail/devaluing-the-think-tank.
Williams, Brooke and Ken Silverstein. 2013. "Meet the Think Tank Scholars who are also Beltway Lobbyists." *The New Republic*, 10 May.

6 Germany
The think and the tank

Josef Braml

Introduction

The reconfiguration of global power, whose central feature is the unfolding bipolarity between China and the United States, forces German foreign policy elites, especially think tanks, to think beyond their traditional transatlantic mantra. Yet the nationalistic overkill of the Nazi era makes it difficult for today's policy thinkers in Germany to cope with the geo-politics of major powers. It is important to consider Germany's historical experience in order to understand why German think tanks' attributes and activities have only slowly and carefully been changing over time.

A sketch of German think tank history

The history of German think tanks[1] begins with the foundation of four of today's seven large economic research institutes: the Hamburg Institute of International Economics (1908), the Kiel Institute of World Economics at the University of Kiel (1914), the German Institute for Economic Research (1925), and the Rhine-Westphalia Institute for Economic Research (1926). Also in 1926, the Association for Efficient Public Administration assumed the task of enhancing communication between the business world, academia, and public administration. Attempting to bring economic principles and efficiency to the government, the association had a mission similar to the one which inspired the National Bureau of Economic Research and the Brookings Institution during the same post-World War I period in the United States. Similarly, the Center for Public Finance at the University of Cologne (1927) assumed its mission to improve the performance of government in financial matters. This period of initial growth was followed by a period of zero growth. The Nazi dictatorship did not allow for independent research organizations. For example, the Social Democratic Party's Friedrich Ebert Foundation, established in 1925, was banned in 1933, and it was only able to resume its activities after the war, in 1947.

In the aftermath of World War II, German think tanks witnessed a period of considerable growth which was markedly stronger than in the United States. From 1946 to 1967, the number of newly founded institutes was double that in the United States (Braml 2004: 276, 285). In general, the think tanks which emerged during this post-war period were either special interest oriented advocacy tanks,[2] politically oriented party foundations/think tanks (of which there were a handful), or, for the most part, organizations which were less politically or special interest driven, but rather mandated or funded by the government – either directly in the form of contracts or through other intermediate funding mechanisms – in order to improve matters at home and abroad.

With the exception of a few interest oriented advocacy organizations – such as the Institute for Economic and Social Research of the Hans Böckler Foundation of the German Trade Union Federation (1946); the Cologne Institute for Business Research (1951), which is supported by the employers' and industrial associations; the Walter Raymond Foundation of the Confederation of German Employers' Associations (1952); the Research Institute of the Protestant Churches in Germany (1957); and the Karl Bräuer Institute of the German Taxpayers' Association (1965) – the organizations emerging after the war were mainly creatures of the government and were not driven by special interests. The German government spurred the growth of think tanks to rebuild the domestic infrastructure and to re-establish the country's international credibility.

The federal and state governments' domestic efforts to rebuild economic and human resources in the aftermath of World War II become visible with the creation of the Academy for Regional Research and Regional Planning (1946), the Dortmund Social Policy Research Center (1946), the Institute for Economic Research (1949), the German Institute for International Educational Research (1951), the German Youth Institute (1963), the German Institute for Distance Learning (1967), and the Institute for Employment Research of the Federal Employment Services Agency (1969). Encouraged by a pro-government intellectual environment and a corresponding economic (Keynesian) reasoning, the German government assumed a more active role in shaping social and economic developments. This was paralleled in the United States, where the government also became more involved in research both on domestic matters and foreign policy after the war.

The German government's increased foreign policy efforts, engaging in "quiet" or "second track diplomacy," became evident with the creation of organizations such as the Franco-German Institute (1948), the Research Institute of the German Council on Foreign Relations (1955), the Institute of Asian Affairs (1956), the German Foundation for International Development (1959), the Arnold Bergstraesser Institute for Socio-Cultural Research (1960), the Federal Institute for Russian, East European and International Studies[3] (1961), the German Institute for International and Security Affairs (SWP; 1962), and the German Development Institute (1964). Karl Kaiser, former research director of the German Council on Foreign Relations, explains the Council's origins:

> The society was founded with the Royal Institute of International Affairs (Chatham House) and the Council on Foreign Relations as role models in mind. The idea was to create an organization in the Federal Republic – which in 1955 was, with a few exceptions, given full autonomy in terms of foreign

policy – to bring together those elites in Germany which contribute to the foreign policy dialogue. The Federal Republic wanted to catch up in terms of foreign policy discussions and expertise which had already been established in other countries; people wanted to improve the bipartisan foreign policy consensus, including many participants exchanging ideas based on mutual trust; and people wanted to make the public debate on foreign policy, security and defense matters more informed and rational. (Interview with Karl Kaiser, former Director of the German Council on Foreign Relations, 25 May 1999; for the Council's history see Eisermann 1999).

During the same period, political parties which had not already established their political foundations created such organizations to advance their objectives and to be able to receive government funding beyond the increasingly limiting mandate the Federal Constitutional Court imposed upon them. With the Political Academy in Eichholz (1958), which in 1964 evolved into the Konrad Adenauer Foundation, the Friedrich Naumann Foundation (1958) and the Hanns Seidel Foundation (1967), three additional foundations were established by their respective political parties: the Christian Democratic Union, the Free Democratic Party, and the Christian Social Union. Particularly after the Federal Constitutional Court explicitly ruled out the political parties' role – and with it the financing – of "political education" in 1966, political party foundations/think tanks became the organizational vehicle for carrying out this important role. Beyond their domestic mission, political parties also became a legitimizing means for the German government to re-establish its international standing, since "the provision of foreign political aid to developing countries and emerging democracies is in full keeping with Germany's preferred self-image as a 'civilian power' in international affairs, employing 'soft power' resources in foreign policy" (Thunert 1999: 32).

In the post 1968 period, the influence of different levels of government remained a significant driving force. These governing bodies helped the creation of both non-university-based think tanks – like the Research Institute for Regional and Urban Development (1971) and the German Institute of Urban Affairs (1973), which was founded by the German Association of Towns and Cities – and research institutes affiliated with a university, like the Institute for Development Planning and Structural Research at the University of Hannover (1972), as well as funding organizations which can be considered "universities without students," notably the Social Science Research Center Berlin (1969). As was the case in the United States, the German government became involved in urban and regional planning and other domestic issue areas, providing contracts and research opportunities for think tanks. Furthermore, as the names of the Eduard Pestel Institute for Systems Analysis (1975) and the Institute for Technology Assessment and Systems Analysis at the Research Center for Technology and Environment in Karlsruhe (1977) indicate, "R&D" (research and development) and "systems analysis" also became a hard currency in the German context. Similar to its influence in the American context, RAND became a role model and its methodology was seen as something to be emulated both by foreign policy[4] and domestic think tanks in Germany.

At the same time, the ideologically tense climate in the aftermath of 1968 became visible in the form of the advocacy-oriented species of think tanks, which grew during this period. The Centre for Cultural Research (1969) was "initially conceived as a kind of counterpart to 'think tanks' in the USA" by its founders, hence the center "became known . . . for its often unconventional methods (e.g. 'action research')."[5] At the end of the 1960s, with the creation of the German Association for Peace and Conflict Research (1968), the Peace Research Institute Frankfurt (1970), and the Institute for Peace Research and Security Policy at the University of Hamburg (1971), the first advocates of peace research appeared on the German think tank scene. Together with the Research Institute of the Protestant Churches in Germany, the latter two institutes annually co-edit the "Peace Assessment" (Friedensgutachten), a yearbook monitoring and documenting events and trends in peace matters worldwide. Meanwhile, the German Association for Peace and Conflict Research includes about 250 members (most of which are peace research institutions and other institutional members). It coordinates research efforts, holds annual conferences, and seeks to engage political decision makers as well as the general public in a constructive dialogue. As a lobby group for peace research, it facilitates fundraising and advocates peace research with policy makers.

With the creation of the German Society for Peace and Conflict Research in 1970, peace research obtained a more "official" status and also funding from the government. This mandate was short lived, however. In 1983, the society was dissolved after conservative governments at both the state and federal levels withdrew public funding. Together with the Association for Peace Research in Bonn, the German Society for Peace and Conflict Research remained, but with a much reduced mission of coordination and information. A subsequent change of government at the national level created some renewed momentum for peace research, with the SPD-Green coalition explicitly stating in its coalition agreement on 20 October 1998 that German foreign policy was *a priori* a policy of peace, thus creating some hope for future state financial support for the peace research community. Two years later, in October 2000, the government appropriated DM 50 million to establish the German Foundation for Peace Research (Deutsche Stiftung Friedensforschung) whose mission is to promote applied peace research in Germany. These developments indicate that peace research had become an established discipline in Germany, well anchored in the think tank community.

In the early days, prior to their ascendance into the governmental realm, peace research institutes had much common ground with environmentally oriented advocacy organizations such as the Öko Institute for Applied Ecology (1977), the German Association for Environmental Education (1983), the Institute for Ecological Economic Research (1985), the Institute for Social-Ecological Research (1989), and the Hamburg Environmental Institute: Center for Social and Ecological Technology (1989) – organizations which would bit by bit also manage to establish themselves in the political framework. Particularly in the aftermath of the Chernobyl nuclear accident in 1986, and with the concurrent electoral successes of the Green Party, environmental issues were catapulted to the public and political forefront.

Also in the late 1970s and the 1980s, another set of advocacy institutes that included the IWG Bonn (Institute for Economic and Social Research,1977) and the Frankfurt Market Economy and Policy Institute (1982) began to advocate for a stronger emphasis on the "market" in Germany's social market economy. By contrast, the Institute for Work and Technology at the Science Centre North Rhine Westphalia (1988) was established to place a stronger emphasis on the "social" aspects of policy. Their differences in political principles notwithstanding, both the Frankfurt Market Economy and Policy Institute and the Institute for Work and Technology were admittedly inspired by the more proactive advocacy style of think tanks in the United States.

The post-reunification period brought another significant boost to the German think tank industry. The advocacy model would be the pattern in the 1990s. Institutes as different as the Research Institute for Philosophy in Hannover: Christian Public Foundation (1989), the Brandenburg-Berlin Institute for Social Studies (1990), the Bureau for Future Studies (1990), the Institute for Market–Environment–Society at the University of Hannover (1991), the Wuppertal Institute for Climate, Environment and Energy (1991) at the Science Centre North Rhine Westphalia, the Oswald von Nell-Breuning Institute for Ethics in Society and Business (1991), the UNI Enterprise Institute of the Association of Independent Entrepreneurs (1993), the Bonn International Center for Conversion (1994), and the Schleswig-Holstein Institute for Peace Research at the University of Kiel (1995) share a common organizational feature in that they advocate their quite different interests and causes in the German marketplace of ideas. In 1989 the Green Party established the Stiftungsverband Regenbogen, which evolved into the Heinrich Böll Foundation; and the Party of Democratic Socialism (now Die Linke, "The Left") set up its Rosa Luxemburg Foundation in 1999, formerly referred to as the Political Foundation for the Analysis of Societies and Political Education (1990). They too, not surprisingly, adopted the advocacy model in order to promote their respective policy agendas and draw upon government funding.

During the most recent period of German think tank history, the federal and state governments have continued to shape the development of these organizations. In order to cope with the enormous challenge of the reunification, the different levels of the German government either created new organizations or "reinvented" those which had existed in the German Democratic Republic (GDR). Many of these institutes were included in the organizational framework and funding scheme of the Gottfried Wilhelm Leibniz Scientific Society (Wissenschaftsgemeinschaft Gottfried Wilhelm Leibniz, WGL).[6] An example is the Institute of Regional Geography in Leipzig: re-established in 1992 as a member of the WGL, it carries on the tradition and research of the German Institute of Regional Geography and its predecessor institutions, which date back as early as 1896, as well as the regional studies and regional geographic work of the Institute of Geography and Geo-ecology at the former Academy of Sciences of the GDR. In addition, newly founded organizations of the WGL, such as the Institute for Regional Development and Structural Planning (1992) and the Halle Institute for Economic Research (1992) were also instrumental for regional development, both in the eastern states of the Federal Republic and in Germany's neighbor countries which have also embarked on a transition process toward democratic governance combined with socially and environmentally sound market economies. Also a member of the WGL, the Institute of Agricultural Development in Central and Eastern Europe was founded in 1994, following the proposal of the Science Council (Wissenschaftsrat)[7] to provide an academic framework for the transformation processes in the countries of Central and Eastern Europe. Its location is again characteristic for this type of think tank. According to the founders of the institute, the location of Halle in the part of Germany formerly belonging to the GDR was chosen for two reasons: first, because of the long-established links between the eastern German states and the countries in Central and Eastern Europe; and second, because the location provides the opportunity for close cooperation in the areas of research and teaching with the Faculty of Agriculture of the Martin Luther University. In 1992, another member of the WGL, the Institute for Ecological and Regional Development, was created on the recommendation of the Science Council to address issues relating to the ecological regeneration of heavily polluted industrialized regions and other matters relating to regional development and housing in eastern Germany. The UFZ Centre for Environmental Research (1991), which is a part of the Hermann von Helmholtz Community of German Research Centers and is mainly funded by the Federal Ministry for Education, Science, Research and Technology, focuses – from an interdisciplinary angle including both natural and social sciences – on the environmental regeneration of polluted areas. For a more global environmental assessment, the Potsdam Institute for Climate Impact Research (1992) was also created within the government-funded framework of the WGL.

Although most of the WGL institutes that were established after the reunification in the eastern states, also referred to as the New Länder, are instrumental for the economic, social, and environmental revitalization of their respective regions, these organizations, like the older institutes of the WGL, have also a supra-regional focus and work in the national interest. This twofold mission – which reflects the governance structure of the Federal Republic of Germany – is reinforced by the funding scheme of the WGL. The institutes are jointly funded by the federal and state governments, providing the respective state governments with the immediate responsibility for "their" institutes while also ensuring the involvement of the federal government.

Exemplifying a rather new trend, namely "German" think tanks assuming a European orientation, is the European Centre for Minority Issues. It was founded in 1996 in Flensburg in the German–Danish border region by the national governments of Denmark and Germany and the (German) state government of Schleswig-Holstein as a non-partisan, bi-national institution. It received a start-up grant under the "INTERREG-II Program" of the EU and draws on regular funding from the German and Danish central governments and the state government of Schleswig-Holstein. This pattern of regional cooperation has become an even stronger political force in the context of a further integrating Europe, characterized by strong regional centers of development in competition with each other in what is often described by the EU as a "Europe of self-confident regions." Lacking neither a strong regional identity nor confidence, North Rhine Westphalia, Germany's most populous state, and Bavaria, which has a very prosperous center in Munich, are other examples illustrating the influence of state governments that are strongly committed to initiating, financing, and shaping the think tank sector in their regions. Political elites in these states make enormous efforts not to be marginalized as political and cultural power-centers in the "Berlin Republic." Furthermore, the creation of the Center for European Economic Research (1990), which became a member of WGL in 2005 to join the club of the big six in economic research; the European Forum for Migration Studies at the University of Bamberg (1993); and the European Academy for Science and Technology Assessment (1996) is an additional indicator of this trend in the German think tank world toward a more European orientation.

In addition to these governmental initiatives, there have been further developments in the German think tank sector which have their origins in the private sector. For example, the Bertelsmann Foundation, both by strengthening its own operating arm with the Bertelsmann (Science) Foundation (1977/1995) and by giving a financial jump start to the Center for Applied Policy Research at the University of Munich (1995), created an interesting new pattern in the history of German think tanks. Another example – of an existing, yet thus far only grant-giving foundation embarking on its own operational think tank venture – is the Schleswig-Holstein Energy Foundation (1993). It finances its operations through an endowment, half of which was provided by the state of Schleswig-Holstein with the other half coming from the energy industry. Additionally, the Otto Wolff von Amerongen Foundation became the founder and shareholder of the Ordoliberal Institute, starting its free market economy advocacy in 1995. The *ordoliberal* (social liberalism) Frankfurt Market Economy and Policy Institute has also "engaged in a joint venture with a non-operating foundation which has the financial means but lacked the personnel resources."[8] Moving its headquarters from Frankfurt to Berlin in 2001, it was relabeled the Market Economy Foundation. With initial funding from George Soros' Open Society Foundations, the European Council on Foreign Relations, a pan-European organization, was established in 2007.

Summing up the history of "German" think tanks, one can identify a few interesting patterns. The initial phase of growth was strongly inhibited by the two wars and the Nazi regime. Only after World War II was there significant growth of the think tank sector in Germany, growth that has been mainly sustained by the state. Very frequently, through contract research but also through (political party) foundations, the government has been the dominant force for the evolution of German think tanks. The species of think tanks established during this period manifest the government's multi-pronged efforts to re-establish its domestic infrastructure and international standing. There were also a few special interest-based initiatives in the think tank sector. In quantitative terms, however, these efforts were relatively small compared to the involvement of the government. This situation changed markedly in the subsequent period, however, when the creation of all kinds of advocacy think tanks indicated a new phase in German think tank history. At the end of the 1960s and in the early 1970s, the growth rate of private sector based and advocacy think tanks became even stronger than that of organizations that were established by the government. German reunification marked another point of inflexion, where the growth pattern of politically/ideologically identifiable advocacy think tanks became significantly stronger. Unlike the previous period, however, the immense challenge of reunification also reactivated a strong – and compared to private institutions, stronger – involvement of the government. At the same time, the German government, shouldering these huge reunification efforts, appears to have sensed the limits of its financial strength. Looking at the data since the mid-1990s, it becomes evident that its exhausted budget did not allow the German government to keep up with the sustained involvement of all kinds of private sector interests in the think tank sector. This has reinforced the advocacy model and created different forms of influence on policy making.

Changing patterns in addressing political decision makers

Rooted in the private sector – particularly in the business world – these newer think tanks have begun to challenge the traditional monopoly of the government as they apply a more public approach of bringing their expertise and interests to the process of policy making. Unlike traditional organizations,which had close and not very transparent relationships with the government, the advocacy think tanks see their mission as the generation of a dialogue with the broader public and attempt to address political decision makers via intermediaries.

Given this fundamental change in the nature of communications between the government, external experts, and the public, media outlets in Germany have become an increasingly important intermediary channel for the activities of experts. With the privatization of the German media landscape, the increase in the number of private broadcast and print media outlets with an immense hunger for information has encouraged think tanks' public relations activities. The increased competition from new entrants in the marketplace of ideas has been a frontal challenge to the traditional foreign policy think tanks, whose preference was for a "Chatham House" style of private interaction with the inner core of the government. These traditional think tanks have adapted their communication patterns to their new environment and have become, of necessity, more media-savvy.

The media can play a key role, especially when it comes to agenda setting. Political consulting services also employ public strategies for influencing policy makers, and think tanks are useful vehicles for placing ideas in the governmental apparatus.[9] There has been a sharp increase in political consulting services, as various lobbies have boosted their efforts to influence decision makers both directly and via public opinion. Many interest groups moved their lobbying activities from the former capital Bonn to Berlin and thus strengthened their presence in the Berlin Republic. In this changing, increasingly competitive, and public context, scientific analysis and interpretation of data have become an important additional source of information or a legitimizing factor helping to substantiate or facilitate political communication, since "the manner in which information and ideas are communicated have important consequences for their credibility and ultimately for the influence that they have on policy conversation" (Brooks 2012: 70). It is an open secret that interest groups therefore also engage experts from public policy research institutes in order to advocate and give intellectual gravitas to their cause. Indeed, in some cases it has even become difficult to distinguish advocacy think tanks from lobbying groups. Since many newer German advocacy think tanks are primarily funded through private initiatives, they have to develop a public approach. In order to demonstrate their relevance and impact to the business interests that finance them, they have to improve their media visibility and increase their perceived impact on public policy making.

What makes it generally difficult to place ideas directly within the government is that, unlike in the United States, Germany does not have a revolving door culture where people leave think tanks and go on to serve in high positions in government. The highly professionalized, permanent, and closed nature of the civil service prevents the temporary recruitment of external advisers and inhibits the exchange between civil servants and outsiders. The German governmental bureaucracies do not offer any incentives to civil servants which would encourage them to leave their position in order to "risk" a research stint at a think tank. Conversely, with only few exceptions, there are not many openings for outsiders to spend some time within the government.

This means that German think tanks, along with other outsiders, must usually be satisfied with trying to influence policy makers externally; they are primarily reliant on influencing the policy debate through publications or op-eds, preferably in the quality media. Placing their ideas in the top media outlets will garner the attention of the relevant decision makers: people at the top of the ministry. Relying on the medium and bottom layers of the media system will, as a rule, have little impact. Reaching officials down the ministerial ladder is also of little value, given their greater distance from the levers of power.

Equipped with huge internal legislative expertise and "in-house" departmental research, the German civil service is quite resistant to external advice. People in the administration are generally suspicious of such advice, since to them every piece of external expertise creates uncertainty. Everything in the political arena has to be seen and evaluated in light of its political implications and public repercussions. Gate-keepers within the state system will therefore always attempt to control their environment as much as possible. Again, the best strategy for making ideas heard in the governmental arena is to convince leaders; "their" idea will then trickle down. Once one has managed to convince the leadership, the lower levels in the administration are more likely to become interested in the idea.

Therefore, experienced think tanks do not provide analysis for the working layer of the ministry or the administration. Instead they try to reach decision makers, meaning the chancellor, the cabinet, ministers, or the leadership within a ministry. This elite audience primarily is inclined to pay serious attention to those ideas that have passed through the gate-keeping of the quality media. This represents a significant change for German policy research that has evolved since the early 1970s

(Reinicke 1996: 17–21; Krevert 1993). Since then, but particularly in more recent years, an increasing number of German think tanks have come to rely increasingly on intermediate forms of communication targeting the attentive public and elite opinion in order to have an impact on public policy making.

Notwithstanding the recent trend of advocacy via intermediaries and the potential for the further growth of this type of think tank influence in the future, it is important to acknowledge that a majority of the German think tank population is not politically or ideologically identifiable, as most of them adhere to academic standards and methodological principles rather than political values or special interests. This is not mere coincidence. Currently, 88 think tanks in Germany are organized under the funding scheme of the WGL (according to its website: <http://www.leibniz-gemeinschaft.de/ueber-uns/>). Engaging in strategic partnerships with "their" universities, WGL institutes can best fulfill their academic mandate and enhance their standing in the academic community. Hence, there are numerous institutes that are close to universities,[10] both geographically and in terms of staffing – that is "at the university of" institutes (An-Institute). This does not preclude other organizations from also cultivating, in some form, strategic relationships with academia and drawing heavily upon government funding that has more often than not been dependent on the academic standing of an institute. The institutional mechanisms whose role it is to distribute government funding or ensure the quality of research funded by the state have an inherently academic bias. As is the case with the WGL, whose funding depends on academic reputation as determined by the Science Council, government funding tends to be channeled into bigger research agglomerates, such as the Foundation of the German Scientific Community (Deutsche Forschungsgemeinschaft, DFG), which disseminate the funding according to their academic standards.

Institutes which seek to provide what might be described as practical policy research, however, complain that policy makers' requests for policy relevant expertise are at odds with the academic control mechanisms associated with governmental funding. "I have a problem not so much with the Science Council itself – although some of its evaluations may be criticized in detail as well," says Gebhard Flaig from the Ifo Institute for Economic Research, "but with the fact that policy makers ask for policy relevant work, which however isn't a criterion at all when the work of research institutes is evaluated by the Science Council. The whole situation is somewhat ambiguous and confusing." (Interview with Gebhard Flaig, Member of the Board of Directors of the ifo Institute for Economic Research, 1 June 1999). The negative verdict of the Science Council to cut off the Ifo Institute completely from state funding could only be averted by the massive intervention of the state government of Bavaria. Nevertheless, as a result of a 45 percent reduction of its government funding in 1999, the Ifo Institute faced a major challenge in order to fundamentally restructure its organization and re-establish its academic reputation. The case of the Halle Institute for Economic Research (IWH) also illustrates the inherent conflict between policy relevant advice and the constraints that accompany state funding. As Hilmar Schneider puts it:

The founding of the IWH in 1992 was in the context of the post-reunification. Faced with major problems of structural adjustment, people decided to establish also in the eastern part of Germany an economic research institute which provides hands-on advice on transformation and regional adjustment issues. We are different from the other economic research organizations because we put a greater emphasis on providing hands-on policy advice. Our statute explicitly points out that we are not expected to conduct basic academic research, and this is in conflict with a more academically oriented mission. . . . That's a problem. Very recently, we received an evaluation by the Science Council, and there is, obviously, a conflict of interest. The Science Council is very rigidly oriented according to academic principles. Although the creation of our institute was recommended by the Science Council, it has also been promoted by policy makers. We are very much engaged in providing policy relevant advice – which is of course based on academic research – to policy makers. And policy relevant expertise is something which academics in the Science Council aren't really familiar with. (Interview with Hilmar Schneider, Senior Fellow at the Halle Institute for Economic Research, 27 May 1999)

If one looks at subsequent evaluations by the Science Council, there is a clear pattern: research institutes are not criticized for being too academic and for being too far away from the political realities, but they are criticized for their lack of scholarliness. Therefore, it is no surprise that the WGL institutes spend most of their energy on academic seminars, conferences, and publications and that their efforts do not carry much weight in the eyes of policy making elites. The DFG, as well, is hesitant to finance policy research, unless one conducts research on policy research. According to Josef Janning, the current head of the Berlin office of the European Council on Foreign Relations:

You can get funding for more abstract and theoretical work on how to best describe the political decision making process, which has an academic value to be sure, but this is not relevant for and sought after by political decision makers. Academics make an effort to heuristically understand political decision making processes, but they don't focus on concrete political decisions. (Josef Janning, then Deputy Director of the Center for Applied Policy Research at the University of Munich, 31 May 1999)

So while the DFG finances research on political processes, the question of how to bring peace to Syria, for example, is, from the point of view of the DFG, an unscientific question.

In sum, and notwithstanding some recent trends toward advocacy research, academic clout and standing is still a very important component of German think tanks' raison d'être. This emphasis on "Wissenschaftlichkeit" more often than not implies what *The Economist* identified as a typically German type of "dull pragmatism" (*Economist*, 1991a; 1991b). In contrast to the US context, where experts have become very much involved in the process of policy making – bearing witness to the Greek root "praxis" in the word "pragmatism" – German experts tend to lack this pragmatic or applied expertise dimension (praxisnahe Politikberatung). Rather than providing policy relevant research, many German academics seem more inclined to indulge in theoretical contemplation about whether and to what extent social science research can be of direct political relevance to begin with. In the United States, "it is not just that [experts] can sit on the sideline and write and talk, but then [they] can also go into government and come back out of government and try to put into practice some of the ideas which [they] have formulated while we have been sitting on the sidelines" (Interview with Bruce MacLaury, President Emeritus of the Brookings Institution, 1 May 1996). In Germany – either through conviction or lack of opportunity or both – the political range of many research institutes seems to be less ambitious; they chiefly seek "to influence the manner in which people talk or write about this or that subject in the future" (Jan Philipp Reemtsma, Executive Director of the Hamburg Institute for Social Research, http://www.his-online.de/).

Predominance of "Wissenschaftlichkeit" and "dull pragmatism"

It is an irony of German history that a lack of practical knowledge about the world facilitated Germany's "Katastrophe," which in turn made German intellectuals even more hesitant to engage in public policy making. It has been argued that insufficient knowledge and simplistic interpretations of the outside world among the German elites caused the two catastrophic wars of the 20th century (Mols 1998: 253). These wars not only had disastrous consequences for the lives and world views of many people in the past, but they have also had implications for the ways and means contemporary political practitioners and experts use to make sense of their world as they lead Germany into the future. The legacy of Germany's history influences the organizational and strategic choices of contemporary German think tanks and the analysts within them.

The ways in which German think tanks view their very organizational identity, their raison d'être, cannot be understood without taking Germany's historic legacy into consideration. Interestingly, the very label "think tank" makes Germans think of tanks, evoking certain memories and pictures in German thinkers' minds, and is therefore probably not the "ideal" label for most Germans to identify with. Generally speaking, it is very common in Germany, especially in the technical, business, and academic worlds, to adopt and integrate anglicisms into the German vocabulary. There certainly is no German equivalent of the Académie Française, whose role is to protect the national linguistic heritage from foreign intrusion and come up with home-made linguistic creations. Yet it is very striking that both German journalists and academics alike are rather hesitant to adopt the label "think tank." What is even more interesting is the fact that the German substitutes for the Anglo-Saxon concept "think tank" all signify or create an allusion to, not so much the history of the wars as the signifier "think tank" may do, but rather the technical advances and economic miracles Germans have accomplished. Hence, two alternative concepts enjoy the status of commonly used linguistic currency in German discourse: "Denkfabrik" (Leggewie 1990), something like a "factory of ideas," and "Ideenagentur" (Gellner 1995), something like an "agency of ideas." Other common variations, like "Denkwerkstatt" (laboratory for thinking) or "Ideenwerkstatt" (laboratory for ideas) obviously also come easier to the German mind when conceiving and making sense of the Anglo- Saxon linguistic term "think tank." While these reflections may be somewhat impressionistic and speculative, they appear to be supported by more concrete and measurable manifestations of Germany's collective memory.

Similarly, the label "ideological" has become somewhat tainted in the German context as a result of the traumatic historical experiences experienced by the country and its people. The rather low standing of "ideology" in Germany seems to correlate with the worship of "Wissenschaftlichkeit." The high esteem in which the latter, connoting scholarship and scientific credentials, is held helps explain the significantly lower esteem in which think tanks with a clear political or ideological profile tend to be held. Most German think tanks do not feel very comfortable with the label "advocacy tank." Only 15 percent of the respondents to a survey of think tank experts accept the label "interest-oriented advocacy think tank" as appropriate for characterizing their mission. The study's author, Martin Thunert, concluded that "in Germany, this label is understood as a stigma, rather than a fair qualification" (Thunert 1997: 4).

This is not to say that there are no politically or ideologically identifiable think tanks in Germany. However, unlike many advocacy organizations in the US context which actively market their political/ideological leanings in the marketplace of ideas, German organizations that are special interest driven or have a clear political agenda are less inclined to fly under their true colors.

In contrast to the open and unashamed advocacy model in the United States, where people within the country's think tank sector are even inclined to view the scientific/scholarly model as a sort of inflated currency, like "paper money in Weimar,"[11] in the Federal Republic of Germany the academic currency appears to be stronger. The high esteem for academic credentials seems to parallel the strength of the D-Mark – a currency which has become one of only a few commonly shared national symbols in post-war Germany, after the traumatic experience of the Nazi regime erased much of the national collective memory. With the German reunification, both of these currencies – academic and monetary – have been embraced, albeit to a different extent, by Germans who were unfortunate enough to live on the other side of the Iron Curtain."

Taking into account the different experiences of the two Germanies since World War II, one might well expect different perceptions of think tanks and their expertise. In fact, Winand Gellner's research (1995: 236–39) illustrates how differently experts and their roles are perceived by political actors representing the views of constituencies in the eastern and western parts of Germany. Expertise generally, and particularly advocacy research, tends to be considerably less appreciated by "Easterners" when compared with the perceptions of "Westerners," who did not live under the ideological experiment of communism. Gellner's empirical findings suggest that the different historical, institutional, and cultural post-war experiences in the eastern and western parts of Germany appear to account for important differences in the perceptions of "Easterners" and "Westerners."

In the aftermath of the "ideological overkill" in the Third Reich and the additional "ideological burden" of Communism in the former East Germany, Germans, both "Westerners" and "Easterners," are more hesitant to accept the label "ideological" or "advocacy" than their US counterparts, who have lived different historical, institutional, and cultural experiences. Germany has developed a strong post-war tradition of consensus, both in foreign policy and domestic matters. Looking at the Anglo-American world from a German perspective, Martin Thunert identifies "a tradition of adversary politics in combination with democratic government that over certain periods encourages vigorous partisanship on the basis of a broad procedural consensus." At the same time he associates the institutional manifestations of post-war political culture in Germany with the specific forms of "coalition-building, corporatist structures of interest mediation, interlocking federalism and consensus orientation on the basic tenets of the German 'social state.' " According to Thunert (1999: 26), "most German [research] institutes have adhered to the organizational patterns, the funding structures and the consensus orientation of the post-war settlement." These features, which *The Economist* identified as "dull pragmatism," can again be explained with reference to "Germany's broken history." As William Wallace (1994: 152) points out, the "re-establishment of democratic government in West Germany after World War II brought an active concern to encourage informed and reasoned debate through state support, far stronger than has been thought necessary in either Britain and France."

It appears that Germany tried very hard to live up to external expectations. For instance, as late as the 1960s, Almond and Verba's (1963, 1989) assessments of Germany's "civic culture" concluded that the state of German democracy was at the mercy of the country's economic prosperity. The very methodology that was used to measure the viability of German democracy revealed a certain bias or preference toward a harmonious way of policy making rather than a more confrontational style of politics. It seems that Germany has internalized the outside world's expectations to the extent that it even tried to avoid any display of controversy that might have generated worries about the success of German "re-education." For instance, the abrupt outburst of conflict in the late 1960s came as a surprise only to those who had not seen, or did not want others to see, the confrontational struggle of Germans grappling with their new identity after World War II. In the 1950s, the decisions regarding re-armament and the establishment of the armed forces, the Bundeswehr, for example, caused enormous political confrontations, not only in the institutional arena but also on the streets among the general public. Those demonstrations, however, did not received much coverage by the state media outlets in order to avoid concern among Germany's neighbors and the United States about Germany's peaceful development and emerging democratic "civic culture."

While Germany has been very busy building and keeping its domestic and economic power house in order, it has also been concerned with cleaning up the expanses of post-war rubble and with building a broad diplomatic foundation on which to re-establish the European house and, thus, its own international standing. There has been both a broad pragmatic consensus on foreign policy and an absence of nationalistic rhetoric in post-war Germany. While there are many US think tanks working on "national defense," or "national security" matters that are not shy to use the word "national," if not in their name then at least in their mission statement, there is an absence of nationalistic rhetoric in the German context. The only thing that has come close to a commonly shared national symbol is the currency, which has arisen in the collective memory of Germans as the symbol of the "economic miracle," the reintegration and re-establishment of Germany in the international system as an important actor and a leader within Europe. Even this valuable asset of the new post-war Germany was traded in for the supra-national integration of Europe. There is a consensus in Germany's post-war foreign policy that no form of German unilateralism is viable, but that greater European and international integration is the only path for Germany to take. Accordingly, most of Germany's post-war foreign policy has been conducted though the means of "soft power" and "quiet diplomacy." In this context, political party foundations were not only important means to promote the political "re-education" of Germans, these foundations also become an important pillar of German development policy abroad. As they were less constrained by historic, constitutional, political, or diplomatic considerations than the official bodies of the state, political party foundations were useful vehicles for conducting Germany's soft power in the realm of foreign policy.

Traditional security and defense foreign policy think tanks oriented their communications toward an elite audience. For a long time in Germany's post-war period, foreign policy has been the domaine reservé of a small elite: "Advising the rulers in an atmosphere of confidentiality and Chatham House rules have been much more important than advising the larger public or advocating specific policy positions in public" (Thunert 1999: 20). For example, the SWP was designed during the Cold War as a security policy think tank after the model of the RAND Corporation in the United States. And even though not much of the work of the SWP was classified anymore, there was an air of secrecy in the splendid isolation of Ebenhausen. Yet the move of the SWP's headquarters from Ebenhausen to the new capital in Berlin indicated in many aspects a strategic reorientation in the German post-Cold War era. As SWP's Albrecht Zunker observes,

> Our mission hasn't changed over the years, but the instruments have changed, the way we perform our mission has changed. In the early years, there was, particularly within the executive, a very different situation; the bureaucracy has over time gradually opened itself to a broader debate. Then it wasn't the case that the foreign ministry was directly represented in discussions, not even at international conferences. The bureaucracy was very much closed off. People used official diplomatic channels, but they didn't engage in the informal pre-processes of discussion in what would be called the Jim and Joe community in the United States. Meanwhile, there has been a learning process, and henceforth the role of the SWP has become very vital, because we have been able to inform the government on what is going on in the community. Today, it's business as usual, because the bureaucracy has learned the lesson that it has to be involved in public discussions right from the start. In

Washington, there are many bilateral events in the policy community where one can now also find representatives from the German Embassy. People have realized how important it is to participate when issues are identified and framed, before they hit the official agenda. (Interview with Albrecht Zunker, former Deputy Director of the SWP, 2 June 1999; for a similar view: Klaiber 1996; Becher 1998)

Needed: Communicating German interests

The competition between "friendly" nation states, which had been somewhat muted by the East–West confrontation, has become more visible in the aftermath of the Cold War. Germany's more self-confident and public approach to bringing its economic, environmental, and peace issues to the table of foreign policy making has brought into question the conventional interpretation of Germany's pragmatic "ideology of smallness" and the absence of national rhetoric in official discourse.

Surely, no serious intellectual in Germany would consider a national "Sonderweg" (special path) in terms of foreign policy. Since Adenauer, all political leaders in Germany have shared the pragmatic political view that re-establishing the standing of Germany can only succeed if undertaken in multi-lateral terms. The Atlantic, East, and European Integration have been fundamental for German re-establishment.

However, this is not the end of the story or even history – as the US scholar Francis Fukuyama (1992) had already "foreseen" after the collapse of the Soviet Union. In fact, a resurgent Russia has called into question the European security infrastructure. Also, within the EU, there is no doubt that the discussions about the design of a new institutional infrastructure in "Euroland" and its international relationships will continue to be led with strong national stands. Germany, as well, has become somewhat less hesitant to define its national interests.

The reconfiguration of global power, especially the unfolding rivalry and bipolarity between China and the United States (Braml 2016), has also forced German foreign policy elites, particularly think tanks, to do what they are supposed to do: think – beyond their traditional transatlantic mantra. "Old Europe", above all its lead nation Germany, will get in even more trouble with its US patron if it continues to cooperate with China to pursue common economic interests. Meanwhile, China has already surpassed the United States and has become Germany's most important trading partner outside of Europe (Statistisches Bundesamt 2015). It will be especially threatening – from a US perspective – if European and Chinese cooperation were to undermine the dollar's "exorbitant privilege," because "dollar dominance" has so far guaranteed the US economic model – the debt-driven business as usual, as well as the funding for its military might. There will be interesting discussions ahead. In order to communicate its interests effectively, Germany will also need more professional and articulate voices, which may provide another opportunity for its think tanks to define their communicative role in the global marketplace of ideas.

Notes

1 According to McGann and Weaver (2000), think tanks are "third sector"/"civil societal" organizations which are not-for-profit in their legal statute, relatively independent/autonomous from the government/state, and dedicated to impacting public policy making.
2 A four-tier typology is used in this study: "academic/university without students;" "contract researchers;" "advocacy tanks;" and "party think tanks." See McGann and Weaver (2000: 6–12); Weaver (1989).
3 In 2000, the Federal Institute for Russian, East European and International Studies was "merged" with SWP.
4 The RAND Corporation served as a role model for the creation of the SWP.
5 This is the self presentation – on an info sheet outlining the history and its mission – of the Center for Cultural Research (Zentrum für Kulturforschung), which was originally named after the German weekly magazine *Der Spiegel*: the Spiegel Institute for Project Studies.
6 The Scientific Association of "Blue List" Institutes (Wissenschaftsvereinigung "Blaue Liste") was established in 1995 with its headquarters in Berlin and a managing office in Bonn. Responding to bylaws that are based in the German constitution, these institutes are jointly funded by the federal and the respective state governments. In 1997, the annual membership meeting in Cologne decided to rename the Association as the Gottfried Wilhelm Leibniz Scientific Society.
7 The Science Council was established in 1957 jointly by the federal and state governments as an advisory body in scientific matters and in matters of higher education. With its recommendations, which determine whether an institute's work is worthy of government funding, the Science Council exerts considerable influence on both the structure of the scientific landscape and the substance of the scientific output in Germany.
8 Interview with Hans Wenkebach, Former Research Director at the Frankfurt Institute for Market Economy and Policy, 7 May 1999.
9 For a conceptual framework illuminating the interaction between lobbies and think tanks, see Abelson (2012).
10 The importance of German think tanks' academic reputation for their (government) funding also explains the typical career patterns. Unlike for their US peers, who are frequently switching between think tanks and government, the only door revolving in Germany is between think tanks and universities.
11 In an interview, Carlyn Bowman of the American Enterprise Institute lamented: "I wonder what is happening sometimes to the think tank currency, whether it is becoming a little bit like paper money in Weimar [Germany] – currency without a lot of value because of the proliferation and because of the open advocacy of some of the think tanks." See original quote in Rich and Weaver (1998: 250).

References

Abelson, Donald 2012. "Theoretical Models and Approaches to Understanding the Role of Lobbies and Think Tanks in US Foreign Policy." In Stephen Brooks, Dorota Stasiak and Tomasz Zyro (eds), *Policy Expertise in Contemporary Democracies*. Farnham/Burlington, Vermont: Ashgate, 9–30.

Almond, Gabriel A., and Sidney Verba. 1963. *The Civic Culture: Political Attitudes and Democracy in Five Nations*. Princeton, NJ: Princeton University Press.

Almond, Gabriel A., and Sidney Verba. 1989. *The Civic Culture Revisited*. Newbury Park, CA: Sage Publications.

Becher, Klaus. 1998. *Praxisorientierte Forschung zur Internationalen Politik. Ein Beitrag zur Diskussion*. Ebenhausen: Stiftung Wissenschaft und Politik.

Braml, Josef. 2004. *Think Tanks versus "Denkfabriken"? U.S. and German Policy Research Institutes' Coping with and Influencing Their Environments*. Baden-Baden: Nomos.
Braml, Josef. 2016. *Auf Kosten der Freiheit*. Cologne/Berlin: Quadriga.
Brooks, Stephen. 2012. "Speaking Truth to Power: The Paradox of the Intellectual in the Visual Information Age." In Stephen Brooks, Dorota Stasiak, and Tomasz Zyro (eds), *Policy Expertise in Contemporary Democracies*. Farnham/Burlington, Vermont: Ashgate, 69–107.
Economist. 1991a. "Think-tanks: The Carousels of Power," 25 May, pp. 23–26.
Economist. 1991b. "The Good Think-tank Guide: The Joys of Detached Involvement," 21 December pp. 49–53.
Eisermann, Daniel. 1999. *Außenpolitik und Strategiediskussion. Die Deutsche Gesellschaft für Auswärtige Politik 1955 bis 1972*. München: Oldenbourg.
Fukuyama, Francis. 1992. *The End of History and the Last Man*. New York: Free Press.
Gellner, Winand. 1995. *Ideenagenturen für Politik und Öffentlichkeit. Think Tanks in den USA und in Deutschland*. Opladen: Westdeutscher Verlag.
Klaiber, Klaus-Peter. 1996. "Politikberatung auf dem Prüfstand. Zielvorgabe: Aktualität, Praxisnähe und Durchsetzbarkeit." *Internationale Politik* 9: 63–64.
Krevert, Peter. 1993. *Funktionswandel der wissenschaftlichen Politikberatung in der Bundesrepublik Deutschland. Entwicklungslinien, Probleme und Perspektiven im Kooperationsfeld von Politik, Wissenschaft und Öffentlichkeit*. Münster, Hamburg: Lit Verlag.
Leggewie, Claus. 1990. "Think Tanks – Wie und was fabrizieren (rechte) Denkfabriken?" *Forschungsjournal Neue Soziale Bewegungen* 8, no. 3: 66–75.
McGann, James G., and R. Kent Weaver. 2000. "Think Tanks and Civil Societies in a Time of Change." In James G. McGann and R. Kent Weaver (eds), *Think Tanks and Civil Societies: Catalysts for Ideas and Action*. New Brunswick, NJ and London: Transaction Publishers, 1–35.
Mols, Manfred. 1998. "Politikberatung im außenpolitischen Entscheidungsprozeß." In Wolf-Dieter Eberwein and Karl Kaiser (eds), *Deutschlands neue Außenpolitik, Vol. 4. Institutionen und Ressourcen*. München: Oldenbourg Verlag, 253–64.
Reinicke, Wolfgang H. 1996. *Tugging at the Sleeves of Politicians: Think Tanks – American Experiences and German Perspectives*. Gütersloh: Bertelsmann Foundation Publishers.
Rich, Andrew, and R. Kent Weaver. 1998. "Advocates and Analysts: Think Tanks and the Politicization of Expertise." In Allan J. Cigler and Burdett A. Loomis (eds), *Interest Group Politics*. 5th ed. Washington, DC: Congressional Quarterly Press, 235–54.
Statistisches Bundesamt. 2015. *Rangfolge der Handelspartner im Außenhandel der Bundesrepublik Deutschland 2014*. Wiesbaden.
Thunert, Martin. 1997. "Thesen und Anmerkungen zur externen Politikberatung in Deutschland in vergleichender Perspektive." Paper delivered at the Workshop "Politikberatung in Deutschland" of the Hanns Seidel Foundation's Akademie für Zeitgeschehen, in Wildbad Kreuth, July 17–18, 1997 (unpublished Manuscript).
Thunert, Martin. 1999. "German Think Tanks as Foreign Policy Resources. Explaining the Changing Landscape of German Think Tanks." Paper Delivered at the Annual Convention of the International Studies Association in Washington, DC, 16–20 February 1999 (unpublished manuscript).
Wallace, William. 1994. "Between Two Worlds. Think-tanks and Foreign Policy." In Christopher Hill and Pamela Beshoff (eds), *Two Worlds of International Relations: Academics, Practitioners and the Trade in Ideas*. New York: Routledge.
Weaver, R. Kent. 1989. "The Changing World of Think Tanks." *PS: Political Science & Politics* 22, no. 1: 563–69.

7 Think tanks and foreign policy in the United Kingdom

Mark Garnett and Simon Mabon

Introduction: Influence and causation

Early in 2015, John de Boer, a senior policy advisor with the UNU Centre for Policy Research, published an article entitled "What Are Think Tanks Good For?". For de Boer, the raison d'etre of a think tank is "to serve as important catalysts for ideas and action" (de Boer 2015).

Academic analysts of the increasingly dynamic and crowded world of policy advice have always faced the seemingly intractable challenge of identifying – and evaluating – "influence". In an ideal scenario for the researcher, the role of policy-oriented institutions like think tanks would be direct and significant; for example, a decision-maker about to embark on a specific course of action would read a think tank publication, change his or her mind, and give the kind of public acknowledgement which is normally confined to Academy Award winners. However, even evidence like this could not be taken at face value; as David Hume warned us, causation is never as simple as it seems on the surface.

De Boer's reference to "catalysts" is useful to all students of think tanks, and is particularly relevant in the context of the present chapter. However, it does not remove the methodological difficulty since in science *every* catalyst is crucial; applied to policy influence, the word still implies a level of input without which decisions would have been different. Richard Higgott and Diane Stone (1994) have argued that evidence of think tank influence should not be confined to instances where decision-makers seem to have changed their minds; such institutes can also perform a "legitimising" role, lending credibility to the decisions and utterances of political actors. However, if taken too far, this approach could lead us to lower the bar for think tank influence to a point where *all* purveyors of policy advice in a specific area can (and often do) claim to have played some role, just by forming part of a relevant intellectual community. A think tank whose recommendations have been ignored could claim inclusion among the "catalysts"; following John Milton's view that "They also serve who only stand and wait", a policy institute which says nothing at all on the subject would also merit a mention.

While acutely conscious of these problems, in this chapter we take a broad view of "influence" rather than focusing exclusively on cases which supply empirical evidence for the role of think tanks. Particularly in the fields of foreign and defence policy, contemporary British think tanks seek to foster rigorous dialogue and an exchange of ideas. The chapter is chiefly concerned with three prominent institutions – the Royal Institute of International Affairs (RIIA, or "Chatham House"); the Royal United Services Institute (RUSI); and the International Institute for Strategic Studies (IISS). It begins with a brief discussion of the long-established British think tank tradition, locating these institutions within a framework of historical interpretation which applies to British think tanks in general. To varying degrees the three organisations owe their existence to the idea that the results of "scientific" enquiry could affect the trajectory of foreign policy, if – and only if – people with expertise enjoy access to those making the policy. The chapter also includes a specific case study – namely, the role of think tanks in the run up to the Iraq War.

The first wave

Although the term "think tank" was unfamiliar to Britons until the 1970s, policy-oriented groups of varying degrees of institutional formality have a long history in the UK. The "Philosophic Radicals" – disciples of Jeremy Bentham's Utilitarian philosophy – exerted significant influence in several key policy fields in the 19th century, either as publicists or as MPs whose energies compensated for their lack of numbers. However, the Fabian Society (founded in 1884) bears a much closer resemblance to the think tanks of today and has a strong claim to be regarded as the first organisation of its kind; its original nine members were connected to an earlier group, "The Fellowship of the New Life", but decided to form a separate society because they wanted to engage more directly in policy-oriented work.

The Fabian Society was thus a self-conscious institution in a way that the Philosophic Radicals never were. Its members were, though, animated by a similar desire to influence policy decisions, and their main impulse came from a sense of ideological certainty. While the Philosophic Radicals were distinctively "liberal", arguing for greater state activity where that seemed to coincide with the self-interest of rational individuals, the Fabians took a more collectivist approach and saw themselves as "socialists"; indeed, the Society was active in the foundation of the Labour Party in 1900 (by which time it boasted nearly a thousand members: Denham and Garnett 2004).

Thus the early exemplars of the British think tank tradition were characterised by loose organisational structures, and a desire to influence policy which arose from clear ideological imperatives. Their numerous and notable successes arose from the fact that, before 1918, the decision-making process in Britain tended to be dominated by individuals who had even less claim to "expertise" in specific areas. Despite reform of the civil service in the late nineteenth century, the cult of the "Gentleman Amateur" still prevailed in Whitehall; and the individuals chosen by a restricted electorate to serve at Westminster tended to owe their places to social status rather than intimate acquaintance with any subject of political relevance. Intellectually, most MPs (and many ministers) were mediocre at best; the exceptions, like Lord Salisbury (Foreign Secretary 1878–80, 1885–86, 1887–92 and 1895–1900;

Prime Minister 1885–86, 1886–92 and 1895–1902), might make a show of independent decision-making, but were usually wise enough to consult people with proven knowledge of topical subjects. In the absence of any overwhelming crisis to shake British complacency in the late nineteenth century, superficially it might look as if the old aristocratic elite was firmly in charge; but serious political operators outside government, who were aware of the growing economic and strategic challenges from Germany and the US, could feel more confident of gaining a hearing, whichever party happened to be in office.

The "second wave" of UK think tanks

World War I shattered the illusions which had bred complacency amongst the British public. The conflict transformed worrying trends for policy-makers into critical dilemmas, demanding careful consideration and well-informed responses. In the years between the world wars, a "second wave" of think tanks emerged in Britain, distinguished from the first in two key respects. First, these bodies were far more "professional" even than the Fabians, whose members had included serious researchers like Beatrice and Sidney Webb as well as the polemical playwright George Bernard Shaw. As its name suggested, Political and Economic Planning (PEP; founded in 1931) focused on the need for more rational policy-making and much more extensive government intervention in industry. The National Institute of Economic and Social Research (NIESR; founded in 1938) sought to provide policy-makers with more accurate statistical data. Second, although these institutions can be seen as key elements of an emerging "Keynesian" consensus on industrial and economic policy, even their detractors would have to concede that they were very different from their "first wave" predecessors, whose policy advice was pre-determined by ideological considerations. For the "second wave" bodies founded between 1918 and 1939, policy recommendations always had a marked ideological bias (usually towards greater state intervention); but the advice had to be based on intensive research, rivalling (if not surpassing) the work conducted in the respective government departments.

From the perspective of the current chapter, it is instructive that PEP and the NIESR were both founded in the 1930s, when Britain's relative weakness (and thus the case for independent sources of advice) had become obvious to any well-informed citizen with an interest in domestic policy-making. By contrast, in the field of foreign policy the lessons of World War I were digested much more rapidly. At the Paris Peace Conference of 1919–20, British officials agreed with their American counterparts on the need for an institute of international affairs. There would be a single "parent" institute, with American and British branches. However, this plan met opposition in both countries, resulting in the formation of separate institutions: the Council for Foreign Relations (1921) in the US and the RIIA (1920; also known as Chatham House, from its occupancy of the former residence of the British Prime Minister William Pitt, Earl of Chatham, in St James's Square, London). Although the twin institutions were thus separated at birth, the main financial backing for Chatham House came from US sources.

The thwarting of this proposed transatlantic think tank partnership was probably fortuitous; the two institutions established amicable relations, avoiding the kind of tensions which might have arisen if they had been forced together. True, Britain and the US shared an overriding foreign policy interest – they both wanted global (particularly European) stability, in which they could pursue their trading interests. But this was a case of key interests coinciding, rather than being the product of a uniform world view based on similar self-images. Britain was a colonial power, whose resources were already overstretched even before the increase in its responsibilities which resulted from the Peace Conference. The US, by contrast, wanted to avoid Britain's mistakes, and to exercise economic dominance without taking direct responsibility in any of the territories which it effectively controlled. It was not difficult to predict that, in time, Britain would become one of those territories which the US hoped to influence (if not dominate) by remote-control. In contrast to the British, who allegedly had become Imperialists through forgetfulness, the US would pretend that it had forgotten to acquire an Empire. The British were now counting the cost of isolationism; most US policy-makers (along with the bulk of public opinion) assumed that their own nation could profit from it. After the years of complacency, British ministers and civil servants needed outside advice because the country's decline was too obvious to conceal from rational observers; the US government needed input from think tanks to help the country adjust to the global great power status which suddenly had been thrust upon it.

Initially established as the "British Institute of International Affairs", Chatham House was awarded a royal charter in 1926 – a remarkable testament to its perceived importance within the UK's policy-making system, which further boosted the prestige of what was now the *Royal* Institute of International Affairs. Its self-adopted mission was to "encourage and facilitate the scientific study of international questions, and to publish or arrange for the publication of works with these objects" (quoted in Wallace 1975: 103). The idea that "international questions" were amenable to *scientific* study was arresting, since it implied that catastrophes like World War I could be avoided if only the "scientists" in question were allowed to influence the decisions of bungling non-specialists. The same mood inspired the establishment of a Department of International Politics at Aberystwyth University, Wales, in the year of the Paris Peace Conference. In the inter-war years think tanks broadly similar to Chatham House were founded in countries which were either self-governing Dominions or still Colonies within the British empire – in Canada (1928), Australia (1932), South Africa (1934), India (1936) and New Zealand (1938).

A "scientific" impulse also lay behind the foundation of RUSI, but in this case the impulse came much earlier; indeed, when Chatham House was founded RUSI (established in 1831) was approaching its centenary year. Initially founded as "The Naval and Military Museum", in 1839 it became "The United Service Institution" and it received the "Royal" seal of approval in 1860 (although the monarchy had been strongly supportive from the outset). However, even the elastic term "think tank" would have to be stretched too far to accommodate RUSI until fairly recently. It was designed as a forum in which members of the armed forces could discuss developments in the "science" of war. As such, like Chatham House, RUSI provided a model for similar bodies worldwide. Only after 1963, on the initiative of a group of officers who wrote to *The Times* on the subject, did RUSI begin to evolve into a more independent and professional organisation with a wider membership.

If RUSI arose from an appreciation of the role of science in warfare, IISS was inspired by a fear that scientific developments were putting the human race in jeopardy. In 1957, the British Council of Churches held a conference to discuss the implications of developments in thermonuclear weaponry, which had become even more relevant to the British public due to Soviet threats of retaliatory action in the Suez crisis of 1956. Discussions among politicians, journalists and retired military officers as well as clergymen resulted in the establishment of an institute whose main purpose should be "the collection and dissemination of information about nuclear weapons and their implications for international relations" (Howard 2008: 8). The decision to establish a think tank, committed to academic research in this sensitive area rather than political campaigning, coincided almost exactly with the formation of a highly political pressure group, the Campaign for Nuclear Disarmament, which was created at a public meeting in February 1958.

The question of influence

As mentioned in Chapter 1 of this volume, even in an age of instant electronic communication geographical proximity to key decision-makers is very useful for think tanks. IISS, Chatham House and RUSI are all based in central London, within walking distance of Westminster and Whitehall. True, if they want to visit IISS MPs, ministers and civil servants might be tempted to hail a taxi; but more energetic policy networkers would enjoy the stroll along the Thames embankment to Arundel Street, the location of IISS. Chatham House is an even more agreeable destination, since St James's Square is adjacent to London's most prestigious clubs as well as being close to Whitehall and Westminster. British foreign secretaries have a private residence in nearby Carlton Gardens; until World War II the German Embassy was situated in Carlton House Terrace. But in terms of deceptively spacious real estate with built-in potential for policy influence, even Chatham House is gazumped by RUSI. The Institute's website informs the first-time visitor that it can be found on Whitehall, "between the Banqueting House and the Welsh Office, diagonally opposite Horseguards". Coyly, it omits to mention that this puts it next door to the obtrusively large building which is home to the Ministry of Defence (MoD).

According to the University of Pennsylvania's authoritative rankings, these think tanks have made the most of their favourable locations. Among think tanks outside the US – of which the survey reckoned there were about 4,500 – RUSI is rated 25th. This is a very respectable showing for an organisation based in a middle-ranking state like Britain. However, RUSI was placed only third among the UK-based bodies, behind IISS (4th) and Chatham House (which came top).

RUSI would have to console itself with a ranking of 10th in the whole world among think tanks concerned with "Defense and National Security" (although this still placed it behind IISS (3rd) and Chatham House (5th)).

These rankings are based on a variety of factors, rather than attempting a crude assessment of direct policy influence. However, it is a reasonable presumption that the British think tanks working in the related areas of foreign policy, security and defence would not have been rated so highly by qualified observers if they were regarded as wholly lacking in such influence. The obvious question is whether this perceived influence can be supported by tangible evidence; and, as so often when think tanks are under discussion, it is difficult to supply a satisfactory answer.

Notoriously, in the crowded and competitive world of think tanks, many organisations have advertised themselves to prospective sponsors by highlighting instances (of varying plausibility) of policy ideas which have been taken up by policy-makers. In Britain, the Adam Smith Institute (founded in 1977) has been a prominent exemplar of this approach, although it also illustrated the potential hazards of self-advertisement since one of its favourite policy ideas (a system of local taxation calculated on the basis of individual residents rather than their financial resources) resulted in a policy disaster which contributed to the forced resignation of Margaret Thatcher (Denham and Garnett 1998: 151–73). This is emphatically *not* the usual style adopted by British think tanks in the area of foreign policy. If such bodies have gained a reputation for policy influence, it is not because they have boasted about it; at most, they tend to include in their publicity a few anecdotes which illustrate their *longevity*. One might say that they have exhibited a stereotypically British style of understatement, which has served them very well in reputational terms. Of course, those whose influence is limited, tend to be guilty of the opposite.

To an extent, however, this reticence has been enforced on Chatham House, RUSI and IISS by the prevailing culture of British decision-making in the fields of foreign policy and defence. While an aggressive ideological "advocacy tank" like the Adam Smith Institute enjoyed a licence to highlight (if not exaggerate) its influence because domestic policy-makers have been hungry for outside advice (particularly since the 1980s), British foreign policy decisions have tended to be taken by a governmental elite which has rarely welcomed external advice. This attitude is reinforced by an unavoidable "knowledge gap" between think tanks and the relevant ministries, which (usually) enjoy far greater resources in terms of information-gathering. A notable exception which reinforces this general rule was the wartime period of 1939–45, when the government's own channels of reliable information were impaired and it turned to Chatham House (temporarily based in Oxford) to help close its own "knowledge gap". Significantly, though, when "normalcy" was restored in 1945 the think tank began to struggle; as the journalist Anthony Sampson noted "it accumulated a lot of dead wood, and was even slower than the Foreign Office in realising the importance of Black Africa and the [EEC]" (Sampson 1965: 280).

Even on the rare occasions when policy-relevant knowledge held within think tanks rivals that of the respective government department, it still has to be translated into terms which are broadly compatible with official thinking. In a 1975 study published under the auspices of Chatham House, William Wallace alluded tactfully to "the difficulty which even the most expert outsider experiences in discovering the terms of debate within Whitehall on his own field" (Wallace 1975: 106). In this scenario, it is difficult for any foreign or defence policy think tank in Britain to influence policy in advance; at best, their analyses of decisions taken without their direct input might help to guide policy-makers when they are faced with similar dilemmas, but even on those occasions their advice is unlikely to divert a government from its preferred course of action.

A second difficulty is that even in cases when influence seems to have been exercised, it is often unclear whether a policy outcome has been affected by the think tanks as *institutions,* or by eminent individuals who have been consulted because of reputations which owe little or nothing to their association with think tanks. This problem can be illustrated by two examples, one taken from the interwar period and the other much more recent. The first is an unusual instance of a foreign policy think tank (in this case Chatham House) drawing attention to its past achievements. Its website mentions its special study group (formed in 1929) on the role of gold in international economics. The website states that the formation of this group "anticipated Britain's decision to leave the Gold Standard two years later". The obvious quibble here is that the decision to decouple the value of sterling from gold was involuntary – because Britain's gold reserves were being depleted at an unsustainable rate – rather than arising from any specific policy advice. Leaving this aside, the study group included many renowned economists, notably John Maynard Keynes, who was well known as a critic of the gold standard long before he joined the Chatham House group (http://www.chathamhouse.org/about/history). The example thus proves that the RIIA was prepared to commission very serious studies of topical questions, and was capable of attracting participants of the highest calibre; but the question of influence remains unanswered (or, indeed, in this instance, unanswerable). Did the connection with the RIIA lend weight to the group's deliberations, or did the participation of luminaries like Keynes make the RIIA's study group seem more important?

The more recent example is more pertinent, because it involves fewer ambiguities in terms of causation. Sir Lawrence Freedman, who had been a significant figure within both Chatham House and IISS for many years, undoubtedly played a leading role in the composition of Tony Blair's momentous speech, delivered in Chicago in April 1999, which outlined the circumstances in which "liberal" governments could (or should) intervene in civil conflicts (http://webarchive.nationalarchives.gov.uk/+/www.number10.gov.uk/Page1297). Whether or not Freedman's input merely added clarity and eloquence to thoughts which were already in Blair's mind, it would be churlish to argue that this should not count as direct influence, heralding not just a change in one particular decision but rather a shift in the framework within which numerous future decisions were taken. However, apart from his well-known work for think tanks, Freedman had been Professor of War Studies at Kings College, London, since 1982. Was he asked to advise Blair on foreign policy issues because of his connection with think tanks, or because of the reputation he had established due to his professorial role (and his authorship of numerous academic books and articles)? The most plausible answer is that without his involvement in think tanks, Sir Lawrence might not have become so prominent as to attract the interest of the Blair government, but that when he provided input to the Chicago speech he was doing so as a private individual.

Although positive examples of direct influence exercised by foreign policy think tanks is elusive, the early days of Blair's "New Labour" government (1997–2007) offer a fascinating piece of *negative* evidence. Blair's first Foreign Secretary, Robin Cook, was antipathetic towards Chatham House, allegedly because it had treated his opinions with inadequate respect; *The Times* reported that he referred to the think tank as "a graveyard of ex-diplomats". Soon after his appointment to the Foreign Office, Cook (and Blair) supported the establishment of a new think tank, the Foreign Policy Centre, with a youthful Director, Mark Leonard. Unlike Chatham House, the new centre was exploring ideas which senior New Labour found highly congenial, particularly in respect of an "ethical dimension" to British decision-making (Little and Wickham-Jones 2000: 13); although it is worth noting that in recent times, the centre identifies as independent, with co-presidents from the two major political parties (FPC, http://fpc.org.uk/about/).[1]

This example could be interpreted as back-handed testimony to the influence of foreign policy think tanks: senior figures within New Labour clearly thought that Chatham House played a significant role, since they took the trouble to promote a new body in the hope that it would perform similar functions in a more congenial fashion. The question remains, however, whether Cook and Blair wanted to contest Chatham House's perceived influence over *policy*, or whether their target was something less tangible – the "climate" of informed opinion.

Informed opinion and foreign policy think tanks

There is considerable support for the notion that, whatever their initial aspirations, British think tanks have long recognised that their most realistic goal in the areas of foreign policy and defence is to influence "informed opinion", rather than hoping for direct decision-making input. Back in the 1960s William Snyder wrote that "The direct influence of the IISS on British defence policy may be negligible; it has however, made an important contribution to the activities of the articulate public" (Snyder 1964: 76). More recently, Robert Self has argued that the think tanks "play a part in shaping the intellectual environment in which policy is made" (Self 2010: 258).

Think tanks can contribute to "shaping the intellectual environment" in two ways. Thanks to the convenient geographical locations of RUSI, Chatham House and IISS, they provide "neutral ground" for invited speakers who can attract audiences which might include policy-makers as well as journalists and prominent academics. Such events, and the ensuing discussions, can lead to specific policy decisions – in which case the think tanks, at least, will have acted as convenient *facilitators* for decisions which may or may not have been made in any case.

Beyond this, conversations at such meetings can inform articles in journals and newspapers, thus contributing to general public discussion.

In addition, the think tanks themselves publish books and journals which enjoy relatively wide circulation among the "informed" public. Chatham House's annual *Survey of International Affairs*, under the inspirational guidance of the think tank's Director of Studies Arnold Toynbee, was an indispensable text for students of British foreign policy between the wars. Its peer-reviewed journal, *International Affairs* (established in 1922) publishes six issues every year. IISS publishes the highly regarded *Adelphi Papers* on specific issues at regular intervals, and its journal, *Survival,* is also well rated. RUSI is responsible for numerous publications, notably its *Whitehall Papers* and the *RUSI Journal*, which first appeared in 1857.

While such publications enjoy considerable academic credibility, they strive to make complex issues seem accessible for the general reader – in contrast to a great number of academic publications, which appear designed to *exclude* a wider audience. However, the think tanks are well aware that their publications will not be consulted beyond the relatively small number of people who interest themselves directly in such matters. Self-consciously, they aim to publish material which will be accessible to journalists; as such, they act as intermediaries between the foreign policy "elite" and the general public. In recent years, many have sought to get their work into the public forum, with an essay from Chatham House's *The World Today* featuring in *The Observer*'s "Worldview" each month.

One can appreciate the success of think tanks in helping to shape the intellectual argument by examining government sponsorship of their various activities. Freedom of Information (FOI) requests lodged by the present authors revealed that the MoD's payments to RUSI have risen from £32,871 in 2010/1 to £226,524 in 2014–15. This funding emanates from across 30 departments within the MoD. In contrast, MoD spending on Chatham House was split across just nine departments. Contrary to this, the Foreign and Commonwealth Office (FCO) is listed as a "partner" of Chatham House and is a corporate member, the cost of which, in 2015, was £13,500. In response to our FOI request for information on FCO funding of Chatham House, the Knowledge Services Manager (responsible for responding to FOI requests) noted that: "As a corporate member the FCO commissions services from Chatham House to assist with various projects around the world that help boost the UK's prosperity and relationships with other countries. These activities are funded by FCO Departments through their devolved budget". This remark, and the details of departmental funding, raises interesting questions about the relationship between government and foreign policy think tanks, especially since these organisations – aside from the value of their properties – are far less affluent than their American counterparts. In their returns to the Charity Commission for 2014–15, Chatham House declared an income of £14.5 million; RUSI declared £5.5 million; the figure for IISS was £16.1 million.

Moreover, the neutral ground provided by think tanks can also serve as a means of communication with other governments, in preference to more official channels. Almost from its inception Chatham House provided an informal diplomatic service, assisting the British government in negotiations with the US over war debts and naval disarmament in the inter-war period. It worked closely with the Foreign Office in dealings with issues relating to the "Pacific Rim", especially through the Institute of Pacific Relations until that body was dissolved in 1960 (Parmar 2004: 23). During the 1980s it played an important role in maintaining communications between the UK government and the Soviet Union – an initiative which bore fruit when Britain was quick to identify the chances of *rapprochement* offered by Mikhail Gorbachev (interview with Lord Wallace of Saltaire). Along with *proximity*, think tanks like Chatham House offer *deniability*; they are close enough to decision-makers to carry credibility as surrogates for serving government officials in contacts of a sensitive nature, while remaining sufficiently detached to avoid causing political embarrassment should such contacts become public knowledge. Such avenues to influence, of course, are not readily available to think tanks working in other fields.

Case study: Think tanks and the Iraq War

In the months before the 2003 invasion of Iraq, think tanks played a prominent role in facilitating debate, but also in creating and shaping perceptions. On 21 February 2003, Jack Straw – then Foreign Secretary – spoke at Chatham House, making the case for military action. Straw prefaced his comments on Iraq by thanking Professor Bulmer-Thomas, the Director of Chatham House, and his team on behalf of the FCO for their efforts over the past 12 months. Straw continued:

> It's hard to overstate the importance of our partnership with Chatham House. As we enter an uncertain new era in international affairs, it's all the more important that FCO staff are able to step back from the day to day vicissitudes of diplomacy and develop a strategic perspective on the environment in which they operate. Chatham House has performed this invaluable service for British diplomats for the past 80 years. (http://www.theguardian.com/politics/2003/feb/21/foreignpolicy.iraq)

Straw's comments stress the importance of Chatham House in several ways. The Foreign Secretary went on to acknowledge the importance of allowing policy-makers to meet with academics to discuss emerging issues.

The selection of Chatham House as the venue for the speech demonstrates the perceived importance of the RIIA. However, it was not the only venue chosen by Straw to outline the case for British action, as he delivered a similar speech at IISS. Six months earlier, the institute had published an 80 page dossier, exploring Iraq's military capabilities. The dossier drew upon the experience of UN weapons inspectors who had been in Iraq but, as *The Guardian* noted, the dossier has as much that can be used to make arguments against military action as it does to advocate it (Norton-Taylor 2002; http://www.theguardian.com/world/2002/sep/10/iraq.politics).

Dr John Chipman, Director General of IISS, echoed this view, stating that the dossier "does not attempt to make a case, either way, as to whether Saddam Hussein's WMD arsenal is a casus belli per se". However other interested parties disagreed. Actors in the media selected material from the IISS dossier and "spun" the report in an attempt to exacerbate the WMD threat. The dossier itself was a considered piece of work, providing scope for interpretation. However, in the coming months the nuances in the document itself were overlooked as the British government exploited it as justification for going to war. As Kim Sengupta (2004) noted in *The Independent*,

> The IISS dossier on Iraqi weapons of mass destruction, published on 9 September 2002 . . . was immediately seized on by Bush and Blair administrations as providing "proof" that Saddam was just months away from launching a chemical and biological, or even a nuclear attack. Large parts of the IISS document were subsequently recycled in the now notorious Downing Street dossier, published with a foreword by the Prime Minister, the following week.

To some denizens of the think tank world, IISS had found itself in a kind of utopia where one of its productions had not only exercised a profound influence on government strategy, but was the subject of intense media discussion. In reality, of course, the incident threatened to damage IISS's reputation for impartial analysis. It came at a time when IISS was seen to be superseding Chatham House as a source of policy advice and a venue for conferences, thanks to its intimate links with the US State Department and the Pentagon as well as the UK's Foreign Office (Dickie 2004: 181). In reality, IISS was receptive to a wide range of views on the Iraq crisis. In 2002 its journal *Survival* published a piece which concluded with the very prescient advice that "If America decides to go into Iraq, it had better do so with its eyes wide open" (Gordon, Indyk and O'Hanlon 2002: 21). To illustrate the Byzantine complexity of think tank activity, the authors were attached to the Brookings Institution rather than IISS. In any event, their warning was ignored by the US, even if it was not entirely lost on the British.

Conclusion

If the story of IISS and the Iraq dossier suggests that when think tanks sup with governments they should use long-handled cutlery, the fact remains that a close relationship is indispensable. For think tanks in this field, a desire for complete independence equates to total impotence. Economic think tanks (for example), can criticise government programmes with virtual impunity, so long as their arguments have a sound statistical basis. Thus, for example, the Institute for Fiscal Studies has enhanced its reputation in the UK through its unflinching analysis of government proposals, particularly in the current "age of austerity". However, issues relating to war and peace evoke a quite different response; criticism of government decisions, however well founded, can lead to accusations that a think tank is "unpatriotic", threatening to deprive it of its audience among the wider public as well as decision-makers.

Foreign policy think tanks are sufficiently distinctive from other policy institutes to require different standards of appraisal on the question of institutional independence. But if the British institutions truly deserve lofty reputations, they can still negotiate these delicate relationships to the advantage of all parties; they will attract well-placed speakers and contributors to their publications, and act as venues for informed discussions, without compromising their intellectual integrity. Thus, the announcement in 2015 that the former Conservative Foreign Secretary Lord (William) Hague was to assume the chairmanship of RUSI in September that year was unlikely to endanger its reputation; while RUSI would benefit from association with a senior member of the ruling Conservative Party, Hague augmented his image as a statesman whose insights into global developments transcended mere party politics.

No one who reads the numerous publications of the British foreign policy think tanks could dismiss them as elitist bodies who consciously address themselves to a closed world of decision-makers. In this respect, they are clearly committed to the transmission of knowledge in digestible form, either through their own organs or through media outlets, including radio and television as well as serious newspapers and magazines. If they have not succeeded in expanding the sphere of "informed opinion" in matters of foreign policy, it has not been for want of trying, especially in recent years when they have made their publications freely available on the Internet. Ultimately, the British foreign policy think tanks have been trying to gain traction with two unheeding audiences – policy-makers who (usually) assume that they can do their work without help from non-governmental bodies, and a public which (usually) only recognises its need to be better-informed when government decisions have already been taken. Faced with these ingrained attitudes in the British context, it is not surprising that the think tanks have failed in relation to their original objectives; the wonder is that, in spite of everything, they keep on trying to fulfil them.

References

de Boer, J. 2105. "What Are Think Tanks Good For?" United Nations University. http://cpr.unu.edu/what-are-think-tanks-good-for.html.

Denham, A., and Garnett, M. 1998. *British Think Tanks and the Climate of Opinion*. London: UCL Press.

Denham, A., and Garnett, M. 2004. "A Hollowed-Out Tradition? British Think Tanks in the Twenty-First Century." In D. Stone and A. Denham (eds), *Think Tank Traditions: Policy Research and the Politics of Ideas*. Manchester: Manchester University Press, 232–46.

Dickie, J. 2004. *The New Mandarins: How British Foreign Policy Works*. London: I.B Tauris.

Gordon, P., M. Indyk and M. O'Hanlon. 2002. "Getting Serious about Iraq." *Survival* 44: 9–22.

Higgott, R., and D. Stone. 1994. "The Limits of Influence: Foreign Policy Think Tanks in Britain and the USA." *Review of International Studies* 20: 15–34.

Howard, M. 2008. "Present at the Creation." *Survival* 50: 5–8.

Little, R., and M. Wickham-Jones (eds). 2000. *Labour's Foreign Policy: A New Moral Crusade?* Manchester: Manchester University Press.

Norton-Taylor, R. 2002. "The Iraqi Threat: Real or Imagined?" *The Guardian*, 10 September.

Parmar, I. 2004. "Institutes of International Affairs." In D. Stone and A. Denham (eds), *Think Tank Traditions: Policy Research and the Politics of Ideas*. Manchester: Manchester University Press, 19–33.

Sampson, A. 1965. *The Anatomy of Britain Today*. London: Hodder and Stoughton.

Self, R. 2010. *British Foreign & Defence Policy since 1945*. London: Palgrave Macmillan.

Sengupta, K. 2004. "Occupation Made War Less Safe, Pro-War Institute Says." *The Independent*, 26 May. Available from http://www.independent.co.uk/news/world/middle-east/occupation-made-world-less-safe-prowar-institute-says-6169169.html.

Snyder, W. 1964. *The Politics of British Defence Policy 1945–1962*. London: Ernest Benn.

Wallace, W. 1975. *The Foreign Policy Process in Britain*. London: Royal Institute of International Affairs.

8 Chinese think tanks' influence on foreign policy making

A case study of the role of CIIS and SIIS in the making of China's Europe policy[1]

Xin Hua

Introduction

Faced with a volatile external environment and forced to handle foreign policy issues beyond their expertise and analyzing capacities, Chinese foreign policy decision makers increasingly rely on think tanks as a kind of "external brain" offering policy advice. The modalities through which these think tanks influence policy, and the nature of their relationship to political power in China, are the concerns of this chapter.

Our analysis proceeds through a number of steps. It begins with a categorization of China's overall think tank system, including the methods used by Chinese think tanks to exert policy influence. It then provides case studies of two elite Chinese foreign policy think tanks, the China Institute of International Studies (CIIS) and the Shanghai Institute of International Studies (SIIS), and analyzes their role in the making of China's policy towards Europe. The chapter concludes that CIIS and SIIS do indeed have an effect on the shaping of China's policy positions with respect to three major issues in its relations with Europe. They have long-term indirect influence through their research projects, as well as short-term direct influence. This more direct influence may be observed through a survey of their high-level forums and symposiums as well as small-scale bilateral meetings with state officials. They also have long-term direct influence through the unique Chinese-style "revolving door" mechanisms that are described in this chapter. Finally, after a review of three sets of theoretical paradigms for explaining think tanks' policy influence, this chapter adopts the paradigm of "central space of the four fields of power" to summarize the role of CIIS and SIIS in China's foreign policy making.

The emergence of China's think tank community

As a result of its rapid economic development over the past three decades, China has become increasingly integrated into global and regional networks of interdependency. China's political leaders find themselves confronting an unpredictable international environment in which new and complex issues test the limits of their analytical capacities. These circumstances have led to the emergence of Chinese foreign policy think tanks, which goes back to the early 1990s. In more recent years, their numbers have proliferated, and they have become an important and influential sector in China's policy community and policy making process. In a largely authoritarian regime with a lack of open policy debates involving competing interests and a tradition of concentrating policy consultations within an inner circle of elites, the significant role of Chinese think tanks may not be obvious. Nevertheless, Chinese foreign policy think tanks, particularly the country's highly specialized foreign policy research institutes, are now playing a very influential role in China's foreign policy making. Indeed, they may be said to have real clout in China's foreign policy community. For this reason, they deserve serious attention by those intent on understanding China's foreign policy making process.

Foreign policy think tanks within the current political and bureaucratic system

China's political system is vastly different from those found in liberal democracies in the West. Within China, most think tanks are solely or mostly funded by government, and very few of them can achieve real independence. Nevertheless, just like any substantially separate policy research institution evolving in a complex policy community shaped by a fluid international environment, Chinese foreign policy think tanks have gradually developed a series of characteristics that are similar to their counterparts in the West. First, Chinese policy makers are increasingly viewing think tanks as an indispensable part of an "external brain" that can generate reliable and professional policy advice. In an official document jointly issued by the General Offices of the Central Committee of the Chinese Communist Party (CCP) and China's State Council in January 2015, China's top leadership referred to think tanks as an important source of the state's governance capacity, and even acknowledged that they are a starting point to build China's international competitiveness.[2] Second, as the most developed of all think tanks in the country, Chinese foreign policy research institutions have already established relatively clear structures of governance and complete teams of experts. Their expert teams and standards for enrolling experts are very similar to those of their counterparts in the US, Europe, and Japan, although their governance structures are quite different, shaped by China's unique social and political environment. Third, there is a "revolving door" mechanism apparent in several elite foreign policy research institutions which enhances their influence on China's foreign policy making. Some leading experts in several elite foreign policy research institutions of China, such as CIIS and the China Institutes of Contemporary International Studies, have been appointed as ambassadors in Chinese embassies, while some senior leaders from China's Ministry of Foreign Affairs (MFA) became executive officers of these research institutes. In this sense, elite Chinese foreign policy think tanks share certain characteristics with some of their western counterparts.

On the other hand, the current Chinese political and social system has some structural continuities with its communist and totalitarianism past that still largely shape China's foreign policy process and the role of its think tanks within this system. One of these continuities that has the largest effect on Chinese foreign policy think tanks is the so-called "stove-piping" structure of bureaucracy (Shambaugh 2002: 580; Glaser 2012).[3] The entire bureaucracy of China's foreign policy decision making is still compartmentalized into several parallel systems of top-to-bottom vertical hierarchies, which is a very prominent feature of Leninist political structures. Inside this structure, China's foreign policy research institutions are positioned as specific and professional policy advice providers affiliated with different vertical hierarchies ("xitong" in Chinese), and having different bureaucratic statuses ("xingzheng jibie"). They are allocated different resources and funding in relation to the specific vertical bureaucratic hierarchies to which they belong. Furthermore, their ability to make their voices heard, and the success they enjoy in having their ideas taken seriously by those in top leadership positions is determined by the significance and competence of the vertical bureaucratic hierarchy to which they belong. For example, CIIS is affiliated to China's MFA and therefore both its resources and influence are confined within the MFA system, whose responsibilities mainly involve normal diplomacy. Therefore, CIIS can do little to influence military-related security policy, which is largely the domain of the General Staff Department of the Chinese People's Liberation Army. Likewise, its influence and research capacity in matters of foreign economic policy, which is under the authority of the Ministry of Commerce, are also relatively weak,

The lack of a public sphere for policy debates and policy advocacy

China still lacks a cultural and institutional environment for open public debates on foreign policy, and any harsh criticism or over-active campaigning in regard to the top leadership's major foreign policy decisions are unacceptable to the ruling elite. Consequently, Chinese foreign policy research institutions are passive in their interactions with the top leadership and often act as interpreters and advocates of the foreign policy orientations of China's paramount leaders in the standing committee of the central political bureau of the CCP. Moreover, Chinese foreign policy research institutions do not have substantial connections with China's nascent non-official organizations in civil society. Although some economic think tanks will sometimes speak in bold terms to the top elites in Beijing in defense of certain social groups on some economic and public policy issues, particularly on a few issues related to rural areas, it is safe to say that Chinese foreign policy think tanks do not have the capacity or conditions to play this sort of advocacy or lobbying role.

A review of current literature relevant to Chinese think tanks

Chinese and foreign scholars have contributed to a growing literature on Chinese think tanks' unique role in the country's social and political system. Among domestic scholars, Zhu Xufeng (2013) has conducted the most systematic and detailed statistical surveys of Chinese think tanks. He divides Chinese think tanks into three categories: official, semi-official, and non-official. Applying Galtung's "social structure" paradigm, which divides the policy process into three circles – "decision-making nucleus", "center", and "periphery", Zhu Xufeng analyzes Chinese think tanks' influence as it is transmitted through the country's administrative system, social elite circles, and media, with a special focus on think tanks' administrative status, which has an impact on the levels and distributions of resources and prestige among them. He concentrates mainly on China's economic think tanks, without any case study or specific analysis of foreign policy think tanks, and he does not draw definite conclusions on the modalities or degrees of think tanks' influence on policy making.

Among foreign scholars, CSIS analyst Bonnie S. Glaser has for a long-time been an astute observer of Chinese think tanks, particularly those focused on foreign policy. She published articles on Chinese foreign policy think tanks and their policy influence in 2002 and 2012. Covering a period of ten years, these two articles indicate that her evaluation of the Chinese think tank scene evolved in response to the significant development that took place over those years. She identifies persistent characteristics of Chinese think tanks' organizational environment and behavior, such as the "stove-piping" phenomenon and the pivotal role of the General Offices of the State Council and the CCP's Central Committee, and also describes several bureaucratic operational features, such as the unique role played by the secretaries of decision making elites (Glaser and Saunders 2002; Glaser 2012).

The research carried out by Glaser and her colleague, Saunders, is the most systematic and insightful when it comes to understanding China's think tank scene. There are, however, many important contributions made by others who have studied the Chinese think tank phenomenon. In the mid-1990s, Lu Ning provided what may be the earliest description of the role of China's foreign policy research institutions. He concluded that they had "little relevance to the policy process" and had only a "cosmetic" function. He noted that for a long time CIIS had been "used by China's Ministry of Foreign Affairs (MFA) as a place to dispose of the undesirable and untrustworthy elements from the MFA in a thinly veiled 'internal exile' " (Lu 1997).

Since the end of 1990s, however, Chinese studies experts have gradually paid more attention to think tanks and have come to assign more importance to them than in the past. David Shambaugh (2002: 575–96) made a case-by-case survey of the organizational structures of seven elite foreign policy think tanks established and supported by China's central government. He Li (2002) pointed out that the "copy-cat" effect might be a major force contributing to the organizational and operational streamlining of Chinese foreign policy think tanks. Moreover, Barry Naughton (2002) examined the origins and evolution of China's top economic think tanks before and after the launch of China's important market reforms in 1992. And Zhao Quansheng (1992; 2013) described the changes and trends in Chinese think tanks using an analytical framework of information and expertise exchanges between "inner circles" and "outer circles", based on his central idea that China's political structure has been converted from Mao's "vertical authoritarianism" to Deng's "horizontal authoritarianism". Liao Xuanli (2006) created the "pluralistic elitism" approach to understanding foreign policy think tanks' influence on the making of China's Japan policy. He argues that think tanks form a unique and significant part of the pluralistic policy inputs that are filtered upward to the exclusive inner circle of decision makers. In fact, this "pluralistic elitism" paradigm is similar to the concept of "fragmented authoritarianism" offered by Kenneth Lieberthal (1992).

All of these scholars have observed and described foreign policy think tanks and their role in China's foreign policy making. Their research does not, however, offer detailed case studies of specific Chinese foreign policy think tanks or specific foreign policy fields. Furthermore, their categorizations of Chinese think tanks lack clarity. This chapter will endeavor to provide a more detailed and accurate picture of China's foreign policy research institutions, their positions in China's foreign policy community, and their influence on China's foreign policy decision making.

Foreign policy research institutes within the overall think tank system

In order to have a clear understanding of the function and role of research institutions in China's foreign policy decision making, it is first important to establish a precise and comprehensive categorization of the entire, complex system of Chinese think tanks. The following three factors add to the complexity of this system. First, in China's past, policy advice, the training of experts, and academic research were not clearly differentiated or divided from each other, so a variety of teaching and research institutions have come to be involved in policy advice. Second, the Chinese communist ruling elites copied the whole organizational structure of academic research from the Soviet Union in the 1950s, including the academy of social sciences system and the Party school system, which form an integral part of the core of China's policy-related academic researches. Third, because China's communist ruling elites are pragmatic and traditionally prefer short-term analysis and case-by-case problem-solving to long-term strategic research, they entrust a large proportion of policy research work to the small in-house policy advice organs of the Party's committees and government bodies at various levels. These in-house sources of policy advice can be controlled directly and operated by policy elites. They represent a particular type of think tank that has functions similar to those performed by such public institutions as the US Congressional Research Service.

Contemporary Chinese think tanks can be organized into five major types in accordance with their proximity to the core of top-level decision makers and their access to information. Of the five categories, the in-house research organs of the Party and the government are the closest to the decision makers and have the most direct influence; they have convenient access to largely confidential information and are in daily contact with political and policy elites, attributes that place them first in terms of proximity. The specialized foreign policy research institutions rank second; they maintain regular and intimate communications with top-level

Table 8.1 The overall system of Chinese think tanks

Category \ Level	Central	Provincial	Below provincial
I: In-house research organs of the Party and governments	Policy research offices of the CCP's Central Committee and the State Council, DRC[1] of the State Council	Policy research offices of CCP's provincial committees and provincial governments, DRC of provincial governments	Policy research offices of city-level and county-level governments
II: Specialized foreign policy research institutes	CIRIR, CIIS, CIISS, CCIEE[2]	SIIS[3]	none
III: The system of Party schools	Party school of the Central Committee of the CCP, China's National School of Administration, the four major central-level cadre schools[4]	Party schools of CCP's provincial committees	Party schools at city and county levels
IV: The system of the Academy of Social Sciences	CASS[5]	Provincial-level academies of social sciences, such as SASS[6]	none
V: Research institutes affiliated to universities	Research institutes affiliated to the universities of the "985 List" and "211 List"	Research institutes affiliated to universities controlled by provincial governments or ministries other than the education ministry	none

1 Development Research Center.
2 China Institute of Contemporary International Relations; China Institute of International Studies; China Institute for International Strategic Studies; China Center for International Economic Exchanges.
3 Shanghai Institute of International Studies.
4 These are located in Shanghai, Yan'an, Jingangshan and Dalian.
5 Chinese Academy of Social Sciences.
6 Shanghai Academy of Social Sciences.

leaders on major foreign policy issues due to their professionalized expertise and skills in conducting foreign policy related analyses. The Party schools rank third; based on their privilege of approaching the inner circle of policy elites – a privilege that is derived from the fact that they train high-ranking cadres before they are further promoted in the Party and the government – the Party schools are able to play an active role in policy advice. After the Party schools is the academy of social sciences, ranking fourth. The category of think tanks most distant from the center of political power and with the weakest links to decision makers includes the university-affiliated research institutes. Their relatively marginal status is due to the CCP's longstanding tradition and innate distrust of public intellectuals and the usual communist bureaucratic pattern of exponentially decreasing the amount of policy-related information that is distributed among lower levels in the state hierarchy.

The five categories of Chinese think tanks and their distribution at the various administrative levels are indicated in Table 8.1. In fact, these think tanks are not only differentiated by their position relative to the center of political power and their connections to decision makers, they also vary in terms of their levels of professional expertise and policy advice capacities. For example, the academies of social science have more expertise and are more professionally skillful in conducting policy research and offering advice than are the Party schools on the same administrative levels. This is the case despite the fact that the latter may be much closer to the core of decision makers than the former. Even within the same category, think tanks on different geographical administrative levels are differentiated because of the dramatic imbalance in the distribution of resources and information between the center and the periphery of China's communist bureaucracy. The academies of social sciences provide an example of this. The Chinese Academy of Social Sciences (CASS), which is on the central level, is infinitely closer, and more influential, in relation to China's top political leadership than provincial-level academies of social sciences. The same holds true for the system of Party schools. Therefore, think tanks in the five categories of Table 8.1 can be reorganized into the coordinate system of Figure 8.1, structured along two dimensions: the "expertise–ideology orientation" continuum and the "center–periphery" continuum.

Figure 8.1 depicts a comprehensive, but static picture of Chinese think tanks using a two-dimensional framework of categorization. It does not tell us how Chinese think tanks exert their influence in the policy making system. In the field of think tank studies, western scholars have been exploring the American, European, and Canadian think tanks' operating strategies for quite some time and have established a rather clear and widely accepted typology on the issue of influence strategies (Abelson 2002, 2006; Weidenbaum 2009). Some western China experts, such as Bonnie S. Glaser (2012), have offered a rough division of the channels and methods that Chinese think tanks may adopt to transmit their advice and influence policy makers, but it still lacks precision. I propose a two-dimensional system, shown in Figure 8.2, which locates the various methods employed by Chinese think tanks to exert influence along a "short vs long term" continuum and a "direct vs indirect" continuum.

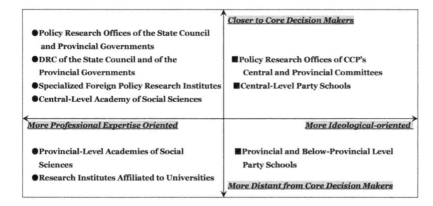

Figure 8.1 The two-dimensional division of the Chinese think tank system

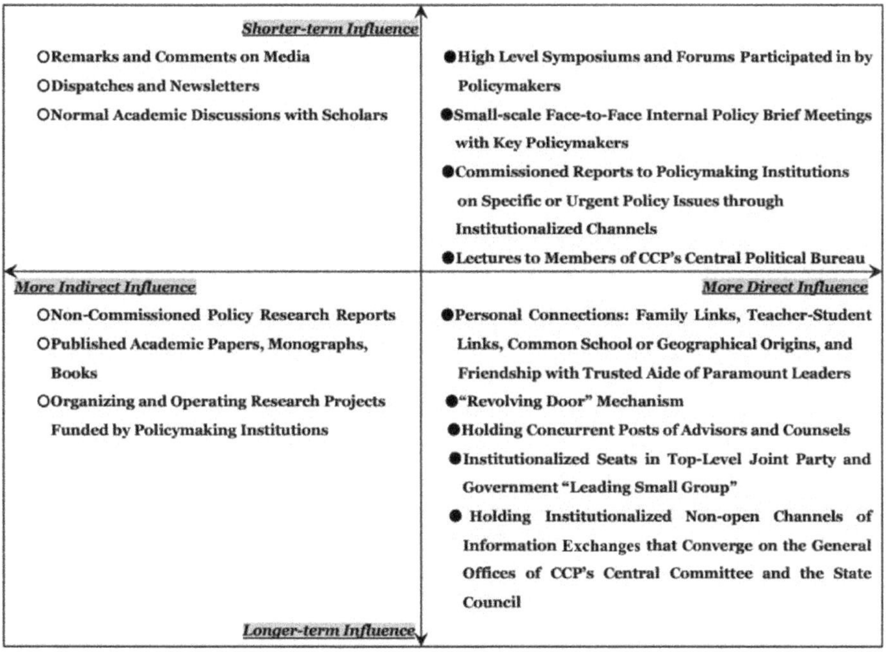

Figure 8.2 Chinese think tanks' methods to exert policy influence: a two-dimensional framework

All the 14 methods (or strategies) of Chinese think tanks are included in this two-dimensional structure. Some of them are unique but rather effective strategies, specially developed within and adapted to China's largely authoritarian and centralized political system. These include the personal links between think tank executives and researchers and trusted aides of high-level leaders, particularly with the secretaries serving these leaders, and think tanks' personal links with some leaders through teacher–student relations formed when these leaders were in the higher education system of the Party schools. These are the culturally unique ways through which Chinese think tanks may influence the center of political power. It is difficult, of course, to document and pinpoint precise instances where these channels of influence have been successful.

Case study: The role of CIIS and SIIS in forming China's policy toward Europe

The categorizations in Figures 8.1 and 8.2 present what we believe to be a useful clarification of the position of foreign policy research institutes within China's overall think tank system and their methods for achieving policy influence. An in-depth study is necessary to reveal a more finely grained picture of their activities and relationship to political power. For this purpose, I have chosen two important examples of China's specialized foreign policy research institutes: CIIS and SIIS. The focus is their efforts to influence China's policy making towards Europe (the EU and its member states). CIIS and SIIS are two of the most professionalized and best funded foreign policy research institutes in China. They are affiliated to China's MFA and the Shanghai Municipal Government, respectively. CIIS is controlled by China's central government and SIIS by a provincial-level government.

The general effect of CIIS and SIIS on China's policy toward Europe

The first issue is the key one: How effective are these two think tanks in shaping China's policy making in regard to Europe. It is difficult, as many of the chapters of this volume have pointed out, to locate a "smoking gun" or direct linear relationship between a think tank proposal, study, or other intervention and state action. This is certainly true in the case of both CIIS and SIIS and the relationship between their proposals and new policy initiatives adopted by China's top political leaders. Moreover, finding clear relationships is even more difficult in the case of China than in the other countries studied in this volume, because of the lack of transparency in the Chinese policy making process and the lack of public access to the documents and records of China's top-level political activities.

Nevertheless, traces of the policy ideas generated by CIIS and SIIS and new ideas and policy initiatives embraced by the country's leaders can still be found. Since the beginning of the European sovereign debt crisis in 2010, several issues have dominated the attention of Chinese policy makers and China's relations with Europe have become more delicate and less stable. After scrutinizing official and media records of these major issues, I collected the open research publications of CIIS and SIIS on major policy issues related to China's relations with Europe, including media comments and citations, dispatches and newsletters, and published academic papers and books. I then summarized their major viewpoints on particular issues. When the viewpoints proposed by CIIS and SIIS are compared to changes in the Chinese leadership's policy initiatives and/or expressed ideas in the same field, it may be inferred that there is a possible causal connection. In the case of three major issues relating to China's policy towards Europe, there is a chronological time sequence from ideas and proposals generated by CIIS and SIIS and Chinese leaders adopting policy initiatives consistent with these ideas and proposals (see Table 8.2). In other words, it can be shown that the viewpoints of CIIS and SIIS appeared first, after which Chinese policy makers initiated new policies that very much resembled what was generated by the experts at CIIS and SIIS. In light of the regular and institutionalized exchanges of information between CIIS and SIIS and the country's top foreign policy makers through the joint Party-government organ of the Foreign Affairs Leading Small Group, it is very likely that CIIS and SIIS had some degree of influence on the Chinese leadership.

The long-term and indirect influence of CIIS and SIIS: Their relevant research projects

In Figure 8.2, research projects are considered to be one of the longer-term and indirect methods whereby Chinese think tanks may exert policy influence. Thus, it is useful to survey those research projects that are relevant to European studies and China–EU relations. Table 8.3 lists the four major research projects of CIIS that are focused on these matters. Three of them were funded by the MFA and launched since 2010 against the background of the European debt crisis. This demonstrates the close ties between CIIS and the concerns and activities of the MFA. The resources for policy-related research flow from the MFA and the reports and papers produced by project-specific funding are inevitably submitted to and noticed by the top leaders of the MFA, although this is usually a long and perhaps slow process. Through these projects CIIS has played an indispensable role since the beginning of the European debt crisis in shaping the agenda and the consideration of options as the MFA has developed its response.

The short-term and direct influence of CIIS and SIIS: High-level forums and symposiums and small-scale bilateral meetings

In Figure 8.2, high-level forums and symposiums that are attended by policy makers are identified as the method by which Chinese think tanks' achieve short-term and direct policy influence. In practice, some high-level forums and symposiums have become fairly regular, so that they may now be considered institutionalized mechanisms linking think tanks to top government leaders. Even for China's most elite foreign policy research institutes, including CIIS and SIIS, which enjoy some access to policy makers through informal channels, the high-level forums and symposiums are still important. They are important embodiments of China's public diplomacy or what has been called "track-II diplomacy". In recent years, Chinese leaders have come to realize that it is far more efficient to transmit diplomatic

Table 8.2 The perceptional links and time sequences between CIIS and SIIS and Chinese policy-makers on three major issues related to China's policy towards Europe[1]

Policy issue		China's policy towards the European sovereign debt crisis	China's stand on the EU–China Bilateral Investment Treaty (BIT) negotiations	China's proper measures to let Europe accept the "One Belt One Road" Initiative
Specific policy point of the issues		China may consider increasing its purchase of EU's debt bonds and participate in the European Stability Mechanism.	China will regard EU–China BIT as the founding framework for China's economic growth in the next ten years.	China may consider integrating "One Belt One Road" initiative into the "European Strategic Investment Fund" Plan
Proposals of the policy points by CIIS	Time	13 May and 18 July 2011	November 2011 and June 2012	February, March, and early June 2015
	Form	Blue-cover Year Book and speech on symposium	Published monographs and newspaper comment	Published articles and newspaper comment
Proposals of the policy points by SIIS	Time	10 November 2011	March 2013	March and April 2015
	Form	Newspaper comment	Article published in academic journal	Published articles and newspaper comments
Chinese Policymakers' Endorsement of the Policy Point	Time	February 15th of 2012	November 21st, 2013	May and June of 2015
	Form	Chinese Premier WEN Jiabao's press declaration	Joint Statement for the 16th China-EU Summit: the EU China 2020 Strategic Agenda	The Joint Statements for the 2015 China-EU Strategic Dialogue and the 17th China–EU Summit

1 Sources on which the "Proposals of the policy points by SIIS" and the "Chinese Policymakers' Endorsement of Policy Point" are based are available from the author.

Table 8.3 The major research projects of CIIS on EU–China relations

Project titles	Funding source	Person in charge of the project	Funding period	Form of achievements
EU's adjustment of its Africa policy and its influence on China	China's national fund for social sciences	Jin Ling, researcher, European Studies section	2008–11	Papers published in CSSCI journals
European public opinion towards China	China's MFA	CUI Hongjian, head of the European Studies section	2010–11	Special reports
EU reform against its debt crisis	China's MFA	Jin Ling, researcher, European Studies Section	2011–12	Published papers and special reports
Post-crisis public debt issues of developed countries	China's MFA	HU Dawei, researcher, European Studies section	2011–present	Special reports and published papers

signals or collect policy-related information through these "track-II diplomacy" events than through fully official and formal diplomatic channels. This is particularly true in the case of some highly confrontational and controversial issues. As Table 8.4 indicates, CIIS and SIIS operate a series of institutionalized and regular high-level forums and symposiums for academic, diplomatic, economic, and political exchanges between Chinese institutions and their European counterparts. These have become major and, one might say, almost official connecting mechanisms between China and Europe.

The majority of these forums and symposiums are jointly organized by elite European think tanks and governmental institutions, and thus they become important channels for understanding the political and policy trends and perceptions of the EU and its member states. It is for this reason that China's MFA and other governmental institutions are actively involved in organizing these opportunities for the exchange of ideas and the statement of policies. The interpretations of European experts at CIIS and SIIS of the speeches, statements, and remarks made by European officials and think tank experts become an important source of information for Chinese foreign policy makers.

The regular high-level forums and symposiums are always in the media spotlight and attract the most attention from the general public. Nevertheless, it is in the more day-to-day activities of think tanks, including small-scale bilateral meetings with policy makers and politicians, particularly internal bilateral policy

Table 8.4 Institutionalized high-level China–Europe forums and symposiums operated by CIIS and SIIS

Items Titles	Regularity	Chinese organizers	European joint organizers	Chinese governmental participants and supporters
Symposium on "Sino-EU relations and the Taiwan question"	Annual	SIIS	FES, SWP[1]	MFA, Taiwan Affairs Offices of the State Council and provincial governments
Stockholm China Forum	Biannual	SIIS, CIIS	Swedish Foreign Ministry, USGMF[2]	MFA, PLA officers from the military academy and institutes
High-Level symposium of think tanks from China and Central and Eastern European Countries	Annual	SIIS, CIIS, CFISS[3]	Central and Eastern European political leaders	MFA, Ministry of Commerce, China's Half-Official Business Interest Groups
China–France roundtable	Annual	CIIS	Victor Segalen Foundation	MFA
China–Europe think tank roundtable	Annual	CIIS	EPC, EU-Asia Centre, and KAS[4]	MFA
Workshop for European diplomats	Annual	CIIS	None	MFA, provincial governments
NATO studies project team's field research meetings	Annual	CIIS	European think tanks	Chinese military establishments

1 Friedrich-Ebert-Stiftung; German Institute for International and Security Affairs.
2 United States German Marshall Foundation.
3 China Foundation for Internatinoal Studies.
4 Konrad Adenauer Stiftung.

briefings with key decision makers, that a more direct and substantial influence over policy making may be achieved. The number, frequency, and bureaucratic level of these small-scale bilateral meetings between think tank personnel and policy makers within a certain period may tell us much about the true importance of that think tank in the policy community and the real degree of its policy influence. The open records of CIIS do not include a complete record of these meetings, but SIIS's public information about this kind of bilateral meeting is detailed and explicit. Based on that information, Table 8.5 lists the bilateral small-scale meetings of SIIS in descending order of these meetings' policy influence level. The data suggest the existence of strong daily structural links between SIIS and China's political system and administrative bureaucracy, and also suggest the exceptional position of SIIS in China's foreign policy making toward Europe.

The long-term and direct influence of CIIS and SIIS: The "revolving door" mechanism

As early as 2002, some experts in Chinese studies had already noticed that there existed a Chinese "revolving door" mechanism between diplomats and elite think tank researchers (He Li 2002). Nevertheless, the continuing prevalence of vertical compartmentalization in China's bureaucratic hierarchy ensures that the personnel exchanges between specific Chinese foreign policy research institutes and China's huge and complex bureaucratic policy making systems are concentrated in very narrow sectors. The "revolving door" of western and especially US think tanks may open wide and allow traffic back and forth, whereas "the revolving door" of Chinese foreign policy think tanks only opens in a single direction most of the time. Tables 8.6 and 8.7 present a full list of the institutions of China's formal bureaucratic system in which the executives and researchers of CIIS and SIIS worked in the past, or hold concurrent posts at present.

Table 8.5 Small-scale bilateral meetings by SIIS from September 2014 to September 2015

Types of small-scale bilateral meetings by SIIS	Number
Bilateral meetings with central-level Chinese officials outside MFA (institutions of CCP's Central Committee and the State Council)	9
Bilateral meetings with officials from MFA	9
Bilateral meetings with China's military officers	2
Bilateral meetings with officials of Shanghai Municipal Party committee and government	13
Bilateral meetings with other provincial-level party and government officials	2
Bilateral meetings with Chinese domestic business circle (chamber of commerce, trade associations, corporations)	4
Bilateral meetings with other Chinese think tanks and universities	10
Bilateral meetings with delegates from the EU and its member states	14
Bilateral meetings with diplomats from the EU and its member states stationed in China	10
Bilateral meetings with scholars from European think tanks and universities	17

Source: Calculation by Xin Hua based on interviews and information on the SIIS official website.

Table 8.6 The "revolving door" mechanism of CIIS: Official institutions of China's bureaucratic system that provide past work or present concurrent posts to employees of CIIS

Types and numbers of Employees Institutions offering past work or present concurrent posts	Executives	Researchers		Associate and assistant Researchers		Percent of the CIIS Total
		Total	Specialized in European Studies	Total	Specialized in European Studies	
Institutions of CCP's Central Committee		1				1.2%
MFA	5	10	3	20	6	41.2%
Other ministry-level institutions of China's State Council	1					1.1%
China's military system		1		1		2.3%
State-owned corporations and banks				1		1.2%
Chinese media	2			1		3.5%
Other Chinese think tanks		2		10	4	14.1%
Chinese universities				1	1	1.2%
International organizations (UN, IMF, World Bank)	1	3	2	3		8.2%

Source: Calculation by Xin Hua based on interviews and information on the CIIS official website.

The total number of executives and researchers in CIIS is 85. This includes 20 who have the formal senior professional title of "researcher", 23 associate researchers, 32 assistant researchers, and 10 research assistants. As Table 8.6 shows, a significant number of these researchers have backgrounds or current connections with the system of China's MFA, other Chinese think tanks, or international organizations. The system of the MFA occupies a particularly important position in the "revolving door" mechanism and overall external personnel connections, with 41.2 percent of CIIS's team of experts coming from or holding concurrent posts in the MFA. CIIS has a specially invited senior advisory board of around 11 advisors, all of whom are retired ambassadors from the MFA. Therefore, nearly half of the total researchers of CIIS are closely associated with the MFA system. Specifically, 9 of the 12 experts in the European studies section of CIIS have experience as diplomats for the MFA. On some occasions, CIIS may present itself as a separate and independent policy research institute; in the bureaucratic organizational chart of the State Council, however, CIIS is a subsidiary institution of the MFA and occupies the bureaucratic status of a "bureau". The data in Table 6 largely confirms this close connection to the state apparatus.

Therefore, the most institutionalized and reliable channel for CIIS to influence top-level foreign policy decision makers is through its close and complex connections to the MFA. Indeed, leaders of the MFA are the major targets of CIIS's influence on specific foreign policy issues, particularly on issues related to China's policy towards Europe. At the same time, Table 8.6 also reveals that CIIS, a central-level elite think tank, has very weak connections to universities. This corroborates the rather peripheral position of universities in China's policy advice system. Nor does CIIS have significant links with the Party's central committee, the military establishments, or the systems of other ministries of China's State Council. This is consistent with the phenomenon of "stove-piping" in the Chinese bureaucracy, a prominent feature of Leninist political power structures.

Table 8.7 shows that the situation at SIIS is somewhat different from that at CIIS. As is true of any institution within the system of a provincial-level government, SIIS is actually under a form of "dual leadership" (referred to as *shuangchong lingdao*). More specifically, it is under both the direct control of the Shanghai Municipal Government when it comes to financing and personnel appointment (termed as "horizontal leadership" in Chinese bureaucratic jargon) and also the strong guidance of China's MFA with respect to its professional work (termed as "vertical leadership"). In the bureaucratic organizational chart, SIIS is both a subsidiary of the Shanghai Municipal Government with the administrative status of "bureau" and a node on a line extending down from the MFA in Beijing.[4]

In such circumstances it is inevitable and understandable that the Shanghai Municipal Government and the MFA in Beijing rank first and second, respectively, when it comes to past employment or concurrent posts held by SIIS experts. Researchers at SIIS are regularly seconded to full-time posts at the Foreign Affairs Office of the Shanghai Municipal Government for periods of one to two years. Closer examination reveals that SIIS researchers who worked for

Table 8.7 The "revolving door" mechanism of SIIS: Official institutions of China's bureaucratic system that provide past work or present concurrent posts to employees of SIIS

Types and numbers of employees / Institutions offering past work or present concurrent posts	Executives	Researchers Total	Researchers Specialized in European Studies	Associate and Assistant Researchers Total	Associate and Assistant Researchers Specialized in European Studies	Percent of the SIIS Total
Institutions of CCP's Central Committee	2	1				1.4%
MFA	1	3				6.8%
Other ministry-level institutions of China's State Council	1					1.4%
Shanghai Municipal Government		4	1	5	2	13.5%
China's military system		1				1.4%
International organizations (UN, IMF, World Bank)		2				2.7%
Chinese media		1	1	2		4.1%
Other Chinese think tanks		4	3	1		6.8%
Chinese universities		4	2	3		9.5%

Source: Calculation by Xin Hua based on interviews and information on the SIIS official website.

the MFA in the past are mostly senior ones, while those who have worked at the Foreign Affairs Office of the Shanghai Municipal Government are the younger generation. This means the "revolving door" between SIIS and the MFA has become less significant in recent years for young researchers. SIIS connections with universities are much stronger than in the case of CIIS. Furthermore, at least one-third of all the SIIS researchers have no experience of holding a post of any kind in the Chinese bureaucratic system. All of this suggests that SIIS is more oriented towards longer term specialized academic research. It also indicates that SIIS occupies a more peripheral position in China's foreign policy decision making system relative to CIIS.

Theoretical implications

Scholars have proposed several theoretical paradigms to explain the role of think tanks in the policy making process and their relationship to the overall political system more generally. The three theoretical paradigms most frequently used and cited by scholars are explained below.

Elitism vs pluralism

Scholars have used the elitist framework to emphasize that think tanks, and particularly foreign policy research institutes, are highly professionalized in policy research and very capable of offering expert advice. They occupy a location contiguous to the inner circle of policy decision making and therefore deserve to be considered part of the ruling elite (Domhoff 2006; Dahl 1967; Lukes 2004; Fischer 1990; Truman 1951). Scholars adopting the pluralist approach, however, emphasize the complexity of the policy process and the multiple forces that shape policy makers' perceptions and affect agenda-setting. Liao Xuanli (2006) has bridged these differences by suggesting that Chinese foreign policy think tanks' unique position in the country's political system should be conceptualized within a framework of "pluralized elitism".

The network, system, or institutionalism paradigms

(Teichler 2007; Hass 1992; Sabatier and Weible 2007; Rhodes 1997; Smith 1991) Elitist or pluralist approaches may be able to offer an overall framework for explanation, but they are unable to capture the details of the interactive relationships between the various forces in the policy process and the linkages and channels through which think tanks may exert their influence. Therefore, the concept of "epistemic community", proposed by Peter Hass (1992), became frequently used in research on think tanks' policy influence. Employing this concept and similar ones such as "policy network", "policy community", or "advocacy coalition", scholars are able to construct a more finely grained picture of how and when think tank activities influence policy (Teichler 2007; Hass 1992; Sabatier and Weible 2007; Rhodes 1997; Smith 1991).

"Social space" and "field of power" paradigm

Using Pierre Bourdieu's concept of "social space" – where the convergence of different social forces occurs, shaping the evolution of a political system – Thomas Medvetz (2012) argues that think tanks can be viewed as occupying a central space at the confluence of four fields of power. These fields include the political and bureaucratic field, the economic field, the cultural production field, and the media field. The strategies and frequencies of think tanks' interactions with these four fields of power determine their role and position in the policy making system.

This third paradigm might be particularly useful in theorizing about the role and influence of foreign policy think tanks in China. Such concepts as "elitism", "pluralism", or "epistemic community" are derived from systems of liberal democracy such as those of the US and UK, while China remains an authoritarian and unitary state with a comparatively underdeveloped civil society. Moreover, the political activities that are described by western political scientists using such terms as "policy debates" or "interest representation" are either non-existent or confined within a very small and inaccessible circle in China. Medvetz's paradigm that conceptualizes the think tank as occupying the central space of four major "fields of power" has the virtue of capturing some common features of any social and political system.

Conclusion

This chapter has analyzed the position of Chinese foreign policy research institutes within China's overall think tank system. As Table 8.1 shows, among the five major categories of Chinese think tanks, foreign policy research institutes rank second in terms of their proximity to the center of political power and key policy makers. A more specific analysis of two of the most elite foreign policy research institutes, the central-level CIIS and the provincial-level SIIS, reveals several features of these two institutes that help us understand the role that they play in the foreign policy making process.

First, after comparing their policy research publications and the record of new policy initiatives and ideas of Chinese top leaders, it can reasonably be concluded that they do play a role in shaping the opinions and attitudes of these leaders when it comes to China's policy towards Europe. Within Medvetz's analytical paradigm of "central space in the fields of power", we may conclude that CIIS and SIIS form an integral part of this "central space" that strongly affects the surrounding "fields of power".

Second, analysis of the meetings and symposiums of CIIS and SIIS reveals that these two institutes are not located at the geometrical center of the general system of the four major "fields of power". They appear to be closest to the "political and bureaucratic field" and most distant from the "economic field". As a matter of fact, and because of the lack of open and regular mechanisms for interest representation and policy debates, the various social and business interest groups in China cannot count on think tanks as channels through which their demands and ideas on foreign policy issues can be communicated to top-level political leaders. Chinese think tanks simply do not have the capacity to conduct any policy advocacy.

Third, CIIS has stronger and closer connections to the top-levels of political power in China than does SIIS. At the same time, Tables 8.6 and 8.7, as well as other evidence, demonstrate that CIIS has stronger linkages to the "media field" but is much less connected to the "cultural production field" than SIIS. More specifically, compared to SIIS, CIIS enjoys much stronger connections to the inner circle of China's political power and more media exposure, but has much weaker connections to universities. These features not only reflect the relatively marginal position of Chinese universities in China's political and policy making system, but also relate to the political system's dominance over the media in China.

Generally speaking, elite foreign policy research institutes in China, such as CIIS and SIIS, have been dramatically increasing their relative position and strengthening their importance in China's foreign policy making system, particularly since the beginning of the 21st century. In the 2015 global think tank rankings published by the Think Tanks and Civil Societies Program of the University of Pennsylvania, CIIS and SIIS ranked 33rd and 64th, respectively, in the list of the "Top 100 Non-US Think Tanks Worldwide". This is quite impressive, given that China's think tank sector is comparatively young. At the same time, however, the roles and influence of think tanks in China's political and bureaucratic systems, and the mutual relations between different categories of Chinese think tanks, remain insufficiently and inconsistently researched both inside and outside China. More efforts in this research field will be meaningful and enlightening.

Notes

1 This chapter is part of the output of three research projects on think tank studies supported by the Education Commission of the Shanghai Municipal Government, the Shanghai Municipal Office for the Planning of Philosophy and Social Sciences, and China's Education Ministry respectively. (The registration numbers of these three projects are:13YJCGJW013, 2012FGJ001, 13ZS048.) It is also a part of the post-doctorate research project of the Shanghai International Studies University on the role of think tanks in foreign policy making.
2 *"Viewpoints on How to Strengthen the Constructions of the New-Type Think Tanks with Chinese Characteristics"*, Official Document issued by the General Offices of the Chinese Communist Party's Central Committee and the China's State Council, 21 January 2015. Available at http://news.xinhuanet.com/zgjx/2015-01/21/c_133934292.htm.
3 Some mainland Chinese and Taiwanese researchers mentioned this point without using the term of "stove-piping".
4 The bureaucrats in charge of practical work in provincial-level governments know this "dual leadership" far too well. Astonishingly, most of the academic works on China's bureaucratic system, English or Chinese, do not mention this point. An exception is John Bryan Starr, who mentions this phenomenon explicitly and terms it a "power grid" (Starr 2010: 60).

References

Abelson, Donald E. 2002. *Do Think Tanks Matter? Assessing the Impact of Public Policy Institutes*. Montreal: McGill-Queen's University Press.
Abelson, Donald E. 2006. *A Capitol Idea: Think Tanks and US Foreign Policy*. Montreal: McGill-Queen's University Press.
China Institute of International Studies. 2011. *International Situation and China's Foreign Affairs 2010–2011*. Beijing: Current Affairs Publishing House, 210–11.
Cui, Hongjian. 2012. "Perspective on the China–EU Relations Against the European Debt Crisis." *The People's Daily*, 28 November.
Dahl, Robert A. 2004. *Pluralist Democracy in the United States*. Chicago: Rand McNally, 1967.
Domhoff, William G. 2006. *Who Rules America? Power, Politics, and Social Change*, Boston: McGraw Hill.
Fischer, Frank. 1990. *Technocracy and the Politics of Experience*. Newbury Park, CA: Sage Publications.
Glaser, Bonnie S. 2012. "Chinese Foreign Policy Research Institutes and the Practice of Influence." In Gilbert Rozman (ed.), *China's Foreign Policy: Who Makes It, and How Is It Made?* New York: Palgrave MacMillan, 125–49.
Glaser, Bonnie S., and Philip C. Saunders. 2002. "Chinese Civilian Foreign Policy Research Institutes: Evolving Roles and Increasing Influence." *China Quarterly*, August 2002: 597–616.
Gong Ting. 2015. " 'One Belt One Road': Responses of the Press and Public Opinions of the International Community and Policy Advice." *External Communication* 3.
Gong Ting. 2015. "Leading Not Directing: China Leads the Era of 'Win-Win' Pattern." *The People's Daily* (overseas edition), 22 June.
Hass, Peter M. 1992. "Epistemic Communities and International Policy Coordination." *International Organization* 46, no.1 (Winter): 1–35.
He Li. 2002. "The Role of Think Tanks in Chinese Foreign Policy." *Problems of Post-Communism* 49, no. 2 (March/April): 33–43.
Jin, Yingzhong. 2015. " 'One Belt One Road' Is the Common Development Strategy for Europe, Asia, and Africa." *Global Review*, March/April.
Liao Xuanli. 2006. *Chinese Foreign Policy Think Tanks and China's Policy towards Japan*. Hong Kong: Chinese University Press, 3–7.
Lieberthal, Kenneth. 1992. "Introduction: The 'Fragmented Authoritarianism' Model and Its Limitations." In Kenneth Lieberthal and David Lampton (eds), *Bureaucracy, Politics, and Decision Making in Post-Mao China*. Berkeley, CA: University of California Press.
Lu, Chuanying. 2011. "How Should China Respond to the European Debt Crisis?" *Jiafang Daily*, 10 November.
Lu Ning. 1997. *The Dynamics of Foreign Policymaking in China*. Boulder, Colorado: Westview Press, 130–31.
Lukes, Steven. 2004. *Power: A Radical View*. 2nd edition. New York: Palgrave MacMillan.
Medvetz, Thomas. 2012. *Think Tanks in America*. Chicago: University of Chicago Press.
Naughton, Barry. 2002. "China's Economic Think Tanks: Their Changing Role in the 1990s." *China Quarterly*, September: 625–35.
Rhodes, R.A.W. 1997. *Understanding Governance: Policy Networks, Governance, Reflexivity and Accountability*. Buckingham: Open University Press.
Sabatier, Paul A., and Christopher M. Weible. 2007. "The Advocacy Coalition Framework: Innovations and Clarifications." In Paul A. Sabatier (ed.), *Theories of the Policy Process*. London: Westview Press.

Shambaugh, David. 2002. "China's International Relations Think Tanks: Evolving Structure and Process." *China Quarterly*, September.

Shoup, Lawrence H., and William Minter. 1977. *Imperial Brain Trust: The Council on Foreign Relations and the United States Foreign Policy*. New York and London: Monthly Review Press.

Smith, M.J. 1991. "From Policy Community to Issue Networks: Salmonella in Eggs and the New Politics of Food." *Public Administration* 69 (Summer): 234–55.

Starr, John Bryan. 2010 *Understanding China: A Guide to China's Economy, History, and Political Culture*. 3rd edition. New York: Hill and Wang.

Teichler, Thomas. 2007. "Think Tanks as an Epistemic Community: The Case of European Armaments Cooperation." Paper presented at the annual meeting of the International Studies Association 48th Annual Convention, Chicago, Illinois.

Truman, David B. 1951. *The Governmental Process: Political Interests and Public Opinion*. New York: Alfred A. Knopf.

Weidenbaum, Murray. 2009. *Competition of Ideas: The World of the Washington Think Tanks*. New Brunswick, NJ: Transaction Publishers.

Wen, Jiabao. 2012. "China Has Been Prepared to Increase its Intensity to Participate into the Effort to Resolve the European Debt Crisis," 14 February, http://news.sina.com.cn/c/2012–02–14/220923933304.shtml.

Yin, Chengde. 2013. "Achievements and Challenges of China's Diplomacy in 2012." *New Trends and Situations of International Security and the New Responses of China's Diplomacy*, May: 25–40.

Zhang, Haibing. 2013. "New Trends of Global Economic Governance from the Perspective of European Debt Crisis." *European Studies*, April.

Zhang, Haibing. 2015. " 'One Belt One Road Blueprint and Action' Indicates China's Grand Measure for Its Opening Strategy," 30 March 30. Available at http://www.siis.org.cn/index.php?m=content&c=index&a=show&catid=22&id=617.

Zhao Quansheng. 1992. "Domestic Factors of Chinese Foreign Policy: From Vertical to Horizontal Authoritarianism." *Annals of the American Academy of Political and Social Sciences* 519 (January): 159–76.

Zhao Quansheng. 2013. "Moving between the 'Inner Circle' and 'Outer Circle': The Limited Impact of Think Tanks on Policy Making in China." In Gilbert Rozman (ed.), *China's Foreign Policy: Who Makes It, and How Is It Made?*

Zhu Xufeng. 2013. *The Rise of Think Tanks in China*. London and New York: Routledge.

9 Still lagging behind?
Foreign policy think tanks in Poland: origins and contemporary challenges

Monika Sus

"The missing link of Polish politics" – this is how Wawrzyniec Smoczynski (2009), a young Polish publicist defined think tanks in his article six years ago and not much has changed since then. In the 2014 Global Go To Think Tank Index rankings, Poland was placed fourth in Central and Eastern Europe (CEE) in terms of the number of think tanks (McGann 2015: 58). The 2014 report indicates that there are 41 such institutions in Poland, 112 of them in Russia, 54 in Romania and 47 in the Ukraine. Poland lags far behind the Western countries – in Great Britain there are 287 think tanks, in Germany 194, and in France 177. The US remains the Mecca of think tanks with 1,830 such institutions, followed by China which has 429 think tanks (McGann 2015: 58).

The relatively small number of Polish think tanks combined with, as this chapter shows, their limited influence on policy-makers, illustrates well the stage of development of the think tank community in Poland. It is definitely still in its infancy, as is scholarly activity on the topic.[1] Furthermore, Polish think tanks struggle with the problem of financing their activities, a problem that has become particularly acute in view of the economic crisis in the EU, and also due to the fact that demand for their expertise from state institutions is weak. Improving the expert sector in Poland is a necessary and ongoing stage toward the further modernization of the country and establishing a firmer position in the EU.

The aim of this chapter is to shed light on Poland's foreign and globally oriented think tanks and to understand the opportunities and limitations of their influence on policy. In the comparative spirit of this book, this analysis is undertaken in the context of other countries that constitute a point of reference for the think tank scene in Poland (both independent from and associated with the state in one way or another).

The chapter begins with an examination of the origins of the Polish think tank community and the current state of affairs in the marketplace of ideas relating to foreign policy and global issues. Next, we examine four think tanks that, according to their reputation and the frequency with which their experts are cited and interviewed in the media, dominate the scene in Poland. Based on these four cases we elucidate both the pathways of influence and the challenges for think tanks in Poland. Finally, the chapter addresses three issues of special significance, identified in the introduction of this book: the importance of think tanks for foreign policy-making, the question of foreign funding for think tanks and its possible consequences, and the innovation that has been used in order to be heard and relevant in the crowded world of foreign and global policy think tanks.

With regard to data and sources, the chapter is primarily based on my own research of the Polish marketplace of ideas, research that has been ongoing since 2007. Since then I have published a book and two chapters on the topic, for which I conducted a large number of interviews with experts and policy-makers, and analysed the websites, documents and instruments that think tanks use to influence foreign policy in Poland. I also draw on secondary literature, including newspaper articles and documents from the Ministry of Foreign Affairs in Poland (MFA). For the purposes of this chapter I conducted updated interviews with some staff members at Polish think tanks. All interviewees were guaranteed anonymity.

1. The emergence of Polish think tanks

The focus of the study is primarily the development of Polish foreign policy think tanks since 1989, when Poland gained independence from the Soviet Union and started to make its own foreign policy. However, it should be noted that the first institutions resembling what we think of as think tanks developed in Poland in the middle of the twentieth century (Sus 2011: 62–74). Under the communist regime three institutions were established that continue to play an important advisory role to this day when it comes to Polish foreign policy. An analysis of the origins of Polish think tanks needs to begin with these institutions.

Forerunners of contemporary Polish think tanks

The oldest institution of a think tank nature is the Institute for Western Affairs,[2] which dates back to 1941 and operates from Poznan. Its original mission was to analyse issues related to the new territorial structure of post-war Poland as well as the historical, cultural and socio-economic matters of the country's Western and Northern Territories. In the years 1945–89, in spite of being under the control of the Communist Party, the Institute survived all the political changes and tried to serve the Polish *raison d'état*. The collapse of communism and improvement in Polish–German relations brought about changes in the structure and nature of the Institute's activities; its research became focused on Poland's relations with Germany and with Europe, particularly the EU. After many years of struggling with financial and organisational problems the Institute was reorganized in December 2015 as a part of the Chancellery of the Prime Minister. From 2016 it will receive annual funding of US$700,000–900,000.[3]

The second think tank that emerged after World War II was the Polish Institute of International Affairs (PISM, Polski Instytut Spraw Miedzynarodowych),[4] established in 1947 by a decision of the state elites. Located in Warsaw, PISM was virtually the only scientific institution in the Polish People's Republic focusing on international relations, while also engaged in generating information and advice to the state institutions responsible for implementing foreign policy. Many currently respected researchers began their careers in PISM. After the collapse of communism and the change of regime, PISM was confronted with funding problems and temporarily closed in 1993 due to financial insolvency. In 1996 the Polish Parliament decided to re-establish PISM and it has been functioning since that time.

Another institution that arose before the transformation from communism to democracy and has been recognized in Poland as a think tank is the Stefan Batory Foundation.[5] It was created in 1988 and continues to be active. Its founder and sponsor is George Soros, an American financier and philanthropist, who initiated the creation of a network of foundations operating in over 30 countries. However, it is important to point out that influencing policy-makers is only part of the broader scope of the Foundation's activities. Its main activities involve providing grants to non-governmental organizations that are engaged in promoting the progressive goals of Soros' Open Society Foundation in Poland and across CEE.

The think tank wave after 1989

The year 1989 was a breakthrough in terms of the formation of an independent Polish foreign policy. The new post-communist priorities included the normalization of relations with Germany, achieving Polish accession to the EU and membership in NATO. The possibility as well as the necessity of defining new foreign policy directions and structures resulted in the creation of numerous new centres of expertise.

In October 1989, at the request of the Presidium of the Senate, the Centre for International Studies was created as an advisory body in matters of foreign policy (Hajnicz 2006: 57–58). The Centre cooperated with the Polish government, the president and political parties, as well as with foreign scientific centres such as the RAND Corporation, whose experts were invited by the Centre to discuss the possibility of Polish membership in NATO. The Centre contributed to the conscious shaping of a new and independent Polish foreign policy. Since 1993, a conflict between a part of the Senate and the employees of the Centre has arisen. In 1995 the Centre was removed from the structures of the Senate but continued its activities within the Polish Robert Schuman Foundation, which does not operate as a classic think tank.

Another research institute established in post-communist Poland is the Centre for Eastern Studies (OSW, Osrodek Studiow Wschodnich),[6] created by a resolution of the Council of Ministers in December 1990. One of its founders was a prominent historian and sovietologist, Marek Karp. From the beginning the Centre's activity was financed from the state budget, initially under the Ministry of Foreign Economic Cooperation and later the Ministry of Economy (Koscinski 2007). Its main area of interest has been related to the countries of the former USSR and Polish foreign policy. In 2004, the Centre was given the Jerzy Giedroyc Award for long-term creative realization of the political thought of Jerzy Giedroyc and for building bridges between Poland and its eastern neighbours. Eastern Europe and post-Soviet countries also have been the research focus of the Institute of Central Eastern Europe,[7] which was established in Lublin in 1991. This university-affiliated institute examines the processes shaping the identity of Central Europe and promotes the history and culture of that region (Kloczkowski and Gil 2006: 174). In 1993 another university-affiliated think tank was established – the Institute for Strategic Studies[8] (formerly known as the International Centre for the Development of Democracy). Since its creation this institute has dealt mainly with Euro-Atlantic security issues. The Natolin European Centre[9] was also created in 1993, based in Natolin near Warsaw. Its main founder was the State Treasury and the Minister of Finance, acting on its behalf. Its statutory objectives include fostering knowledge on European integration, conducting scientific research and inviting experts interested in the European idea. It has established its position among Polish think tanks primarily because of the reputations of the experts who work there and its ties to the College of Europe in Bruges, Belgium.

Two years later, in 1995, the Institute of Public Affairs[10] was founded. It aims to provide a scientific and intellectual basis for the modernization of the country and the ongoing policy debates in Poland. It is a non-governmental and independent organization whose areas of research are very broad and indeed cover the spectrum of issues relating to the public life: from the problems of migration and social policy, through education and the development of civil society, to international affairs. It also has a small European programme whose focus is on foreign policy matters. During that same year a non-governmental analytical organization whose aim is the monitoring of foreign policy, the Centre for International Relations (CSM, Centrum Stosunkow Miedzynarodowych),[11] was established in Warsaw. Its founder is Janusz Reiter, Polish Ambassador to Germany in the years 1990–95 and to the US in the years 2005–08. In 1999 the Institute on Research of International Affairs[12] was established with the aim of publishing a monthly periodical on international relations. In 2000, at the initiative of persons connected with the Jagiellonian University, the Kosciuszko Institute[13] (operating under the name Institute for European Integration until 2007) was founded. Since then it has been dealing with the support of Polish activity in the EU, focusing on energy issues and relations between Poland and its Eastern neighbours. It played an important role in the preparations for the Polish EU Council presidency.

After this period of intense development of the think tank sector in the 1990s, the dynamics weakened considerably at the beginning of the twenty-first century, notwithstanding a number of challenges that confronted Polish foreign policy. Preparations for the EU accession, taking a stand on the attacks of 11 September 2001, and deciding whether to participate in the military interventions in Afghanistan along with the US were just some of these challenges. Given the turmoil on the international scene it might seem astonishing that no significant centre for policy advice emerged until 2004, when the Sobieski Institute[14] was established by Pawel Szalamacha, vice minister in the Ministry of State Treasury between 2005 and 2007 and minister of finance since November 2015. The Sobieski Institute deals with a broad range of issues such as economic development, education, promotion of democracy and external policy. Witold Waszczykowski, foreign minister of Poland since November 2015, has been affiliated with this think

158 *Monika Sus*

tank. The Kazimierz Pulaski Foundation[15] was also founded in 2004; its central mission is to provide strategic analyses and solutions for state decision makers, the private sector and civil society. This think tank focuses mainly on security issues, transatlantic relations and the Eastern Neighbourhood.

In mid-2006, demosEuropa, also known as the Centre for European Strategy,[16] was created. The initiator of this new think tank was Pawel Swieboda, who in the years 1996–2001 was an expert in the Chancellery of the President of Poland and in the years 2001–06 was the director of the Department of the EU in the Polish MFA. The focus of demosEuropa involves challenges currently faced by the EU and Polish responses to them. It is one of the 16 European think tanks which contribute to the Think Global – Act European programme, which is coordinated by the Jacques Delors Institute and aimed at facilitating a broader discussion on the new challenges faced by the EU's external policy and the instruments at the EU's disposal. Within the last decade demosEuropa has become one of the most recognizable Polish advisory bodies when it comes to EU issues.

In summary, two observations need to be made. First, and as these short descriptions of Polish think tanks reveal, only a few of them are focused solely on foreign and global policy issues. The majority of actors in Poland's marketplace of ideas deal with various topics that have a primary domestic character such as social policy, economics and finance or infrastructure. Foreign policy constitutes just one strand of their research, and oftentimes a rather limited one. The think tanks which focus solely on foreign global policy issues will be examined in a more comprehensive way in the following section of this chapter. The second observation involves newcomers to the think tank community. Although in recent years, due to low barriers to entry into the market, some new think tanks have been established, none of them has yet gained a reputation comparable to that of those which came into being earlier.[17] These newcomers to the scene, which have yet to establish their policy relevance, are not analysed here.

2. Foreign policy think tanks: The current state of affairs

Among the research institutions funded directly by the state, there are currently five that deal with foreign and security policy issues (see Table 9.1).

Of these five institutions, two of them – the Institute for Western Affairs and the Institute of Central Eastern Europe – carry out activities which focus more on scientific research than on providing advice on current foreign policy challenges. In the case of the Natolin European Centre, its activities have been very limited over the last five years and it is hard to estimate its current role and influence within the Polish foreign policy community. PISM and OSW stand out as the two state-funded think tanks whose activities and influence are most relevant to the policy conversation on Polish foreign policy.

The non-governmental privately funded think tanks, which raise resources for their activity from foundations, companies or individuals, are listed in Table 9.2. The number of such organizations clearly exceeds that of research institutes that

Table 9.1 Foreign policy think tanks financed by state assets

	Name	Year of foundation and headquarters	Source of funding
1	Institute for Western Affairs	1945, Poznan	Chancellery of the Prime Minister
2	The Polish Institute of International Affairs (PISM)	1947/1996, Warsaw	Ministry of Foreign Affairs
3	Centre for Eastern Studies (OSW)	1990, Warsaw	Chancellery of the Prime Minister
4	Institute of Central Eastern Europe	1991, Lublin	Ministry of Science and Higher Education
5	Natolin European Centre	1993, Natolin	Ministry of Foreign Affairs

Table 9.2 Non-governmental foreign policy think tanks in Poland

	Name	Year of foundation and headquarters
1	The Stefan Batory Foundation	1988, Warsaw
2	The Institute for Strategic Studies	1993, Cracow
3	Centre for International Relations (CSM)	1995, Warsaw
4	Institute of Public Affairs	1995, Warsaw
5	Institute for Research on International Relations	1999, Warsaw
6	The Kosciuszko Institute	2000, Cracow
7	The Sobieski Institute	2004, Warsaw
8	The Pulaski Institute	2004, Warsaw
9	Institute of Foreign Affairs	2005, Warsaw
10	demosEuropa – Centre for European Strategy	2006, Warsaw

are directly tied to the state. However, it is worth noting that the majority of these private sector think tanks generate at least part of their revenues from contracts or other activities financed by the state.

Among these ten private think tanks, there are two that deal entirely with foreign and global policy issues – CSM and demosEuropa. The others encompass a broader scope of policy areas in which foreign policy is only one and not necessarily the dominant concern of the organization. So, for example, the Institute of Public Affairs more strongly emphasizes matters connected with social and migration policy than those related to foreign policy. Similarly, in the case of the Sobieski and Kosciuszko Institutes, experts deal principally with topics such as the economy, state finances and energy and climate policy.

Of the 15 think tanks listed in Tables 9.1 and 9.2, all of which include foreign policy and geo-political affairs within the scope of their activities, PISM, OSW, CSM and demosEuropa stand apart from the others in terms of reputation in these fields. This is evident from media mentions of their experts and activities but also from discussions with policy-makers. This opinion is also confirmed by the results of the *Global Go To Think Tank Report 2014*: among the best non-US think tanks worldwide, PISM ranked 57th; and in the ranking of top think tanks in Central and Eastern Europe, PISM occupied 3rd position, demosEuropa 17th, OSW 24th and CSM 53rd (McGann 2015: 66, 85). PISM and OSW were also mentioned under the top think tanks which deal with foreign and international policy – PISM in 19th place and OSW in 36th (McGann 2015: 101). Moreover both institutes were ranked among best government affiliated think tanks – PISM in 7th place and OSW in 15th (McGann 2015: 117). Finally, PISM was acknowledged as the best think tank with an annual operating budget of less than US$5 million (McGann 2015: 152) and was also ranked in third place with regard to the best policy study/report produced by a think tank in 2013–14 (McGann 2015: 125). Together with Istituto Affari Internazionali, Real Instituto Elcano and the Swedish Institute of International Affairs, PISM co-authored a report entitled "Towards a European Global Strategy: Securing European Influence in a Changing World",[18] which was widely discussed and considered to be quite influential among policy-makers and experts.

These four research institutions clearly dominate the marketplace of foreign and geo-political policy ideas in Poland. It is, indeed, quite an oligopolistic market. Also noteworthy is the fact that all of the most recognizable Polish think tanks are located in Warsaw. Sharing the same physical space with policy-makers, civil servants and journalists make the activities of a think tank more accessible for them. Among the other reasons why these particular think tanks have become most successful is the issue of funding. The state provides PISM and OSW with a stable financial position that enables them to conduct intensive research and organize numerous meetings. Because of their close institutional and legal ties with the MFA (in case of PISM) and the Chancellery of the Prime Minister (in case of OSW), both institutions have easier access to decision makers than do other think tanks. In the case of demosEuropa, its reputation for influence has undoubtedly resulted from its connections to the highest levels of the state elite, which its founder Pawel Swieboda cultivated during many years of work in the MFA, but also from the skilful selection of research topics and the competence of its experts. The same may be said for the Centre of International Studies. Its early influence was built on the reputation and connections of its co-founder and first director, Janusz Reiter. His name was a door opener not only to the Polish state elite but also to the foreign (mainly German) foundations that provided the centre with generous funding for its project. Barriers to entry into Poland's think tank universe might indeed have been relatively low, but having financial stability and an extensive as well as prestigious network of potential clients are prerequisites for playing in the big league.

3. Current challenges

The question of demand

One of the biggest challenges for Polish think tanks is demand for their services from policy-makers. Taking into account the relatively short period during which

Poland has been in control of its own foreign policy – barely a generation – the limited size of the marketplace for policy ideas in the country, and the fact that, unlike in the US, there does not exist a longstanding tradition of looking outside the state for policy advice, it is not surprising to find that demand is limited. For example, expert opinions were requested from PISM, an MFA think tank, by the MFA only six times in 2013 and five in 2014. In 2014 PISM's analysts were asked to participate in closed consultations at the MFA, other ministries and the Parliament as well as in the offices of Prime Minister and the President on 39 occasions.[19] Bearing in mind how turbulent 2014 was in the world affairs – it was, among other things, the year that saw the beginning of Russian military intervention in Ukraine, leading to the independence of Crimea, and also the escalation of the civil war in Syria – these numbers suggest a rather limited interest on the part of Polish foreign policy-makers in advice from one of the most prestigious think tanks in CEE.

Investigating demand over the last eight years, I would argue that this limited interest on the part of state elites has been characteristic for some time. The willingness to solicit expert opinion increases when an unexpected crisis breaks out: when anti-government protests broke out in Kiev in November 2013, OSW analyses were requested frequently by Polish policy-makers. But when such crises abate, so too does the state's interest in the views and advice of think tank experts.[20] Consequently, Polish think tanks have been looking for other possible ways of influencing foreign policy-making. The instruments that many of them rely on are oriented toward influencing public opinion, which is seen as an indirect way to have an impact on foreign policy-makers. For example of the flagship instruments of PISM are short, written analyses, including bulletins (262 issued in 2014), and longer studies called "strategic files" (27 in 2014) and "policy papers" (19 in 2014), which are published on PISM's website in Polish and in English. Similar papers that focus on Eastern countries are issued by OSW. In 2014 it published a total of 211 expert reports, comments and studies. The two privately funded think tanks, demosEuropa and CSM, also issue comparable publications. Due, however, to the significantly smaller pool of experts they have at their disposal, the number of publications produced annually by these two think tanks is significantly smaller than for their public sector rivals for the ears of policy-makers. Another strategy used by demosEuropa and CSM to influence the foreign policy debate in Poland is the organization of public events, discussions, conferences and seminars. Indeed, PISM and OSW, notwithstanding their formal ties to the Polish state, also use this strategy and PISM has been the most active in this respect (40 events in 2014). Interestingly, due to the participation of politicians and experts from abroad, an increasing number of such meetings are held exclusively in English. Moreover, all think tanks try to gain as much media attention as possible as this visibility is one of the key elements in building their reputation. It is particularly important for the non-state funded think tanks, of course, given that private foundations want the outcomes of the research they pay for to be promoted in the media.

Revolving doors

The American phenomenon of movement between the policy-making and think tank worlds (Haas 2002: 7–8) is still very limited in Poland. There are two main reasons for this. The first is the professionalization of the Polish civil service, which makes it difficult and often not financially rewarding for officials from the MFA to leave their positions to join think tanks. Quitting a position in the state administration means abandoning the status of a civil servant and the return to such a position is very difficult, if not impossible. Revolving doors can exist, however, between think tanks and high ranking positions that are political and depend on the party in power. There are a few high officials who have their career from a think tank to the administration; one leading example is an excellent Polish expert on Russia, Katarzyna Pelczynska-Nalecz, a one-time director of the OSW who moved to the MFA to become the Polish ambassador in Moscow in 2014. Another example is Pawel Szalamacha, the founder of Sobieski Institute, who recently became minister of finance. Another case is that of Radoslaw Sikorski, who served as deputy defence minister in 1992 and as deputy minister of foreign affairs from 1998 to 2001, then from 2002 to 2005 worked as a journalist, as an expert at the American Enterprise Institute and as director of the New Atlantic Initiative; he returned to the policy-making world as Polish foreign minister (2007–14). Sikorski's example illustrates how the revolving door mechanism may contribute to an increased demand for think tank expertise. Knowing the think tank universe very well, Sikorski was the first Polish foreign minister who regularly mentioned think tanks as an important instrument of foreign policy-making (Sikorski 2013). He also sought advice from foreign think tanks, in particular during the preparations for Poland's Presidency in the Council of the EU. At the same time, think tank experts who have worked in the administration are better able to understand the nature of the policy-making process, which is a pre-condition for effective advice.

Competition from transnational think tanks

Another key challenge in the Polish marketplace of policy ideas is the growing number of foreign think tanks that have opened branches in Warsaw. In 2011 the European Council on Foreign Relations (ECFR)[21] opened its Polish office. ECFR is the first pan-European think tank, with offices in Berlin, London, Madrid, Paris, Rome and Sofia, and greatly profits from its international network by combining different national perspectives on European matters. The fairly small Warsaw office (five staff members) has become an important player on the Polish think tank scene because of its ability to draw on resources from other offices, publishing papers that they produce and organizing joint events. Also in 2011, the German Marshall Fund (GMF)[22] opened its Warsaw branch. As a think tank operating on both sides of the Atlantic it deals with the promotion and strengthening of transatlantic ties. The Polish office focuses particularly on issues critical to Poland, the Baltic States and CEE. Although the Warsaw offices of ECFR and the GMF are small, they are able to leverage their visibility and influence as a result of belonging to a much larger network of think tanks, both of which are internationally recognized and quite prestigious.

4. Conclusions

The emergence and growth of the Polish think tank sector began just over two decades ago and thus the process of developing a diverse and influential marketplace of policy ideas is still under way. With 15 foreign-policy-oriented research institutes, Poland is among the countries in CEE with the greatest number of think tanks that through various channels and strategies attempt to influence policy-makers and public opinion on current foreign policy and geo-political issues. Thinking about the way forward for the Polish think tank sector, one of the key steps would seem to be finding more effective ways to access the policy-making policy, and thereby establishing the relevance and value of think tank expertise in the eyes of political elites, as well as greater financial stability. This would enable think tanks to compete with other sources of policy analysis and advice, including the transnational think tanks that have become active in Poland. Better coordination of the research agendas of state-funded think tanks so that their activities involve not only the current priorities of Polish foreign policy but also global and emerging challenges might also enhance the value of think tank advice in the eyes of policy-makers and in the wider policy community. Non-governmental think tanks with limited financial resources should consider specialization in one or a smaller number of regions or thematic areas. If the Polish think tank sector is to expand and its influence grow, a pre-condition would seem to be not only, or perhaps not even principally, greater financial support from the state, but from the business community as in the case in Germany (Lada 2016, forthcoming).

Without such business sponsorship, some mechanisms enabling better and more secure medium-term financial support from the state would significantly benefit private think tanks. The existing system of grants and contracts awarded by ministries seems to be insufficient, such funding often being only enough to cover the expenses connected with a particular project. More secure funding that would help cover the ongoing costs of think tanks, and not simply the particular projects supported by contracts and grants, would go a long way toward providing the stable financial basis that, as the American, German and British examples illustrate, is a pre-condition for the development of a reputation for quality research and relevance. The contract and grant funding model also, of course, reduces the independence of think tanks. A more diverse revenue model, as exists in the US and Germany, helps to reduce such dependence.

With regard to the three issues mentioned in Chapter 1 of this book, there are several observations to be made. First of all, due to the very young tradition of think tanks in Poland, their importance in the national foreign policy conversation and ultimately their influence on the decisions of state officials does not compare with the case of the US or, for that matter, other Western countries with long democratic traditions. Awareness of think tanks and the willingness to see them as legitimate and relevant sources of policy advice are not yet firmly established among Polish state officials. Secondly, the revenue model of those Polish think tanks that are privately founded is often based on foreign money, mainly American and German. This money generally comes from foreign private foundations whose motivation is to support the development of a marketplace of policy ideas as an element of an established democracy and perhaps also to raise awareness of particular issues and encourage ways of thinking about policy issues. Thirdly, the world of foreign policy think tanks is not very crowded in Poland, as is the case in some other countries. This reduces the need for Polish think tanks to be innovative in their influence strategies, relying instead on well-known methods of policy advising such as publications, websites, debates, roundtables and conferences.

Bulgarian political scientist Ivan Krastev has written that "in post-communist societies, a think tank is something everybody hears about but nobody actually knows much about" (2002: 142). Until fairly recently he might have been talking specifically about Poland. There are signs that matters are changing but, for the reasons explained in this chapter,Poland continues to lag behind longer established democracies when it comes to making use of what think tanks can offer.

Notes

1 So far four books and one article in an academic journal have been published on Polish think tanks. Additionally, a few scholars have contributed to edited volumes about think tanks worldwide and presented the Polish market of ideas.
2 See the website: http://www.iz.poznan.pl/index.php?lang=ang&v=1 (accessed 3 January 2016).
3 Interview with a member of staff from the Institute of Western Affairs, 7 January 2016.
4 See the website: http://www.pism.pl/en#1 (accessed 3 January 2016).
5 See the website: http://www.batory.org.pl/en (accessed 3 January 2016).
6 See the website: http://www.osw.waw.pl/en (accessed 3 January 2016).
7 See the website: http://www.iesw.lublin.pl (accessed 3 January 2016).
8 See the website: http://www.iss.krakow.pl/en/index.php (accessed 3 January 2016).
9 See the website: http:// www.natolin.edu.pl (accessed 3 January 2016).
10 See the website: http://www.isp.org.pl/index.php?id=1&lang=2 (accessed 3 January 2016).
11 See the website: http://csm.org.pl/en/(accessed 2 January 2016).
12 See the webiste: http://www.stosunki.pl/?q=node/4 (accessed 2 January 2016).
13 See the website: http://ik.org.pl/en/ (accessed 2 January 2016).
14 See the website: http://www.sobieski.org.pl/en/ (accessed 2 January 2016).
15 See the website: http://pulaski.pl/en/home-2/ (accessed 2 January 2016).
16 See the website: http://www.demoseuropa.eu/?lang=en (accessed 2 January 2016).
17 An example of a newcomer is the Civic Institute (pol. Instytut Obywatelski) which has been established 2010 as a party think tank of the Civic Platform (pol. Platforma Obywatelska), http://www.instytutobywatelski.pl/about-us (accessed on 6 January 2015).
18 See the report: http://www.iai.it/sites/default/files/egs_report.pdf (accessed 4 January 2016).
19 Interview with a member of staff from PISM, 4 January 2016; detailed data is also available in an annual report of PISM: http://www.pism.pl/files/?id_plik=19852 (accessed 5 January 2016).
20 Interview with a member of staff from the OSW, 10 November 2015.
21 See the website: http://www.ecfr.eu/warsaw (accessed 2 January 2016).
22 See the website: http://www.gmfus.org/offices/warsaw (accessed 2 January 2016).

References

Bakowski, T., and J.H. Szlachetko (eds). 2012. *Zagadnienie think tanków w ujęciu interdyscyplinarnym.* Gdansk.

Czaputowicz, J. 2010. "Rola ośrodków eksperckich w procesach decyzyjnych polityki zagranicznej Polski." In S. Bielen (ed), *Polityka zagraniczna Polski po wstąpieniu do NATO i do Unii Europejskiej. Problemy tożsamości i adaptacji.* Warszawa, 216–28.

Czaputowicz, J., and D. Stasiak. 2012. "Political Expertise in Poland in the Field of Foreign Policy and the Emergence of Think Tanks." In S. Brooks, D. Stasiak, T. Zyro (eds), *Policy Expertise in Contemporary Democracies.* Surrey, 165–82.

Haas, R.N. 2002. "Think Tank and US Foreign Policy: A Policy-Maker's Perspective." *US Foreign Policy Agenda: An Electronic Journal of the US Department of State*, Vol. 3.

Hajnicz, A. 2006. *Meandry polskiej polityki zagranicznej w latach 1939–1991.* Warszawa.

Kancelaria Prezesa Rady Ministrów. 2011. *Podniesienie jakości procesów decyzyjnych w administracji rządowej poprzez wykorzystanie potencjału środowisk naukowych i eksperckich.* Warszawa: Kancelaria Prezesa Rady Ministrów.

Kloczkowski, J., and A. Gil. 2006. *Rocznik Instytutu Europy Środkowo-Wschodniej.* Lublin.

Koscinski, P. 2007. "Nasz wschodni Think Tank." *Rzeczpospolita*, 12 September, p. 11.

Krastev, I. 2000. "Post-Communist Think Tanks. Making and Faking Influence." In D. Stone (eds.), *Banking on Knowledge: The Genesis of the Global Development Network.* London, 145–63.

Lada, A. Forthcoming. *Cooperation between Business and Think Tanks in Poland: Motivations, Challenges, Recommendations.* Warsaw.

McGann, J.G. 2015. *Global Go To Think Tanks Report 2014.* University of Pennsylvania, Philadelphia.

Sikorski, R. 2013. "Expose Ministra Spraw Zagranicznych Radosława Sikorskiego," 21 March. Available at http://londyn.msz.gov.pl/pl/aktualnosci/expose_ministra_spraw_zagranicznych_radoslawa_sikorskiego (accessed 27 December 2015).

Smoczynski, W. 2009. "Myślą i rządzą." *Polityka* 4: 38.

Stasiak, D. 2014. "Think Tanks in Poland: Policy Experts at the Crossroads." *Polish Journal of Political Science* 2, no. 1: 95–140.

Sus, M. 2008. "Foreign Policy Think Tanks: The Example of Poland and Germany." In J. Elvert and S. Schirmann (eds), *Changing Times: Germany in 20th-Century Europe.* Brussels-Bern, 321–39.

Sus, M. 2011. *Doradztwo w polityce zagranicznej Polski i Niemiec. Inspiracje dla Polski na przykładzie wybranych ośrodków eksperckich*, Wrocław.

Sus, M. 2012. "Think tanki w polskiej polityce zagranicznej. Wspolczesne wyzwania." In A. Bąkowski and J. Szlachetko (eds), *Think tanki jako fenomen swiatowy.* Gdansk, 116–41.

Zbieranek, P. 2011. *Polski Model Organizacji Typu Think Tank.* Warszawa.

Ziętara, W. 2010. *Think tanks. Na przykładzie USA i Polski.* Lublin.

10 Foreign policies in Spain

The role of think tanks in the battle between the central state and Catalonia

Olivier Urrutia

Introduction

According to two recent surveys, there are between 50 and 60 think tanks in Spain.[1] The absence of either a proper legal framework or academic consensus on a hard definition of the term "think tank" makes it extremely complicated to accurately map the Spanish think tank environment. Indeed, as several of the preceding chapters have demonstrated, the concept is elastic, the term carries multiple meanings and think tank ecosystems are multifaceted and changing. These are all obstacles to a definitive analysis and understanding of the think tank phenomenon. In the past 30 years, numerous studies on think tanks – often led by British or American researchers – have been conducted. These studies are essential tools in coming to grips with the complexity of this research topic. Think tanks are the product of their own socio-political environment which speaks to their idiosyncratic nature (Rich 2004). This is certainly true for the relatively young Spanish think tank scene. By the end of World War II, think tanks dealing with international relations, defense and security matters were an established part of the policy scene in the US (Abelson 2006), as well as in Western Europe and Russia. Spain, however, was a latecomer on the global think tank scene. Thorough analyses of the Spanish international relations think tank community have yet to be carried out. That said, the ongoing confrontation between the Spanish government, whose capital is Madrid, and the independence-seeking autonomous community of Catalonia, whose capital is Barcelona, offers a unique and exciting opportunity to analyze how effective Spanish think tanks are at exerting influence on those who make foreign policy. It also provides an opportunity to understand the role and space think tanks have carved out in Madrid and Barcelona; however, it is important to recognize that Spain is more of a state of nations than a typical European nation-state.

Spanish think tanks have developed expertise in the fields of international relations, security, defense, governance theory and regional integration in the context of many regime changes and competition between regional centers of power fueled by domestic separatist tensions in the Basque Country and Catalonia. This chapter aims to describe the emergence of the Spanish foreign policy research institute scene in the post-Franco era, including the role that these institutes currently play in relation to the project of Catalonia's independence. It will examine the nature of their research activity and public policy production, as well as the strategies they employ to communicate with the public and with policy-makers (Requejo et al. 1999).

Spain: A state of nations

When Francisco Franco died on 20 November 1975, a 39-year military dictatorship ended. Three years later, in November 1978, a new constitution, supported by 88 percent of Spaniards, marked the starting point for the decentralization of power through a system of 17 autonomous regions and the return of individual freedoms, including the rights to assembly and association. This marked the rebirth of civil society in what had long been a fascist state. Francoism survives in two founding elements of contemporary Spanish society: a non-aggression pact between supporters and opponents of the defunct military regime and a guarantee of unity for Spain, one and indivisible. The dissolution of the military dictatorship also signified the return of Spain to the international stage, including integration into NATO (1982) and the EU (1986). The Spanish state had to develop a new foreign policy in order to assume and affirm its position in the world. An interconnected world built on treaties, supranational bodies, interaction and interdependence requires states to maneuver with increasing technocratic expertise in order to manage international issues that have an impact at a national level. Thus, multinationals, NGOs, lobbying agencies and think tanks have become central players in the setting and management of public policies, both nationally and internationally.

Two axes have structured political thought in Spain since the eighteenth century: the nature of the state and the choice of political regime. Indeed, the question of the central state's powers and the manner in which society regulates the choice of political regime are two central topics of debate in Spain's past and present. These two issues are closely linked. Progressive and conservative forces – depending on the period and the countries concerned – will sometimes be partisans aiming to reinforce the central state, and at other times, pushing for a federal system composed of autonomous regions with significantly expanded powers. Contemporary Spain is composed of many nations, some of which, and for diverse reasons, have demanded their independence.

Since 1978, a succession of governments in Catalonia have been increasingly aggressive in their pursuit of independence, leading to the 2015 proposition of unilateral secession following a public referendum. From the Reconquista (718–1492) to the War of Succession (1701–14), through the Spanish Civil War (1936–39) to the current political battle over the secession of Catalonia, the many internal struggles punctuating the history of Spain illustrate the difficulty of constructing a sense of community and national cohesion. The War of Independence (1804–14) against Napoleon's French army of occupation is an historical episode of relatively exceptional unity in Spain's history. As a general rule, however, the national union of Spain has always been fragile, being subject to very deep religious, cultural, linguistic and legal strife.

The Nueva Planta Decrees (1706–16) made Castile the veritable backbone of the idea of a centralized Spain. The decrees aimed at uniting the various kingdoms of the Iberian peninsula in politico-administrative, linguistic, legal and economic respects, giving concrete form to the national project. In general, laws and specific institutions that existed in each kingdom were abolished and replaced with those of Castile. "Vertical Spain," writes Ricardo García Cárcel (2002), "that is to say, centralized and structured around a central axis – Castile – and a concept, that of the homogeneous and intensive Spanish identity, ended federalist Spain whose national reality was built around an aggregate of national territories with the primary common concept of a plural and extensive Spanish identity."

This is the main point of conflict between centralists and federalists, who have competing conceptions of the state and nation and who have fought over horizontalism versus verticalism over the course of Spain's history. Centralism has identified the nation with its center, forgetting the identity and history of its provinces (Ortega y Gasset 1999). Two events in the history of Spain established strong markers of Catalan identity and proto-nationalism: the war against France (1635), which resulted in the permanent loss of the Catalan territory north of the Pyrenees, and the military disaster against the US (1898), which was seen as a sign of the inefficiency and weakness of Spain.

Contemporary Spain's model of political organization, heavily criticized in recent years by Catalan and Basque leaders, is the culmination of a very deep-rooted process initiated in 1976. Catalonia has tried to promote the creation of a federal state in opposition to the existence of a centralized one whose powers radiate from Madrid (Navarro 2014). Since 1978, many instances of conflict between the Spanish government and the Generalitat[2] have been provoked by these opposing visions. Proponents of a federalist vision consider that the regional autonomies should not be limited to the delegation of some powers by the central state. Rather, they believe that these powers should *belong* to the autonomous regions. In pursuit of this goal, the autonomous community of Catalonia has developed since 1978 an increasingly aggressive foreign policy. The policy, which is part of a larger project of national independence, relies on the projection of official diplomatic representation by Catalonia's public institutions[3] and a soft power strategy undertaken by civil society actors, including think tanks. Needless to say, this policy, which is based on a disputed interpretation of the Spanish Constitution, is a sensitive subject. In this politically charged context, think tanks have a legal status and freedom of expression, and operate in a manner that sensitizes and mobilizes Catalan civil society around its political leadership. This largely explains their integration into the foreign policy of the autonomous community of Catalonia and the multiple sources of funding they receive, both public and private.

History of the Spanish think tanks scene

In Spain, the majority of think tanks were created after 1980. This is primarily a consequence of the European processes of political and administrative decentralization and the end of the Franco dictatorship. This allowed for the return of the rights of assembly and association, an indispensable condition for the development of civil society and the legal existence of think tanks. Nevertheless, the think tank phenomenon in Spain is in its infancy especially when compared to similar institutions in the US, Britain, Germany, Italy and France. Indeed, unlike in these countries, think tanks in Spain are just beginning to integrate themselves into the policy-making process and into broader public discussions.

The earliest roots of think tanks in Spain go back over a century. The Instituto Nacional de Estadística (1877) and the Junta para Ampliación de Estudios e Investigaciones Científicas (1907) were the first organizations dedicated to planning, management and information on government policies in Spain. These early organizations do not fully correspond to the modern meaning of think tanks, but they laid the conceptual basis, constituting the historical substrate for what would eventually develop. One could describe them as "proto-think tanks." The Franco regime, rather than banning centers of research and information, centralized them within public administration to exercise more control over them. Thus, the creation of the Instituto de Estudios Políticos (1939), the Instituto de Estudios agrosociales (1947) and the Instituto de Estudios de Opinión Pública (1964) responded to the main objective of support for the regime, a far cry from the research activities and innovative reforms that, in America for example, were associated with think tanks. There followed two major milestones in the development of the think tank scene in Spain. From the 1970s to the 2000s, two think tanks in particular appeared to have a moderate impact on the formation of public policy, the Círculo de Empresarios (1970) and the Instituto de Estudios Económicos (1979). The aims of these institutions were to oversee the integration of Spain into the EU and advocate for Spain's future role in the EU (Ponsa and González Capitel 2015). In the twenty-first century, organizations appeared in Spain that approached the North American model of *advocacy* (Weaver 1989), but with much more modest resources. These included: the Club of Madrid (2001), the CITpax (2004), the Instituto Juan de Mariana (2005), the Fundación Burke (2006) and the Instituto Choiseul (2008).

The factors that have contributed to the emergence of a more diverse and rich think tank environment in Spain in the post-Franco era may be summarized as follows:

- recognition of the fundamental rights of assembly and association;
- a diverse political society at both the national and regional levels;
- the autonomous system through which power has been decentralized to the state level;
- laws granting certain tax benefits to the foundations of political parties and to non-profit associations;
- the economic crisis that weakened the central state and the autonomous regions, allowing and encouraging civil society to become more involved in the formation of public policy;
- the political commitment of the state to these organizations, including government subsidies;

- media coverage of think tanks;
- the complexity of increasingly technical public policy, requiring greater expertise;
- the policy of openness and Spain's commitment to international relations;
- democratization since the 2000s, which has allowed for access to and communication with the Ministry of Education and social networks.

At the same time, however, there are contextual, cultural and infrastructural obstacles to the rise of Spanish think tanks, some of which are linked to Franco's legacy:

- the general de-politicization of the population and a patriarchal society (Sastre García 1997);
- the strong presence of the state and public administration;
- the crushing weight of political parties inherited from the democratic transition (Morodo 1979);
- the lack of a culture of philanthropic tradition;
- the relative unfamiliarity with think tanks, including a media exposure deficit (Hallin and Mancini 2008);
- the economic crisis;
- the lack of credibility of many organizations (political party foundations, advocacy organizations, empty shells) that to some degree discredit think tanks;
- provincialism – many think tanks confining themselves to parochial issues;
- the absence of the revolving door practice that in some countries, most notably the US, serves to connect the think tank scene to policy-makers.

In Catalonia, most think tanks emerged between 1990 and 2000. That said, it is actually the fight for independence, the issue that overshadows everything else, that has fueled the more recent boom of the Catalan think tank scene. The emergence of many so-called *advocacy tanks* aimed at pushing for independence is both a consequence of, and, a catalyst for, the greater involvement of citizens in the local political scene. If the Catalan local political and think tank scene has become increasingly dynamic over the last couple of decades, this is because of the crises and tensions between Catalonia and the Spanish state. These tensions and the project of independence have shaped and inspired the activities of think tanks in Catalonia. There is now quite a vibrant and specialized think tank scene in the region. With regards to their main research topics, the Fundació Rafael Campalans (1979) deals with the socialism; the Fundació Pi i Sunyer Carles (1986) specializes in research and knowledge sharing on local issues and regional autonomy; Nous Horitzons (1992) focuses on ecology; CatDem (1994) deals with Catalan nationalism; and the Fundació Josep Irla (1997) advocates for separatism (Ponsa and Xifra 2012). They all prefer organizing conferences and publishing media opinion pieces over more academic-oriented research and publishing. Their more *engagé* orientation distinguishes Catalan think tanks from the foreign policy research institutes in Madrid, which tend to be much more traditional and less connected to civil society.

Foreign policies in Spain 171

When it comes to the factors that have contributed to the emergence of a more diverse and rich think tank environment in the post-Franco era, in the specific context of the Autonomous Region of Catalonia the following could be added:

- a highly mobilized Catalan civil society (businesses, chambers of commerce, universities, media, citizens) when it comes to the issue of independence, which has translated into continuously increasing popular support for independence;
- Catalonia's foreign policy strategy, whose goal is greater autonomy and ultimately independence from the Spanish state;
- strong political and financial interdependence between think tanks and pro-independence political parties, whose members now control Catalonia's policy-making apparatus.

Think tanks as actors in territorial struggles and public diplomacy

Most Spanish think tanks have integrated ideas of territoriality into their main topics of research and advocacy and struggle fiercely through their publications and conferences to promote their ideology: the union of Spain around a strong state on the right, and greater decentralization to the regions on the left. The main points of disagreement include all of the traditional functions of government, including education, natural resources (water), taxation, employment, immigration and citizenship, defense, justice and more. In order to understand the integration of think tanks into the foreign policy process, one must first examine the more general relationship between think tanks in Madrid and the central government and its agencies, and those between Catalan think tanks and the Generalitat.

Since the beginning of this century, political foundations and so-called advocacy tanks have multiplied, a development facilitated by the tax code. In this environment, these institutions jostle with each other to be heard in the dense and confused circumstances that have existed in Europe since the beginning of the economic crisis in 2007, and in Spain particularly since 2010. In fact, even traditional Spanish political foundations are shifting towards becoming advocacy tanks. Instead of hiding behind some academically neutral discourse, their ideological orientations are becoming increasingly clear, stated and known. At the same time, the think tanks that have the most extensive networks and the strongest international reputations are those that operate on the model of "universities without students." A number of Spanish think tanks appear in the Global Go To Think Tank 2014 rankings, most of them specializing in international relations. The Real Instituto Elcano, Fundación para las Relaciones Internacionales y el Diálogo, Fundacion para el Análisis y los Estudios Sociales (Foundation for Social Studies and Analysis) and the Fundación Alternativas are included in this ranking, all of them Madrid-based think tanks. CIDOB (the Barcelona Centre for International Affairs) is the only one on the list that is not based in Madrid. The reputational methodology of the McGann annual ranking certainly has an impact on which

Table 10.1 Typology of think tanks specializing in IR

Profile #1 Universities without students	Profile #2 Public research organizations
Fundación para las Relaciones Internacionales y el Diálogo (4)* Instituto de Cuestiones Internacionales y Política Exterior (INCIPE) Real Instituto Elcano (5)*	CIDOB (6)* Instituto Español de Estudios Estratégicos (IEEE) L'Institut Europeu de la Mediterrània (IEMED) UAH-Instituto Franklin
Profile #3 Political foundations	Profile #4 Advocacy Tanks
Fundacion para el Análisis y los Estudios Sociales (2)* Fundación Alternativas (1)* Fundació Catalunya Europa	Instituto de Estudios Sobre Conflictos y Acción Humanitaria (IECAH) Grupo de Estudios Estratégicos (GEES) Council on Foreign Relations (Madrid office)

*GGTT 2014 mentions

Source: Table prepared by O. Urrutia. Categories #1 and #2 are from R. Kent Weaver (1989).

think tanks make the rankings. In turn, however, expert awareness of these think tanks, and assessment of their influence, is affected by their financial resources, the volume of their output, their communications strategies and the nature of the state and civil society networks to which they are connected.

History

Over the past 30 years, three periods are evident in the emergence and evolution of the Spanish international relations think tank environment. The first corresponds to the last years of the Franco regime, as the country prepared for its return to the international stage. The administration fostered the creation of the IEEE in Madrid, which deals with defense and security issues, and allowed the Barcelona-based CIDOB to focus on geo-political affairs in the Mediterranean, a natural focus in view of its location. The second period stretches across the 1980s and the 1990s and was influenced by the process of integration into NATO and the EU. Private and public research centers including UAH Instituto-Franklin, GEES and INCIPE with its Atlantic orientation, as well as IEMED, which reinforced the role of the central state in the Mediterranean zone. Relations with the US became increasingly important during this period, as did closer relations with Latin America and with Spain's traditional partner, Morocco. The appointment of a Secretary of State for Cooperation and Relations with the Ibero-American region was a clear sign of Spain's more active foreign policy and strategic projection outside its borders. Beyond the usual and familiar tools of foreign policy-making, the creation of Real Instituto Elcano and IEMED as part of the Spanish state's public diplomacy initiative, as well as the state's more general support for think tanks, were important innovations in foreign policy formation. The third period, since the late 1990s, has been marked by the explosive growth of new information technologies, the emergence and travails of the Eurozone and the war against terrorism. FRIDE, IECAH and the Real Instituto Elcano have all been prominent

Table 10.2 Growth of the foreign policy think tank sector

	Date	Location	Status	Main topics	Languages	Transparency
IEEE www.ieee.es	1970	Madrid	Ministry of Defense	Security & Defense Competitive intelligence Geopolitics	Spanish English	
CIDOB www.cidob.org	1973	Barcelona	Public Foundation	Security Migration Development Regions	Spanish English Catalan	Not listed
GEES www.gees-spain.org	1987	Madrid	Nonprofit organization	Against proliferation Transatlantic relations War against terrorism Regions	Spanish English	Not listed
UAH Instituto-Franklin www.institutofranklin.net	1987	Alcala de Henares (Madrid)	University center	History Politic Economy Sociology Arts & Culture Science & Technology	Spanish English	
IEMED www.iemed.org	1989	Barcelona	Public Consortium	Euromediterranean politics Socioeconomics development Mediterranean cultures Cultural action Arab & Mediterranean world	Spanish English French Catalan	Not listed
FAES www.fundacionfaes.org	1989	Madrid	Nonprofit foundation	Economy/Public policy Constitutions/International institutions	Spanish English	Not listed
INCIPE www.incipe.org	1991	Madrid	Nonprofit private foundation	European Union Atlantic Alliance Russia Against Proliferation & Disarmament	Spanish English	Not listed
OPEX Fundación Alternativas www.fundacionalternativas.org	1997	Madrid	Private cultural foundation	Europe International relations of Spain	Spanish	Not listed

(continued)

Table 10.2 (continued)

	Date	Location	Status	Main topics	Languages	Transparency
FRIDE www.fride.org	1999	Madrid Brussels	Private foundation	European foreign policies New global order Eastern Europe, Caucasus & Central Asia Middle East & North Africa, Asia, Americas	Spanish English	Recorded (7 May 2014)
IECAH www.iecah.org	2000	Madrid	Private entity	Humanitarian action	Spanish	Not listed
Real Instituto Elcano www.realinstitutoelcano.org	2001	Madrid	Private foundation	Security & Defense Foreign Affairs of Spain Energy International economy Demography International Cooperation & Development	Spanish English	Not listed
ECFR www.ecfr.eu	2007	Madrid	N.C.	Asia & China Europe Middle East & North Africa	Spanish English	Recorded (14 January 2015)
Fundació Catalunya www.catalunyaeuropa.net	2008	Barcelona	Nonprofit private foundation	Economy Governance & Democracy Society & Culture Cities & territories	Spanish English French Catalan	Recorded (7 July 2010)

Source: Table prepared by O.Urrutia

during this period. The Fundació Catalunya Europa (2007) was created during this period, giving voice to a more aggressive Catalan nationalism with the aim of establishing direct links to the EU through public diplomacy.

The Spanish political system explains the relative fragmentation of the think tank ecosystem. However, as is true of Washington and New York, two clear centers of power emerge in the country: Madrid and Barcelona. The creation of international think tanks in Madrid, such as ECFR and the Club de Madrid, highlight the strong appeal of the city and its status as a political, economic and administrative capital. Built on the model of the Council on Foreign Relations in the US, ECFR is a pan-European research center that operates in a rather perplexing manner through its offices in London, Paris, Rome, Sofia, Berlin, Madrid and Warsaw. FRIDE is one of the founders of the ECFR, which also received major funding from the Soros Foundation.

The Spanish state has a strong interest in the geo-strategic role of the autonomous community of Catalonia, situated as it is at the northwestern corner of the Mediterranean zone. This was evident in the involvement of the Spanish state in the creation and governance of CIDOB and IEMED, and negotiations conducted at the time by the Spanish government with its European counterparts, leading to the choice of Barcelona as the seat of the 43-country Unió per la Mediterrània (Union for the Mediterranean). There exists a collaborative public diplomacy relationship between the central state and the autonomous community of Catalonia that allows Catalonia to develop and assume leadership in the Mediterranean through representing Spain. The government in Madrid retains ultimate control through its financial and political participation in all of these organizations.

There exists, therefore, a certain equilibrium in the distribution of organizations dealing with international relations between Castile and Catalonia, especially when it comes to some aspects of international relations and a willingness on the part of the central state to concede a leadership role to the authorities in Catalonia. This is particularly true when it comes to some of the Mediterranean matters that are of obvious importance to that region. At the same time, however, there has been growing support for advocacy tanks in the autonomous community of Catalonia, signaling increasing militancy in favor of secession. The stated objective of think tanks in Madrid is to serve the public interest through a better understanding of international issues and the role of Spain in the international sphere. By contrast, the Catalan advocacy tanks have as their main objective the increasing autonomy of Catalonia from the Spanish state and the projection of an image of Catalonia that will make international actors both aware of, and, prepared for, the region's independence. They operate as instruments of soft power whose targets lie outside of Spain in support of the independence movement.

The physical occupation of space is another way to exert influence. Spain has greatly benefited from its integration into the EU and has become one of its leading members. However, there are no think tanks in Madrid dedicated exclusively to the European question. Only the Catalan political foundations have a major interest in these matters. Finally, the presence in Brussels – and more widely overseas – of

Spanish think tanks is marginal. Only FRIDE has physical representation – as in a real office with specific objectives – outside Spain, including a Brussels office. This lack of representation outside the country could be attributed to the relative economic and logistical weakness of Spanish think tanks – and also to their leaders' lack of strategic vision – leading to lost opportunities for Spanish public diplomacy. The physical encounters that permit the direct exchange of ideas and the building of personal relationships, the ability to host events and to influence the EU media conversation that radiates from Brussels, the capacity to be recognized by decision-makers, and to systematically integrate into transnational working groups: none of these are open to Spanish think tanks because of their modest presence outside of the country's borders.

A matter of language

All research centers use at least English and Spanish to communicate to multiple target audiences. The use of these languages also offers a much better referencing of published works on the Internet. Catalan think tanks, because of their strategy of nationalist orientation and desire to maintain and deepen connections with French Catalonia, also communicate in French and Catalan. Language is used as a strategic tool to occupy a virtual or printed space, to develop emotional links and to advocate specific ideas and goals. The majority of advocacy tanks in Catalonia use Catalan exclusively as the language of communication on their websites and for their publications and local conferences. This is a strategic choice that profoundly reduces the dissemination of the ideas generated and advocated by these advocacy tanks. At the same time, however, it sends an important message and may contribute in some degree, within Catalonia, to the status and influence of these organizations. "Language always accompanies Empire," observes Antonio de Nebrija (1492), "the two are always born, have always grown and prospered together." Indeed, by highlighting the Catalan language and using it to discuss important issues instead of relying on the language of another community, these advocacy tanks express to the people of Catalan, to Spain and to the outside world an affirmation that their language and culture are alive and viable.

Organization and financing

Private philanthropy in Spain is not as developed as it is in the US, and private funding is much less important to the revenue model of most Spanish think tanks compared to those in the US. As in Germany, Spanish think tanks are more likely to depend on various sources of state funding. Indeed, some are almost or entirely dependent, statutorily and financially, on the state. The possible downside in terms of their independence is obvious. On the other hand, having stable and predictable finances enables these think tanks to employ well-qualified and permanent teams of researchers. By contrast, private research organizations are characterized by a good deal of unevenness in their access to public and private funding, resulting in quite a lot of variation in the quality and quantity of their output and activities. The think tanks with the healthiest budgets generate a consistently high volume of output, including organizing events, and tend to be characterized by greater diversity in the range of subjects they cover. CIDOB, the Real Instituto Elcano Royal and FRIDE, all of which have stable finances, provide leadership in the think tank community through the quality and quantity of their research and analyses, and are regularly cited in the media and acknowledged by policy-makers.

The ability to organize conferences, seminars and working groups, both nationally and internationally, can create a community of ideas and expertise, physically integrating civil society at publicly accessible events and disseminating the ideas, values and policy recommendations advocated by think tanks. Spain's private think tanks appear to be more active in this respect, either in partnership with other institutions or alone. This is consistent with their need for visibility in order to develop their networks and attract potential donors to sponsor high-value events. The larger and most prestigious think tanks will also occasionally partner with other organizations to host events; however, this is less crucial in sustaining their visibility and relevance in the eyes of opinion leaders and policy-makers than for smaller, private advocacy think tanks.

A mix of public/private financing is the most common model among Spanish think tanks. Public financing can take the form of ongoing grants, tax breaks, public research contracts or funding tied to single events or programs. Virtually all think tanks depend partially or entirely on state funding. The EU is the other major source of financing for think tanks, providing grants and, more often, contracts tied to particular projects. Political foundations tied to Spain's political parties can receive unlimited private donations from individuals and companies and receive tax benefits. These foundations also receive public funding; the amount is dependent on their representation in the legislature and the assessed quality of their research proposals.

Hard numbers on the finances of think tanks in Spain, as elsewhere, are often elusive. Most think tanks in the US are registered as 501(c)(3) organizations under the Internal Revenue Code. This designation allows American think tanks to receive important tax benefits, but in exchange they are required to make public their annual financial statements. In Spain, however, the choice of legal status allows for various options and there is much less transparency in think tank finances. Researchers, particularly those connected with the think tank transparency group, Transparify, have attempted to collect more information on this subject, so far without much success. Indeed, Transparify's 2015 report states that "data independently compiled by other researchers – and covered by the Spanish media – suggests that [Spain's] think tank scene as a whole is highly opaque." (Transparify 20015:10) This holds true, the report concludes, in Catalonia and in Spain as a whole. FRIDE appears to be something of an exception. CIDOB communicates the names of its patrons, which include some foreign think tanks, international organizations, corporations and state institutions, without specifying the amounts received or the purpose of donations.

Table 10.3 Structure and activities of foreign policy think tanks

	Budget	Staff	Network	Publications	Board
IEEE	N.C.	N.C.	N.C.	Magazine: 2 (120 pages) Panorama: 2 (200–430 pages) Research papers: 9 (40–270 pages) Strategic papers: 20 (4–20 pages)	Ministry of Defense
CIDOB	€2,895,645	2 executives 15 administrative agents 14 researchers 24 associated researchers	**Latin America** CEEIB/LASA/EADI/ REDIAL/RIBEI **Asia** EastAsiaNet/ASEM/ REDIAO/ECAN **Europe** EUROMESCO/EPIN/ EINIRAS **Intercultural** RICEI/RIDEI	Magazine: 3 Working papers: 22 (4 pages) Policy brief: 75 (2–4 pages) Documents: 4 (6 pages) Monographs: 6 (15–20 pages) Yearbook Newsletter Biography: 777	Government of Catalonia Metropolitan area of Barcelona Delegation of Barcelona Barcelona city council MAEC Ministry of Defense Inter-University Council of Catalonia
GEES	N.C.	15	N.C.	Policy briefs: 2 (4–6 p.) Yearbook	N.C.
Instituto Franklin-UAH	N.C.	17 administrative agents 25 researchers	Casa America Fundacion Consejo Espana-USA Instituto Cervantés Fullbright Espana	Working papers: 14 (6 pages) Research papers USA: 3 (45 pages) Newsletter	University Alcala de Henares
INCIPE	N.C.	2 administrative agents 6 researchers	N.C.	N.C.	Former politicians
IEMED	€2,500,000	26 administrative agents	Euromesco ANIMA Investment Network ECEM/EPUF/EMUNI/ FEMEC/FEMISE/FAL/ PNGE/SSN/STRAMED/ RIM/IRSNM	Quaderns: 2 (350 pages) Monographs: (150 pages) Reports: 1 (450 pages) Magazine Afkar/Ideas: 4 Policy Papers: 4 (40 pages)	Government of Catalonia Ministry of Foreign Affairs & Cooperation Barcelona city council

FRIDE	€1,400,000	2 executives 9 administrative agents 9 researchers 13 associated researchers	European Think Tank Group	Papers IEMED/Euromesco: 3 (30 pages)/Yearbook: 1 Joint policy studies: 1 Euromed survey: 1 Focus: 11 (4 pages) Newsletter Commentary: 5 (2 pages) Policy Briefs: 18 (5–7 pages) Working Papers: 1 (21 pages) Challenges: 3 (90–200 pages) Newsletter/book	Former politicians Businessmen
IECAH	N.C.	9 researchers 13 associated researchers 120 contributors	REDHUM	Reports: 1 (70 pages) Note: 1 (36 pages)/newsletter Articles: 34 (1–2 pages) Research papers: 3 (20–80 pages)	N.C.
Real Instituto Elcano	€3,000,000	3 executives 13 administrative agents 14 researchers	EPIN/RIBEI/Euromesco/ Euromed/EADI/EINIRAS/ TGAE/ISN/CSDP MAP	Documents: 18 (45–60 pages) Reports: 4 (+160 pages) Strategic papers: 12 (15 pages) Articles: 40 (12 pages) Policy briefs: 50 (4 pages) Books: 1–2 Magazine CIBER: 12 (30 pages) Magazine Elcano: 6 (80 pages) Barometer: 1–3 Newsletters: 12	King of Spain, Former prime ministers since 1978 Ministers of foreign affairs & cooperation, defense, economy & competitiveness, education, sport & culture Politicians of the opposition party Executives of large companies

(continued)

Table 10.3 (continued)

	Budget	Staff	Network	Publications	Board
Fundacio Catalunya Europa	€200,000	3 executives 6 administrative agents 5 trainees	Barcelona Global Consell Catala del Moviment Europeu	Opinions: 10 (1–4 pages) Editos: 2 (1–2 pages) Collection: 1 (114 pages) Working papers: 1 (15 pages) Policy papers: 2 (12 pages) Cicles Horitzo 2020: 1	Businessmen
ECFR	N.C.	2 executives 3 administrative agents 3 researchers 2 trainees	N.C.	Reports: 4 (6–18 pages) Policy briefs: 10 (6–12 pages) Memos: 4 (9–11 pages) Essays collection: 4 (90–190 pages) Scorecard: 1 (122 pages) Articles Podcast/videos/blogs	Politicians Academics Businessmen
FAES	€5,000,000	2 executives 13 administrative agents 6 researchers	EPIN European Network of Political Foundations European Resource Bank Stockholm Network Hispanic Leadership Network Euromesco RIBEI	Strategic Papers Etudes Policy briefs Livres	Politicians
OPEX Fundacion Alternativas	Global €800,000	2 executives 9 associated researchers		Memorandos: 3 (10–20 pages) Policy briefs: 11 (3–4 pages) Documents: 14 (8–32 pages)	Academics/former politicians/artists/lawyers/doctors/journalists

Networks

In the field of international relations, a think tank's ability to engage in, and make use of, transnational networks is a key advantage in pursuing a strategy of public diplomacy. Participation in transnational working groups and joint publications expands the range of perspectives, experience and reflection, but also has the beneficial effect of increasing a think tank's visibility. In the case of the ecosystems within which Spanish international relations-oriented think tanks operate, three main geostrategic networks emerge: Europe, the Mediterranean zone and Latin America. These, with the US and the Middle East, are the five main geo-cultural spaces that are foremost in the activities of Spanish think tanks; Africa (excluding the Maghreb), Asia and Russia appear to be secondary. Think tanks, most of which have revenue models that make them dependent on the state, serve to some inevitable degree as instruments of soft power policies articulated by the state (Nye 1991). Thus, FAES integrates the Latin American Studies Center and the Centre for Atlantic Studies and hosts programs for researchers from Latin America, the Middle East and North Africa. The Fundación Alternativas, the Foreign Policy Observatory (OPEX) and the Observatory of Culture and Communication do the same at the European level. The Real Instituto Elcano has established its own Observatory of Spain's Image, whose Image Barometer of Spain seeks to assess the impact of the country abroad. INCIPE, born from the merger of the Center for Foreign Policy Studies and the Institute of International Issues, has close connections to the Ministry of Foreign Affairs and Cooperation. FRIDE is one of the founding members of the ECFR in Europe and Spain and is a partner in the Observatory of Strategic Associations of the EU along with the Brussels-based Egmont Royal Institute for International Relations. It is also a participant in several international research programs such as Agora Asia-Europa; the EU-funded CASCADE program, which deals with security issues in the Caucasus region; Futuro Atlántico; EU Central Asia Monitoring; and GREEN, the Global Re-Ordering: Evolution through European Networks, on the role of Europe in a multipolar world. Almost all of these programs are funded by the EU. CIDOB coordinates three European research projects focused on the Atlantic area, a program on the role of youth in the Arab world (SAHWA), and another on the place of women in governance at the European level (MIPEX). The Conflict Observatory of the IEEE analyzes the seven geo-political zones of the world and the Hispa-USA Association of the Instituto Franklin specializes in research on Hispanic society in the US with the aim of encouraging relations between American Hispanics and Spain.

The independence issue

When one searches for the words "Spain" and "Catalonia" in the website of each of the think tanks listed in Table 10.1 the result is unequivocal: 16,589 studies or articles on Spain are listed versus 5,542 on Catalonia.[4] If this same process is applied only to the Catalan think tanks the results are quite different: 11,183 listings for Spain compared to 5,219 for Catalonia. While the search engines of Barcelona-based CIDOB and IEMED highlight many more studies on Catalonia than do the non-Catalan think tanks, the amount of content on Spain remains high. The Barcelona-based Fundació Catalunya Europa, however, is far more likely to focus on Catalonia, a finding that seems consistent with its role as an advocacy tank. Indeed, and in the nationalist spirit of Catalonia's advocacy tanks, the search of Fundació Catalunya Europa's website finds only two studies with the word "España," written in Castilian Spanish, and 866 with "Espanya," written in Catalan. Subjects relating to the relations between Spain and Catalonia are much more likely to be found in the publications and other activities of think tanks located in Catalonia than those based in Madrid. Indeed, Madrid-based FRIDE, GEES, INCIPE and ECFR devote almost no attention to these matters. The same is not true, however, of FAES and Real Instituto Elcano; they have strong links to the conservative Partido Popular, which advocates a united, centralized state. Not surprisingly, therefore, the question of Catalan independence and relations between the autonomous community and Madrid arises in their activities.

A 2015 study predicting positive economic consequences over the medium term for Catalonia in the event of independence was produced by CIDOB in partnership with the Brussels-based Centre for European Policy Studies (CEPS). The study was commissioned and paid for by the separatist Catalan government and presented to the European Parliament, and became an important point of discussion in the ongoing conversation on the future of Catalonia. It also caused some critics to question whether CIDOD was respecting the first of its stated objectives, namely, to be "An independent research centre, plural, without dominant partisan or ideological agendas, and capable of influencing thinking and global political action from within its local reality." Defenders of CIDOB and its association with this study countered that think tanks should be thought of as intellectual embassies, projecting the voice, vision and realities of the places where they are situated and in which their perspectives are embedded.

Conclusion

While it is true that the Spanish think tank scene borrows some features from the German and North American models, it remains uniquely Spanish. The return of democracy after the long Franco era and the adoption of a political model recognizing regional autonomy allowed for the growth and diversification of research centers throughout the country. It was inevitable that they would become concentrated in the two major centers of power, Madrid and Barcelona. Spain, because of its history of cultural-regional division and the current reality of a strong independence movement, does not exhibit the same degree of integration of its think tanks into the foreign policy-making process that one observes in the US (Higgott and Stone 1994). Nevertheless, think tanks have become significant actors in this process. Their dependence on state funding and formal relationship to the state tend to be much greater than in the US, differences that are consistent with Spain's more statist political culture.

It is worth mentioning here that several international affairs oriented organizations that define themselves as think tanks and are featured in think tank directories and included in the Global Go To Think Tank ratings have not been included in this analysis. In some cases this is because they do not deal specifically with matters of foreign policy (this is true, for example, of the Fundación Internacional para la Libertad, the Fundación Europea Sociedad y Educación and the Fundación Ortega-Marañón). In other cases, as with the Casas Asia, Arabic and Africa (a network of houses of public diplomacy that are part of Spain's Ministry of Foreign Affairs), the Club of Madrid, Toledo-based CITpax and the Instituto Choiseul, they simply cannot be considered think tanks. They are more properly thought of as public diplomacy agencies. They are *do tanks* rather than *think tanks*. That said, the line between them and research institutes is not always very clear. All of them have a relationship, to some degree, to the state's public diplomacy strategy.

If Barcelona uses public diplomacy to serve its independence goals, Madrid still retains a certain level of control over Catalan think tanks. Their governance structure, legal status and dependence on state funding ensure this. At the same time, it does not prevent occurrences of the sort that happened in 2015, when the joint CIDOB-CEPS study on the economic consequences of Catalan independence was published and presented to the European Parliament. In Catalonia, research foundations backed by Catalan political parties and advocacy tanks openly publish their independence-oriented research and opinions and have closed strong alliances with the Generalitat. That said, Catalan think tanks' influence abroad is more limited than that of their Madrid-based counterparts due to fewer resources, their clear lack of research neutrality and a general inability to extend the scope of their research and publications beyond purely Catalan issues. Although they try to make the most of their existing relationships with foreign think tanks and European political parties in order to represent Catalonia outside Spain, their impact remains limited. The Generalitat in Barcelona, like the Spanish central state in Madrid, collaborates with local think tanks because of their expertise on international issues and the fact that they support its public diplomacy strategy. For the Generalitat, supporting prestigious think tanks in Barcelona is also intended to send a strong signal to Madrid: Barcelona is a center of power. The political struggle between the Generalitat and the central state finds a parallel in the country's divided think tank scene. These think tanks have been integrated into this longstanding struggle, projecting different visions and identities to the outside world through their research, analysis and policy recommendations.

Notes

1 *2014 Global Go to Think Tank Index Report* (McGann 2015: 57); Guía de los think tanks en España de la Fundación Ciudadanía y Valores (61).
2 The Generalitat of Catalonia is the institution under which the autonomous community of Catalonia is politically organized. It consists of the Parliament of Catalonia, the government of Catalonia and the President of the autonomous community of Catalonia.

3 Department of External Cooperation, Secretariat of Foreign Affairs, Council on Public Diplomacy of Catalonia – Diplocat – and Accio10 were created to serve its international policy.
4 This research was conducted in September 2015.

References

Abelson, Donald. 2006. *A Capitol Idea: Think Tanks and US Foreign Policy*. Montreal: McGill-Queen's University Press.
Abelson, Donald. 2002. *Do Think Tanks Matter? Assessing the Impact of Public Policy Institutes*. Montreal: McGill-Queen's University Press.
Fusi, Juan Pablo. 2012. *Historia mínima de España*. Turner.
García Cárcel, Ricardo. 2002. *Felipe V y los españoles. Una historia periférica de España*. Barcelona: Plaza Janés.
Hallin, Daniel C., and Paolo Mancini. 2004. *Comparing Media Systems. Three Models of Media and Politics*. Cambridge: Cambridge University Press.
Higgott, Richard, and Diane Stone. 1994. "The Limits of Influence: Foreign Policy Think Tanks in Britain and the USA." *Review of International Studies* 20, no.1 (January): 15–34.
Kamen, Henry. 2014. *Brevísima historia de España*. Espasa Libros.
McGann, James G. 2015. *2014 Global Go To Think Tank Index Report*. Think Tanks and Civil Societies Program, University of Pennsylvania. Available from http://repository.upenn.edu/think_tanks/8/.
Medvetz, Thomas. 2012. *Think Tanks in America*. Chicago: University of Chicago Press.
Montobbio, Manuel. 2013. *La geopolítica del pensamiento. Think tanks y política exterior*. Barcelona: CIDOB edicions, Real Instituto Elcano.
Morodo, Raúl. 1979. *Los partidos políticos en España*. Barcelona: Labor.
Navarro, Vicenç. 2014. *Las dos Españas: La monárquica y la republicana*. "Pensamiento Crítico", diario PÚBLICO, 8 April.
Nebrija, Antonio de. 1492. *Gramática de la lengua castellana*. Available from http://www.antoniodenebrija.org/prologo.html.
Nye, Joseph S. 1991. *Bound to Lead:The Changing Nature of American Power*. New York: Basic Books.
Ortega y Gasset, José. 1999. *En España invertebrada*. Barcelona: S.L.U. Espasa Libros.
Ponsa, Francesc, and Jaime González-Capitel. 2015. *Radiografía de los Think Tanks en España*. Madrid: Fundación Ciudadanía y Valores and Observatoire des think tanks.
Ponsa, Francesc, and Jordi Xifra. 2012. *Guía de think tanks a Catalunya*. Barcelona: Sehen.
Requejo, Ferrán, et al. 1999. *Els Think Tanks a Catalunya*. Barcelona: Universitat Pompeu Fabra.
Sastre García, Cayo. 1997. *La Transición política en España: una sociedad desmovilizada*. Revista española de investigaciones sociológicas, no. 80, pp. 33–68.
Sanchez-Albernoz, Claudio. 2000. *España, un enigma histórico*. Edhasa: Edición Slp.
Transparify. 2015. "How Transparent Are Think Tanks about Who Funds Them in 2015?" 17 February. Available at www.transparify.org.
Weaver, R. Kent. 1989. "The Changing World of Think Tanks." *Political Science and Politics* 22, no. 3: 563–78.

11 And the winner is ...
Why measuring think tank performance is inherently problematic: lessons from Canada and beyond

Donald E. Abelson

Over the last two decades, as an increasing number of scholars from various academic disciplines have immersed themselves in the study of think tanks, considerable progress has been made in furthering our understanding of the role these organizations play in policy development. However, despite providing a more detailed and comprehensive explanation as to why think tanks have emerged in significant numbers, and why some regions are particularly well suited for their development, questions surrounding how much or little influence they have in affecting policy change persists. But, interestingly enough, determining how to assess or evaluate the impact think tanks have in shaping public opinion and public policy has not only become a preoccupation of scholars; it has become a pressing concern for directors and presidents of think tanks who must keep their boards of directors and trustees apprised of how their organization has fared relative to their competitors. In addition to satisfying their boards and directors, presidents of think tanks have the added pressure of convincing donors and other key stakeholders to support the work of their institute. To do this, they rely on what are commonly referred to as performance indicators or metrics such as media citations, the frequency with which their staff testify before legislative committees and the number of publications downloaded from their website. What they are trying to measure, albeit indirectly, is their organization's influence on public opinion and public policy.

Some think tank leaders acknowledge how difficult and problematic it is to measure influence; Brian Lee Crowley, Managing Director of the Macdonald-Laurier Institute, readily admits that "it is far from a perfect science." (Interview with author) But Crowley, a recognized veteran in the think tank world who served as founding president of the Atlantic Institute for Market Studies, also appreciates why it is critical for policy institutes to promote themselves and the products they generate. And if this means taking credit (whether deserved or not) for some successful policy initiatives or celebrating a high ranking in a think tank survey, so be it. In the final analysis, as discussed in previous chapters, trying to convince policy-makers, the public and other stakeholders that your institute has been able to shape the discourse around key policy issues is half the battle. For think tanks, it is about creating the illusion of policy influence.

In some respects, think tanks are no different from the corporations and private businesses that fund them. They have a product to sell and an image to project in a marketplace that rarely rewards complacency. As a result, we should be not surprised when think tank directors embellish their institutes' achievements. After all, their reputation and success ultimately depend on how their institute performs. Having said that, it is important for those who study think tanks and read their news releases and publications to understand what motivates them. To this end, I begin by providing examples of how some directors and presidents of think tanks have tried to portray their institute in the most favorable light. I do this, not to castigate or ridicule them (although I would be lying if I didn't acknowledge how much I enjoy doing this), but to remind readers how important it is to read between the lines. Not surprisingly, the examples I have selected are based on the reaction of two think tanks to the favorable rankings they received in the Global Go To Think Tank Report and Index. For think tanks, the annual survey has become their equivalent of the Oscars, Emmys, Tonys, Grammys, Junos and Golden Globe Awards all wrapped in one. The public release of the global rankings may not afford think tank directors an opportunity to schmooze on the red carpet, but for many of them being recognized as one of the world's leading think tanks is worth its weight in gold (or gold plate as is often the case.)

It's all about the rankings: Or is it?

It did not take long for David Bercuson, one of Canada's most renowned military historians and Director of Programs at the Canadian Global Affairs Institute, formerly known as the Canadian Defence and Foreign Affairs Institute (CDFAI), to share the good news he received from the authors of the *2012 Global Go To Think Tank Index Report* (McGann 2013). Indeed, shortly after the preliminary findings of the annual index and rankings of over 6,000 think tanks had been circulated, the CDFAI issued a press release proclaiming, "CDFAI ranked one of the top think tanks in the nation." (CDFAI 2013) On the surface, Bercuson had cause for celebration. His institute, which had been founded in 2001 "to be a catalyst for innovative Canadian global engagement," (CDFAI 2013) had ranked 7th on the list of the top 30 think tanks in Canada and Mexico, (McGann 2013: 61) a considerable improvement over the 30th place ranking CDFAI received a year before. Fourth overall among Canadian think tanks – after the Fraser Institute, the Centre for International Governance Innovation (CIGI) and the North-South Institute (McGann 2012: 44) – CDFAI had clearly made an impression on the over 1,500 experts called upon to rank the world's top think tanks. (McGann 2013: 61) What must have been even more gratifying to Bercuson was the fact that CDFAI placed higher than several larger and more established think tanks, including the C.D. Howe Institute, the Canadian International Council (formerly the Canadian Institute of International Affairs) and the Institute for Research on Public Policy (IRPP).

Bercuson attributed the organization's success to "the many people – Fellows, Advisory Council, Board members and staff – who have worked tirelessly to achieve maximum results with minimal resources." But, interestingly enough, he made no mention of how CDFAI fared in several other categories included in the report. For example, among the "Top 70 Security and International Affairs Think Tanks" in the world, a grouping where one would expect to find CDFAI given its defined areas of expertise, the institute was noticeably absent (McGann 2013: 66–67). Although several American and European think tanks, including the RAND Corporation, the Center for Strategic and International Studies, the Brookings Institution and Chatham House, found themselves atop this star-studded list, no Canadian think tank appeared on the roster. Ironically, it was a Russian think tank that provided the only reference to Canada. The Moscow-based Institute for the United States and Canada Studies ranked 62nd (McGann 2013: 66–67).

The CDFAI was also overlooked in several other categories highlighted in the report. In what the authors of the publication referred to as "Special Achievements," where think tanks were recognized for, among other things, the best use of the media (print and broadcast), best external relations/public engagement, most innovative policy ideas and proposals, outstanding policy-oriented research programs, best use of the internet or social media and most significant impact on public policy, CDFAI did not receive a single mention (McGann 2013: 88–95). However, there was some consolation for the Canadian think tank community as the Fraser Institute, the North-South Institute and IRPP managed to garner some attention. To be fair, ranking 7th among the top 30 think tanks in Canada and Mexico may have been newsworthy, but Bercuson's comments provided little more than a glimpse of where CDFAI stood relative to its competitors. As is typical for think tanks when they showcase their accomplishments, it is generally what is not said that deserves closer consideration. Interestingly enough, CDFAI, which saw its ranking slip to 8th place among the top think tanks in Canada and Mexico in the 2013 and 2014 editions of the Global Go To Think Tank Report and Index issued a more restrained and somewhat misleading press statement when the report's 2014 findings were released. Indeed, rather than acknowledging that CDFAI placed 8th out of the top 30 think tanks in Canada and Mexico (there is no separate table for think tanks in Canada), CDFAI announced that it "ranked among the top five think tanks in Canada." (CDFAI 2015)

It is true that CDFAI placed among the top five Canadian think tanks listed in this combined category. Still, it is questionable, given the ad hoc, arbitrary and impressionistic nature of the rankings and the less than rigorous process that generates them, that it would have secured a similar position in a category devoted exclusively to Canadian think tanks. Since many of the experts called upon to rank think tanks in this global survey possess little knowledge of think tanks in Canada, it is uncertain where CDFAI would find itself among its competitors. This problem has become particularly acute in surveys of this kind where experts are not required to undertake a detailed assessment of hundreds of institutes, but simply to provide their impressions of think tanks. With little detailed knowledge of what particular think tanks do, or the quality of work they produce, experts often base their decisions on the reputation of policy institutes. This may explain why the Brookings Institution and Chatham House consistently receive the highest rankings in this survey. It would also explain why the Fraser Institute, admittedly Canada's best known think tank, is also consistently rewarded with a favorable ranking.

As noted, think tanks understand the shortcomings of the global think tank survey, and recognize that its findings are not the result of rigorous science, but random selection. However, this has not discouraged CDFAI and others that have received favorable rankings from showcasing their good fortune. As with most think tanks intent on elevating their status in the eyes of key stakeholders, putting a positive spin on the much touted global think tank rankings was a play CDFAI was only too willing to make. In concluding its brief statement following the release of the 2014 report, CDFAI added, "With your help, we look forward to making 2015 an even better year." (CDFAI 2015) But better for whom? For the federal government as it continues its efforts to protect Canada's defense and foreign policy interests, or for CDFAI as it looks to improve its standing in these and other rankings? Perhaps both. As Bercuson observed in the Fall of 2014, "I think we've [CDFAI] had some impact on the way defense and security policy has evolved in Canada over the last 10 years or so." (McCoy 2014) Not surprisingly, Bercuson did not elaborate on what kind of impact his institute has had.

The Fraser Institute was far less modest in publicizing the results of the 2014 survey. In a press release issued on 22 January 2015, a day before the Global Go To Think Tank Report and Index was unveiled in over 60 cities, Fraser Institute president Niels Veldhuis proudly proclaimed that Fraser was "first among the nearly 100 think tanks in Canada for the seventh consecutive year and 19th out of 6,618 think tanks from 182 countries worldwide." (Fraser Institute 2015) He added, "Being recognized as one of the top 20 think tanks in the world and the only Canadian think tank in the global top 40 speaks volumes about the quality of research and programs produced by our diverse staff and senior fellows across Canada and the United States." And if this wasn't enough praise to heap upon his institute, Veldhuis offered the following: "The University of Pennsylvania ranking is validation that the Fraser Institute continues to successfully study, measure and broadly communicate the effects of government policies and entrepreneurship on the well-being of Canadians." (Fraser Institute 2015)

It would be tempting, and frankly justifiable (for some jaded political scientists), to indict Bercuson, Veldhuis and other think tank directors and presidents for exaggerating their institutes' achievements in the press and on their websites. But, as we will discover in the pages that follow, this is exactly what leaders of think tanks are expected to do. In what has become an increasingly competitive marketplace of ideas where think tanks must secure funds to keep afloat, directors have an obligation and, to be blunt, an incentive to cast their organizations in the most flattering light. To dismiss or downplay the kind of public recognition that comes from widely known publications such as the annual Global Go To Think Tank Report and Index would not likely sit well with boards of directors and funders who support the work of these institutes. In fact, to do otherwise would be foolhardy.

This lesson has not been lost on countless other think tanks around the globe who, like their Canadian counterparts, have celebrated the notoriety and visibility that come with high-placed rankings in the Global Go To Think Tank Report and Index. Johan L. Kuylenstierna, executive director of the Stockholm Environment Institute (SEI), noted after the release of the 2014 report that "I am very pleased that SEI continues to be rated among the world's top think tanks. This is strong recognition from our peers and partners on the quality and relevance of our work, and it will spur us to continue our focus on outcome and impacts of what we do. I wish to emphasize that the top-ranking is achieved through the collective commitment to excellence by SEI's staff and through the amazing collaborations we have with hundreds of partners around the world." (Watt 2015) SEI's research director, Måns Nilsson, added, "While rankings can be a bit unpredictable, this result suggests that our approach is succeeding combining robust scientific research with effective decision support to develop new ideas and solutions and solutions to tackle problems that appear increasingly intractable." (Watt 2015)

Professor Lemma Senbet of the African Economic Research Consortium (AERC), which ranked 1st in sub-Saharan Africa and 25th globally in the think tank index, also took great pride in his institute's standing. "We are delighted with the high level ranking because we know that AERC's products are visible round the world. . . . This high ranking is the result of over 25 years of sustained commitment to hard work." (AERC 2015) Not to lose their time in the limelight, the Malaysian-based ASLI's Centre for Public Policy Studies, joined AERC and other think tanks in celebrating their ranking. Tan Sri Dr Michael Yeoh, CEO of ASLI, observed: "We are also pleased that our collaboration and partnership with key stakeholders at various levels of society in Malaysia is recognised. We are indeed grateful for this international recognition." (ASLI 2015)

By pointing out how directors of think tanks can be so cavalier when it comes to highlighting or ignoring data that suits their organizations interests, it is not my intention or desire to cast aspersions on, or in any way to discredit, those entrusted with overseeing the nation's think tanks. There are plenty of political pundits who are willing to take up this cause. Rather, by demonstrating how rankings and other measurements of think tank influence can be easily manipulated, I want to focus attention on one of the fundamental problems scholars and journalists encounter in evaluating the contributions of think tanks to public policy. As we will discuss shortly, influence is, by its very nature, subjective. However, this has not discouraged think tanks, or the various organizations who monitor them, from making unfounded assertions about their efforts to shape specific policy issues and the political environment which they inhabit. We have good reason to be skeptical.

Why is it so important to think tanks to measure their influence?

As a die-hard hockey fan, I regularly browse the National Hockey League website to check on how my favorite players are doing. It's not because I take part in any hockey pools – my son has a far better handle on how they work than I do. I just want to know how many goals and assists Sidney Crosby, Jordan Eberle and Nazem Kadri have tallied. But since hockey is a team sport, why should individual statistics really matter? Why should I not simply focus on the standings? In a similar vein, why have think tanks, as not-for-profit organizations, become so consumed with measuring their performance when ostensibly they are committed, as countless other organizations are, to improving public policy? After all, unlike professional hockey players who have incentive clauses built into their contracts that, if met, could pay handsome dividends, resident scholars at think tanks do not generally receive bonuses for having their publications cited in the press or in academic indices. So why should it matter if some think tanks generate more media citations than their competitors or have staff who testify regularly before legislative committees? As long as policy-makers enact legislation that will serve the public interest, isn't that enough?

The reality is that as much as players are committed to helping their team win and as much as think tanks celebrate positive policy change, they are motivated by competing and often conflicting objectives. For players, it is about posting numbers that will translate into more lucrative contracts. Similarly, for think tanks it is about compiling and massaging performance indicators that will impress current and potential donors. But unlike player statistics, which can be verified, claims about how much influence think tanks wield generally cannot. Still, this has not discouraged think tanks from highlighting their accomplishments. They understand all too well that the more exposure and notoriety they generate, the easier it is for them to attract funding. And with more financial resources at their disposal, think tanks can establish a more visible presence in the political arena. This, in turn, may allow them to establish a stronger platform from which to shape the political climate. But does greater visibility, exposure and favorable rankings in various think tank indices necessarily translate into policy influence?

Presidents and directors of think tanks would like us to believe that performance indicators such as the ones I have referred to are evidence of the policy impact they enjoy, a topic that we will return too shortly. They regularly make such claims in annual reports and rarely hesitate to boast about their institute's achievements in public gatherings. For instance, at the annual Manning Networking Conference, held in Ottawa in March 2014, Veldhuis went to great lengths to extol the virtues of his organization (Veldhuis 2014). During his 30-minute presentation, he claimed, among other things, that while Fraser pays far less attention to influencing policy-makers than it once did, it continues to set its sights on shaping public opinion – something, he argued, his organization has had considerable success doing. However, despite his grand assertions, Veldhuis did not provide a shred of empirical evidence to support his conclusions (since he didn't have any) – something I, as a co-panellist asked to speak about the role and influence of think tanks in Canada and the United States, found rather telling (Abelson 2014). But to be fair, Veldhuis's motivation in constructing a narrative that celebrated and, to be clear, embellished the Fraser Institute's success was not meant to be subjected to close scholarly scrutiny. Rather his comments were intended to encourage the largely conservative faithful in attendance to invest ideologically, and possibly financially, in the efforts of the free-market institute.

Veldhuis's analysis of how the Fraser Institute has become a pillar of the conservative movement in Canada is instructive in so far as it emphasizes the importance of developing a comprehensive and well-coordinated approach to engaging in political advocacy. However, it is questionable whether his statements regarding the influence of his institute would fool even the most basic polygraph. This begs us to ask whether he sincerely believes that Fraser has widespread influence, despite the absence of empirical data to support such claims, or if he has simply adopted a posture that presidents of any corporation, or government agency for that matter, would be expected to embrace.

What rankings and other performance indicators do and do not tell us

When based on concrete data, rankings can prove to be enormously helpful to both public and private institutions. Each year, for example, popular magazines and newspapers such as *US News & World Report*, *Macleans* and *The Globe and Mail* conduct surveys of the best universities in the United States and Canada. Although several university presidents have publicly criticized some of the criteria used to establish rankings, they have also come to rely increasingly on various metrics to assess how their institutions are performing relative to their competitors. For instance, in their strategic planning documents, university administrators pay close attention to how many international students are pursuing advanced degrees on their campus and the amount of tri-council support their faculty receive. They also track completion rates for PhD students and enrollment trends among undergraduates. Although these and other data can be interpreted in different ways, at least the actual numbers can be verified. However, as I have pointed out, the same cannot be said for think tank rankings that have been compiled by the University of Pennsylvania, the Center for Global Development, the UK-based *Prospect Magazine* and other media outlets.

It should come as no shock to anyone by now that I am not a fan of think tank rankings. My concern, as noted, is not that efforts are being made to track the growth of think tanks worldwide. This, in itself, is a worthy endeavor, assuming of course that a consensus is reached on what organizations constitute think tanks. As noted, the problem I have is with the arbitrary and ad hoc manner in which think tank rankings tend to be generated. To put this in perspective, to undertake a thorough and systematic assessment of the work hundreds of think tanks produce in any given year would take teams of researchers several years to complete. A thorough evaluation of even one small to mid-size think tank would consume hundreds of hours. So how is it that the 1,500 or more so-called experts assembled by the University of Pennsylvania to rank what they consider to be the world's most recognized think tanks (which is problematic for other reasons) can complete their work in a matter of hours or days? Since those willing to participate in the rankings are not being compensated, it is difficult to imagine that they would be willing to invest a significant block of time to complete this task. As a result, one must question how seriously they take their responsibility. The problem is that there is no process in place to monitor how experts arrive at their rankings. Or to put it another way, there is no quality control. Individuals who, ostensibly, have some understanding of think tanks (some do but many likely don't) are simply asked to rank policy institutes that appear in different categories. For experts possessing little knowledge of think tanks in particular regions, providing a ranking would be akin to throwing darts at a board. Yet, despite these and other limitations, for the past seven years, as the New Year is ushered in, think tanks anxiously await the results of the global think tank rankings.

For think tanks that consistently receive high rankings, the release of the report is, as I have mentioned, cause for celebration. However, for those of us who have studied these organizations for years, it is cause for dismay. Unless and until a more rigorous process is implemented to properly evaluate the contribution of think tanks to public policy, these and similar rankings should be taken with more than a grain of salt. The authors of the Global Go To Think Tank Report and Index would benefit from looking at how the founders of Transparify conduct their survey of think tank transparency. Concerned that many think tank websites do not reveal financial information regarding their domestic and foreign sources of funding, Transparify established a rating system (similar to a report card) that uses a five-point scale (five being the highest) to assess the extent to which think tanks are transparent. For example, in 2014, the first year in which this rating system was introduced, CIGI received a five-star rating, which it proudly revealed in a news release (Bender 2015). Several other think tanks, however, did not fare as well. Similarly, the authors of the think tank report at the University of Pennsylvania could move from a ranking system to a point scale which evaluates think tanks according to an agreed-upon set of criteria. This system may not be as sexy as the model they now have in place, but the results could prove to be far more accurate. The manner in which think tank surveys and rankings are conducted will undoubtedly generate further discussion as policy institutes continue to compete for recognition and prestige in the policy-making community, but so too will the performance indicators upon which they rely to measure their influence. Should we be sceptical of these as well?

During his appearance on *The Agenda with Steve Paikin* during the Fall of 2014, Jason Clemens, executive vice-president of the Fraser Institute, commented that the motto of his organization – of which, by his own admission, he regularly reminds his researchers – is that "if it matters, measure it" (*Agenda with Steve Paikin* 2014). Although Clemens was referring to a range of social and economic factors that economists often take into account, such as unemployment rates, taxes and social welfare assistance, his advice about measuring what matters has spilled over into performance indicators commonly used by think tanks. In this regard, the motto for many think tanks, including Fraser, appears to be if what we do looks impressive and can be measured, measure it. In short, what matters most to think tanks is whether the target audiences they are trying to reach and win over believe their assertions about the influence they wield. But on what basis do think tanks make such claims? And how do they assess their impact?

Are think tanks as influential as they claim to be?

To take stock of what think tanks do and how they can leverage their influence, CIGI sponsored a conference on 20 September 2011 entitled "Can Think Tanks Make a Difference?" (CIGI 2011) (I gather the title "Do Think Tanks Matter?" was already taken). In the report that was circulated following the day-long event at its Waterloo headquarters, CIGI made several key points about how think tanks can be effective and what they need to do to maximize their influence. Some of these observations are summarized below:

- To maximize their influence, think tanks need to excel at communicating in plain language in order to engage both policy influencers (apparently a new word appropriated from the George W. Bush administration) and citizens at large.
- The role of think tanks should be to influence public opinion. If they can do that, governments will act.
- Think tanks have the most influence on public policy when they establish credibility via high-quality, timely research and understand the political process.
- Effective think tanks need to leverage social media to engage and involve citizens in dialogue. (CIGI 2011: 3)

In a nutshell, the participants in the CIGI conference concluded what scholars who have studied think tanks for years have long observed. In an effort to shape public opinion and public policy, think tanks must engage multiple stakeholders, produce timely and relevant research, and communicate their ideas in a clear, accessible and cogent manner. Just think how much money the conference organizers could have saved by issuing this one statement. In any event, CIGI should be credited for being so candid and honest about its intentions – to influence the policy preferences and choices of policy-makers. But what is missing from this document is whether or not CIGI researchers believe they have succeeded in doing so. In response to the title of the conference, the answer is yes – think tanks can make a difference. The more difficult question is measuring how and to what extent they do.

When it comes to measuring their impact on public opinion and public policy, CIGI finds itself in the same predicament as its competitors. They understand that the various performance indicators do not necessarily provide an accurate assessment of their contribution to key policy debates, but in the absence of a better alternative, CIGI, like most think tanks in Canada, the United States and Europe, feel compelled to draw upon data that speak to their level of engagement and visibility. Yet, as we will discuss below, engagement and visibility should not be confused with policy influence. Although presidents and directors of think tanks have a propensity to equate public exposure with policy influence, establishing a causal relationship between the two is inherently problematic.

Among the most common performance indicators upon which think tanks rely to impress donors and other key stakeholders is media exposure and their reason for doing this is simple. It is the easiest way for think tanks to convince their target audiences that what they say and do is relevant and important. And what better way to demonstrate this than to maintain records of how often they are referred to in newspapers, on television and on radio. As noted, think tanks regularly monitor the number of times their institute, staff and studies are cited in domestic and foreign newspapers so they can compare their exposure to a select group of competitors. Some, including London's Chatham House, engage the services of a media relations company to perform this function, and the results often make their way into its annual reports and promotional materials (personal correspondence). But monitoring media exposure is more often conducted in-house. Think tanks can take advantage of on-line databases such as the Vanderbilt Television and News Archive to track how often their staff appear on American network newscasts. In addition, they can keep a close watch on how many followers they have on Twitter and Facebook, the number of times their organization has been cited in government publications such as *Hansard* and the *Congressional Record* and the frequency with which their studies are cited in various academic indices. Google Scholar and other search engines are useful in this regard. To provide them with a better sense of how extensive their reach is, think tanks can also record how many visitors access their website, keep a running tally of how many of their studies are downloaded and track the number of people who subscribe to their on-line publications. However, while these and other data are readily accessible and can be used by think tanks to elevate their stature in the eyes of stakeholders, it is important to remind ourselves what the public exposure and visibility of think tanks means.

We know why think tanks covet media exposure, but why have the media become increasingly interested in think tanks? What is it about public policy institutes that journalists find newsworthy? As think tanks have come to occupy a more visible presence on the political landscape (largely because of their growing numbers and strong ties to policy-makers), it is not surprising they have commanded more media attention. At times, think tanks generate exposure because they have released a report (the more controversial, the more exposure) that focuses on an issue of concern to policy-makers and the public such as reforms to health care or post-secondary education. At other times, think tanks may find themselves in the news because they have received a high-placed ranking in a think tank survey or because they are being audited by the Canada Revenue Agency. But more often than not, when think tanks are cited in the popular press, it is simply because one of their policy experts has provided his/her take on a given political development. Yet, regardless of the context in which particular think tanks are referenced, what matters to these institutions is not necessarily why they made their way into a news report or newspaper article, but how often they are mentioned. Receiving a high-placed ranking in a global think tank survey is important to think tanks, but so too is being recognized as one of the most talked about and written about policy institutes. This kind of recognition has its own caché. With heightened media exposure, think tanks hope to enhance their credibility in the eyes of the public, policy-makers and other constituencies. And with greater credibility, they might be granted more access to policy-makers – leverage they can then use to attract additional funding.

The amount of media exposure think tanks generate with respect to a specific policy issue may help scholars identify those organizations most invested and engaged in particular policy debates, but it still does not answer the question as to whether their input has mattered. Put simply, being quoted in the press or relying on an op-ed to propose recommendations for changing the substance and direction of various policy initiatives is a far cry from being able to influence what the public and policy-makers think about important policy issues. In fact, just because a think tank makes its views known in the press does not mean that large segments of the public or even a small group of policy-makers are aware of them. And even if they were, it does not mean that think tanks are in a position to effect policy change. As students of public policy understand all too well, there are several factors that reveal themselves at both a micro and macro level that can influence policy decisions. But think tanks know this – they understand the intricacies of the policy-making process, and are painfully aware that it takes far more than media exposure to leave an indelible mark on public policy. Nonetheless, while they may or may not believe their own hype or the spin they put on their public profile, think tanks recognize how critical it is to convince others that they are well-positioned to exercise influence. For think tanks and other organizations that compete for the attention of the public and policy-makers, media exposure is a valuable tool that they can use to elevate themselves in the political arena. As previously discussed, this may explain why some well heeled think tanks in the United States have invested millions of dollars in developing and expanding their own media relations infrastructure. Although few think tanks in Canada are capable of making this kind of investment, they recognize the importance of strengthening their ties to the media.

As important as it is for think tanks to be in the media spotlight, there are other ways for policy institutes and the scholars who participate in their research programs to attract attention, including testifying before legislative committees. Once again, however, it is important to question how this activity may or may not be useful in helping think tanks and the scholars who study them measure their reach and policy impact. But why is this important and of what relevance is this to our current discussion? The reason I bring this up is to emphasize an earlier point. By marketing themselves as institutions comprised of experts engaged in policy analysis, think tanks enjoy a certain status – one that is derived from a widespread belief, nurtured and reinforced by the carefully constructed public relations campaigns they employ, that what they do and how they do it somehow makes them more virtuous. By claiming that they are committed to contributing to better and more enlightened public policies, think tanks wittingly, and at times unwittingly, try to take the high moral ground. Unlike advocacy groups and lobbyists who pursue narrow self-interests, think tanks see themselves as guardians of the public interest. Seen in this light, think tanks take advantage of what many of their competitors appear to lack: respectability and credibility – virtues which they can exploit to gain access to various stages of the policy cycle. At the stage of the policy cycle where the focus is on policy formation, in an attempt to engage multiple stakeholders, policy-makers often turn to various organizations with expertise in particular policy areas. Not surprisingly, policy experts at think tanks who possess an intimate knowledge of the domestic and foreign policy issues that have made their way onto the government's agenda are often invited to share their insights with appropriate legislative committees.

Testifying before high-profile parliamentary or congressional committees provides think tanks with yet another opportunity to showcase their ideas and to enhance their visibility. Still, how much of an impact a single appearance before a committee will have on its members or ultimately on legislation is difficult to measure. However, while the various factors that might have influenced government policy may preoccupy historians and political scientists for years, the answer is of little concern to think tanks that are more interested in gathering data they can use to impress potential supporters. Rather than focusing on who or what ultimately influenced public policy, think tanks are more preoccupied with whether this particular performance indicator can be parlayed into greater financial support.

The purpose of this brief discussion is not to leave readers with the impression that think tanks are being entirely disingenuous when they boast about their accomplishments in the political arena. There are many examples of think tanks that have made valuable contributions to important policy initiatives. I simply want to point out that the narrative think tanks construct around the policy influence they wield must be subjected to closer scrutiny. Performance indicators such as the ones outlined above may allow think tanks to acquire a better sense of how they are doing relative to their competitors and may speak to their level of engagement around particular policy issues, but these and similar data do not provide a clear indication of how much or little policy influence think tanks exercise. Information regarding the media exposure think tanks generate and the frequency with which their staff testify before legislative committees should, along with the kinds of publications they produce and the number of followers they have on Twitter and Facebook, be used as a point of departure, not a landing, for a much broader discussion about the determinants of public policy.

It is understandable why pundits, journalists and scholars are among those who believe that think tanks like the Heritage Foundation, the Brookings Institution, the Fraser Institute and other policy institutes have played a critically important role in shaping public opinion and public policy in the United States and Canada. They have sizeable budgets, enjoy close ties to policy-makers, have become experts in marketing ideas and themselves, and have become permanent fixtures on the political landscape. However, although there is little doubt that in some policy circles they have made their presence felt, they represent but one set of actors competing for policy influence. Scholars who study think tanks are under no obligation, and, in fact, would be foolhardy, to take the claims think tanks make about their impact at face value. When it comes to questioning where true political power resides, our responsibility is to question, to probe and to analyze. Unfortunately, in the study of think tanks, journalists and scholars have been far too complacent. For instance, when Edwin Feulner, the long-serving president of the Heritage Foundation told a reporter in the early 1980s that an estimated 60 percent or more of the hundreds of policy recommendations contained in Heritage's mammoth study *Mandate for Leadership* had been implemented by the Reagan administration, not a single follow-up question was asked. Rather than challenging this claim, Feulner's word was taken as gospel. All the reporter had to do was ask the interviewee two simple questions: how did he arrive at the conclusion that hundreds of Heritage's recommendations had been adopted by President Reagan and his administration, and what empirical evidence did he have to document the extent of his organization's influence? Perhaps it was in the same file containing the material upon which Neils Veldhuis drew when he enumerated the Fraser Institute's successes.

Those entrusted with managing think tanks have an incentive to portray their institutions in the most favorable light even if this means embellishing their achievements. However, scholars who closely follow their activities do not. Our responsibility is not to be publicists or spin doctors, but to expose the multiple layers of the policy-making process so that we can reveal the role think tanks play and the contribution they make to public policy. To do this, however, it is necessary to study think tanks from both a quantitative and qualitative perspective.

A two-pronged approach

Compiling large data sets on the visibility of think tanks, though laborious, is not a difficult undertaking. There are several search engines that allow users to track the media exposure of think tanks in hundreds of domestic and foreign newspapers. Scholars can, for instance, monitor think tank citations by region, topic and date, and depending on the time horizon they select (usually five or ten years) produce a ranking of the most widely cited think tanks. A similar approach can be employed to rank think tanks that are referenced in the broadcast media and on countless internet sites. Moreover, through websites managed by the US Congress and the Canadian parliament, a list of testimonies provided by policy experts at think tanks can also be easily obtained. With this information in hand, scholars can begin to hypothesize as to why some think tanks attract more media exposure than others, and why staff from some policy institutes appear with far greater regularity before legislative committees. Still, while these and related data may help inform discussions about think tank visibility and may speak to the extent to which these institutions are engaged in particular policy debates, they are less useful in assessing policy influence. For example, while there appears to be a direct correlation between the number of times think tanks are quoted in the press and the size of their budget, scholars have been unable to detect a causal relationship between public visibility and policy relevance. To put it another way, the most talked about and written about think tanks are not necessarily those that exercise the most policy influence. Indeed, as noted, some think tanks such as the Caledon

Institute maintain a modest media profile while enjoying considerable access to high-level policy-makers. Other think tanks also prefer to operate with little fanfare and consequently do not assign a high priority to building a public profile, another reason for questioning the utility or futility of media rankings. In short, numbers that reveal how much exposure think tanks attract do not provide the context scholars require to ascertain how and where in the policy-making process think tanks have the greatest impact. On the other hand, qualitative assessments based on surveys, interviews and case studies can prove to be enormously helpful in delving more deeply into the extent and nature of think tank influence.

One of the many challenges scholars of think tanks face is resisting the temptation to make general observations about the organizations they study and the kind of influence they exercise. We have already pointed out that no two think tanks are exactly alike, and, by the same token, the circumstances under which policy institutes are able to contribute to the policy discourse around domestic and foreign policy debates differ dramatically. This explains why Leslie Gelb concluded that assessing the policy influence of think tanks is notoriously difficult – it is "highly episodic, arbitrary, and difficult to predict." (Abelson 2006: 167) For think tanks to achieve policy influence, they need to present the right ideas to the right people at the right time. But even then, their best laid plans may fall upon deaf ears. If there were a five-step program that would guarantee think tanks able to leave an indelible mark on government policies and initiatives, they would trip over each other to sign up. In reality, there is no guaranteed formula for success. At times, think tanks are able to engage policy-makers and the public in ways that afford them opportunities to share their insights about policy issues. However, at other times, their voices are barely heard. As with other non-governmental organizations that remain vulnerable to changing political conditions, much of what happens in the environment think tanks inhabit is beyond their control. They can, as relatively autonomous institutions, establish and implement their research programs, and determine how and in what form to release their policy recommendations; but how well their ideas will be received and whether they will be acted upon is hard to predict. Recognizing this, scholars have published an increasing number of case studies on the involvement of think tanks in various policy debates.

Case studies of think tanks and their efforts to involve themselves in key policy discussions can help shed light on the many factors that may facilitate or frustrate their ability to achieve desired outcomes. Although these avenues of inquiry may only provide a snapshot in time, the picture they reveal at a given moment can go a long way in providing a more systematic examination of public policy institutes. At the very least, a more detailed investigation of particular think tanks and their interaction with key stakeholders may compel scholars to rethink some of the earlier observations they have made about the inner workings of these institutions.

In the process of understanding how think tanks attempt to assess their impact, a healthy dose of scepticism is in order. This is not to suggest that the contribution think tanks make at various stages of the policy cycle should be ignored, or that there is little evidence to suggest that think tanks have left a mark on public policy. On the contrary, there are plenty of domestic and foreign policy debates on which think tanks have had a discernible impact. Rather, I am simply suggesting that to assess more accurately how much influence think tanks wield, it is necessary to pay closer attention to their efforts to educate and inform specific target audiences. Moreover, it is important to keep in mind that influence is exercised in different ways and takes on different forms. Think tanks may not always be in a position to alter specific policy decisions, but this does not mean that their presence has not been felt. In a similar vein, although they may produce a steady stream of publications, occupy the media spotlight and host policy-makers at high-profile functions, it does not mean they are necessarily able to dictate policy outcomes. In short, when it comes to studying think tanks, we should neither exaggerate their influence nor downplay their significance.

References

Abelson, Donald E. 2014. "Ideas, Influence and Public Policy: Think Tanks in Canada and the United States." Presentation given at the 2014 Manning Networking Conference, Ottawa, Ontario, 28 February.

Abelson, Donald E. 2006. *A Capitol Idea: Think Tanks & US Foreign Policy*. Kingston and Montreal: McGill-Queen's University Press.

AFMI. 2015. "AERC among the top in 2014 Global Think Tank Index." AFMI News release, 23 January.

The Agenda with Steve Paikin. 2014. "Think Tanks and Policy Planks." Aired on TVO, 17 November.

ASLI. 2015. "ASLI's Centre for Public Policy Studies (CPPS) Among Top 6 Best Think Tanks in the Southeast Asia and the Pacific Region." Media release, 27 January.

Bender, Tammy. 2015. "CIGI receives highest rating among think tanks globally for financial transparency." CIGI News Release, 17 February.

CDFAI (Canadian Defence and Foreign Affairs Institute). 2013. News release, 23 January.

CDFAI (Canadian Defence and Foreign Affairs Institute). 2015. "CDFAI ranked among top 5 think tanks in Canada." News Release, 23 January.

CIGI (Centre for International Governance Innovation). 2011. "Can Think Tanks Make a Difference?" Conference report, 20 September.

CIGI (Centre for International Governance Innovation). 2015. Fraser Institute Top Think Tank in Canada and Now among Top 20 Worldwide: Annual Global Survey." Press release, 22 January.

McCoy, Heath. 2014. "Centre's Director Dr. David Bercuson Honoured." University of Calgary. Press release, 27 November.

McGann, James G. 2013. *2012 Global Go To Think Tanks Index Report*. Philadelphia: Think Tanks and Civil Societies Program, University of Pennsylvania.

McGann, James G. 2014. *2013 Global Go To Think Tanks Index Report*. Philadelphia: Think Tanks and Civil Societies Program, University of Pennsylvania.

Veldhuis, Neils. 2014. Remarks made during presentation at the 2014 Manning Networking Conference, Ottawa, Ontario, 28 February.

Watt, Robert. 2015. "SEI Ranked No. 2 among World's Environment Think Tanks." SEI News release, 26 January.

Index

Abramowitz, Morton 41
Academy for Regional Research and Regional Planning 102
Adam Smith Institute 92, 124
Addams, Jane 86
Adelphi Papers 127
advocacy tanks 102, 170–1, 175–6, 182–3
Africa Programme 70
African Development Bank Group 74
African Economic Research Consortium (AERC) 189
African Union Convention on Preventing and Combating Corruption 40
Agora Asia-Europa 181
Al-Jazeera 4
Allott, Gordon L. 22
American Enterprise Institute 1, 17, 85, 89, 92, 162
Amnesty International (AI) 3, 13–14, 38, 44, 56
Amsterdam treaty 65
Anderson, Martin 97
Arbour, Louise 41
Arms Trade Treaty 45
Arnold Bergstraesser Institute for Socio-Cultural Research 102
ASLI Centre for Public Policy Studies 189
Association for Efficient Public Administration 101
Atlantic Council 5, 31
Atlantic Institute for Market Studies 185

Barcelona Centre for International Affairs (CIDOB) 171–2, 175, 177, 181–3
Barnett, Richard 89
BBC 8, 11; World Service 4
Becker, Holger 74
Becker, Jo 54
Benenson, Peter 45
Bentham, Jeremy 120
Bercuson, David 186–8
Bernstein, Robert 55
Bertelsmann Foundation 5, 107
Better America 90
Big Four 38
Bill and Melinda Gates Foundation 53
Bill C-51 45
Blair, Tony 125
Bleasdale, Marcus 53
Bliesemann de Guevara, Berit 51
Blitt, Robert 44
Boer, John de 119
Bonn International Center for Conversion 105
Brandenburg-Berlin Institute for Social Studies 105
Bribe Payers Index 49
British Council of Churches 123
Broadbent Institute 34
Broadbent, Ed 34
Brookings Institution 1, 3, 5, 11–12, 20, 22, 24, 31–2, 37, 58, 86–7, 91–3, 95, 101, 112, 129, 187, 196
Brookings, Robert 85–6
Bruegel 10–11
Brzezinski, Zbigniew 88
Buchanan, Pat 89
Budget and Accounting Act of 1921 93
Bureau for Future Studies 105
Bush, George W. 91, 98, 129

C.D. Howe Institute 26, 186
Campaign for Nuclear Disarmament 123
Can Think Tanks Make a Difference? 193
Canada Revenue Agency (CRA) 26, 194
Canadian Centre for Policy Alternatives 26
Canadian Defence and Foreign Affairs Institute (CDFAI) 186

Canadian Global Affairs Institute 186
Canadian International Council 186
Canadian Parliament 197
Carnegie Endowment for International
 Peace 1, 5, 9–10, 37, 41, 58, 86, 93
Carnegie, Andrew 85–6
Carter Center 90
CASCADE program 181
Catalan nationalism 170, 175
Catalonia 166–68, 170–1, 175–8, 181–3
CatDem 170
Cato Institute 1, 10, 46, 53, 83, 89, 92
Center for a New American Security 5,
 90–1
Center for American Progress 5, 34, 85,
 91–2
Center for Applied Policy Research 107,
 111
Center for European Economic Research
 107
Center for Foreign Policy Studies 181
Center for Global Development (CGD)
 9–10, 31, 191
Center for Public Finance 101
Center for Strategic and International
 Studies (CSIS) 1, 5–6, 8, 83, 135, 187
Centre for Atlantic Studies 181
Centre for Cultural Research 104
Centre for Eastern Studies 156
Centre for European Policy Studies
 (CEPS) 70, 73–4, 76, 182–3
Centre for International Governance
 Innovation (CIGI) 186, 192–3
Centre for International Relations (CSM)
 157, 159–61
Centre for International Studies 156
Chatham House 5–6, 9, 15, 37, 50, 92,
 102, 108, 115, 120–129, 187, 194; *see
 also* Royal Institute of International
 Affairs
China-EU Relations 141
China Institute of International Studies
 (CIIS) 16, 132–5, 140–51
China Institutes of Contemporary
 International Relations 5, 133
China's Ministry of Foreign Affairs
 (MFA) 16, 133–5, 140–9
Chinese Academy of Social Sciences
 (CASS) 70, 138
Chinese Communist Party (CCP) 133–5,
 138
Chinese foreign policy 9, 134, 143–5,
 149–50
Chipman, Dr. John 129

Christian Democratic Union 103
Christian Public Foundation 105
Christian Social Union 103
CIDOB (Barcelona Centre for
 International Affairs) 171–2, 175, 177,
 181–3
Círculo de Empresarios 169
Citizens for a Sound Economy 90
CITpax 169, 183
Clark, Julia 9–10
Clemens, Jason 192
climate change 3, 7, 49
Climate Nexus 53
Clinton administration 52
Clinton, Bill 41
Clinton, Hillary 53
Cobham, Alex 47
Cold War 43, 88, 115–16
Cologne Institute for Business Research
 102
Common Foreign and Security Policy
 (CFSP) 63–6, 70, 73, 76
Common Security and Defence Policy
 (CSDP) 64–6, 70
Congressional Record 96, 194
Cook, Robin 126
Cooper, Glenda 53
Coors, Joseph 22
Corruption Perceptions Index 5, 40, 46, 48
Council on Foreign Relations (CFR) 1, 5,
 9, 37, 86, 93–4, 97, 102–3, 107, 111,
 175
Crane, Philip 21
Crimea 16, 161
CrisisWatch 42, 51
Crowe, William 89
Crowley, Brian Lee 185
Cuny, Fred 41

DeMint, Jim 32
Democracy Index 46
Democratic Party 25
demosEuropa (Centre for European
 Strategy) 158–61
Der Spiegel 5, 40
Deutsche Gesellschaft für Auswärtige
 Politik 6
Deutschewelle 5
Development Policy Forum 69–70, 73
Die Linke 105
Die Zeit 5
Dole, Bob 90
Dortmund Social Policy Research Center
 102

Index

Economic Policy Institute 89
Economist Intelligence Unit 46
Edmond J. Safra Center 12, 87
Eduard Pestel Institute for Systems Analysis 103
Egmont Royal Institute for International Relations 181
Eigen, Peter 39, 49
El Mundo 6
El País 6
Empower America 90
EU foreign policy 14, 63–79
EU-China Programme 69–70, 73
European Academy for Science and Technology Assessment 107
European Centre for Minority Issues 106
European Commission 46, 65
European Council on Foreign Relations (ECFR) 107, 111, 162, 175, 181–2
European External Action Service (EEAS) 14, 64–5, 76, 79
European Forum for Migration Studies 107
European Policy Centre (EPC) 70, 73–6
European Political Cooperation 63
European Political Strategy Centre 66
European Union (EU) 51, 70
Evans, Gareth 41–2
Extractive Industries Transparency Initiative 49

Fabian Society 37, 92, 120
Facebook 10, 53, 95–6, 194, 196
Federal Institute for Russian, East European and International Studies 102
Federation of International Football Associations (FIFA) 49–50
Feulner, Edwin J. 14, 20–3, 33–4, 95, 197
Feulner's pendulum 20, 35
Financial Times 51
Finnish Institute of International Affairs 70
Flaig, Gebhard 110
Foreign Affairs Council 65
Foreign and Commonwealth Office (FCO) 127–8
Foreign Policy Centre 126
Foreign Policy Observatory (OPEX) 181
Foreign Policy 51
Foucault, Jean Bernard Léon 20
Foundation of the German Scientific Community (Deutsche Forschungsgemeinschaft, DFG) 110–11
Franco-German Institute 102
Frankfurt Market Economy and Policy Institute 105, 107

Fraser Institute 26, 46, 186–8, 190–2, 196–7
Free Democratic Party 103
Freedman, Sir Lawrence 125
Freedom House 46
Freedom of Information (FOI) 127
FreedomWorks 90
French Agency for Development 69
Friedrich Ebert Foundation 101
Friedrich Naumann Foundation 103
Friends of Europe (FoE) 69–70, 73–6
Fundació Catalunya Europa 175, 182
Fundació Josep Irla 170
Fundació Pi i Sunyer Carles 170
Fundació Rafael Campalans 170
Fundación Alternativas 171, 181
Fundación Burke 169
Fundación Europea Sociedad y Educación 183
Fundación Internacional para la Libertad 183
Fundacion para el Análisis y los Estudios Sociales 171
Fundación para las Relaciones Internacionales y el Diálogo (FRIDE) 171–2, 175–7, 181–2
Futuro Atlántico 181

García Cárcel, Ricardo 168
Gelb, Leslie 97, 198
Gellner, Winand 113
Gentleman Amateur 120
German Association for Environmental Education 104
German Association for Peace and Conflict Research 104
German Democratic Republic (GDR) 105–6
German Development Institute 5, 102
German Federal Enterprise for International Cooperation 69
German foreign policy 101, 104, 116
German Foundation for International Development 102
German Foundation for Peace Research 104
German Institute for Distance Learning 102
German Institute for Economic Research 101
German Institute for International and Security Affairs (SWP) 102, 115–16
German Institute for International and Security Affairs 5, 102

German Institute of Urban Affairs 103
German Marshall Fund (GMF) 162
German Trade Union Federation 102
German Youth Institute 102
Giedroyc, Jerzy 156
Gillmor, Dan 53
Gingrich, Newt 90
Glaser, Bonnie S. 135
Global Corruption Barometer (GCB) 48
Global Go To Think Tank Index Report 3, 5, 9–11, 17, 38, 47, 56
Global Integrity 48
Global Public Affairs 32
Global Witness 48
Gorbachev, Mikhail 128
Gottfried Wilhelm Leibniz Scientific Society 105
Green Party (Germany) 105
Grigat, Sonja 51
Grupo de Estudios Estratégicos (GEES) 172, 182
Guardian 10, 54, 128

Haass, Richard 1
Hague, Lord William 130
Halle Institute for Economic Research 105
Hamburg Environmental Institute: Center for Social and Ecological Technology 104
Hamburg Institute for Social Research 112
Hamburg Institute of International Economics 101
Hanns Seidel Foundation 103
Hans Böckler Foundation 102
Hansard 194
He, Li 135
Heinrich Böll Foundation 105
Hellenic Foundation for European and Foreign Policy 70
Heritage Foundation 5, 10, 13–14, 17, 20–5, 32–4, 46, 83, 85, 87, 89, 92, 94–5, 98, 196–7
Hermann von Helmholtz Community of German Research Centers 106
Herrnstein, Richard 24
Higgott, Richard 119
Hillwatch 32
Hispa-USA Association 181
Hoover Institution 5, 86, 91, 97
Hoover, Herbert 85
HRW Film Festival 53
Hudson Institute 88, 92
Hull House 86

Human Rights Watch (HRW) 3, 13–14, 38–9, 42–4, 51–9
Humanitarian Aid and Civil Protection (H&CP) 64

Ifo Institute for Economic Research 110
Income Tax Act 26, 28, 34
Index of Economic Freedom 46
Institute for Development Planning and Structural Research 103
Institute for Ecological Economic Research 104
Institute for Economic and Social Research 102, 105
Institute for Economic Research 102
Institute for Employment Research of the Federal Employment Services Agency 102
Institute for Government Research 86
Institute for Market-Environment-Society 105
Institute for Peace Research and Security Policy 104
Institute for Policy Studies (IPS) 17, 88
Institute for Regional Development and Structural Planning 105
Institute for Research on Public Policy (IRPP) 186–7
Institute for Social-Ecological Research 104
Institute for Strategic Studies (International Centre for Development of Democracy) 157
Institute for Technology Assessment and Systems Analysis 103
Institute for Western Affairs 155, 158
Institute for Work and Technology 105
Institute of Agricultural Development in Central and Eastern Europe 106
Institute of Asian Affairs 102
Institute of Economic Affairs (IEA) 21
Institute of Economics 86
Institute of Geography and Geo-ecology 105
Institute of International Issues 181
Institute of Law and Comparative Jurisprudence 47
Institute of Public Affairs 157
Institute of Regional Geography 105
Institute on Research of International Affairs 157
Instituto Choiseul 169
Instituto de Cuestiones Internacionales y Política Exterior (INCIPE) 172

204 Index

Instituto de Estudios de Opinión Pública 169
Instituto de Estudios Económicos 169
Instituto de Estudios Políticos 169
Instituto Español de Estudios Estratégicos (IEEE) 172, 181
Instituto Juan de Mariana 169
Instituto Nacional de Estadística 169
Internal Revenue Code 26, 28, 34, 91, 177
International Chamber of Commerce 48
International Criminal Court (ICC) 45
International Crisis Group (ICG) 13, 38, 40–4, 50–2, 54, 56, 58–9, 68
International Institute for Strategic Studies (IISS) 5, 120, 123–9
INTERREG-II Program 106
Iraq 1, 53, 128–9; invasion of 16, 128; war 98, 120, 128
Iron Curtain 113
Israel 54–5
Istituto Affari Internazionali 160
IWG Bonn 105

Jacques Delors Institute 158
Janning, Josef 111
Japan International Cooperation Agency 69
Johnson, Lyndon 88
Junta para Ampliación de Estudios e Investigaciones Científicas 169

Kaberuka, Donald 74
Kahn, Herman 88
Kaiser, Karl 102
Karl Bräuer Institute of the German Taxpayers' Association 102
Karp, Marek 156
Kazimierz Pulaski Foundation 158
Keck, Margaret 38
Keynes, John Maynard 125
Kiel Institute of World Economics 101
Konrad Adenauer Foundation 5, 103, 116
Kosciuszko Institute (Institute for European Integration) 157, 159
Kostić, Roland 51
Krastev, Ivan 164
Kuylenstierna, Johan L. 189

L'Institut Europeu de la Mediterrània (IEMED) 172, 175, 182
L'Institut français des relations internationales 5
Labour Party 120
Latin American Studies Center 181

Le Monde 51
Leonard, Mark 126
Liao, Xuanli 135, 149
Liberales Institut 46
Lieberthal, Kenneth 136
Lisbon treaty 65
Lord Salisbury 120
Lu, Ning 135

Maastricht treaty 65
MacLaury, Bruce 112
Macleans 191
Madariaga – College of Europe Foundation 69
Making Integrity Work 49
Malloch-Brown, Mark 41
Mandate for Leadership 23, 95, 197
Manhattan Project 88
Manning Centre for Building Democracy 34
Manning Networking Conference 190
Manning, Preston 34
Market Economy Foundation 107
McGann, James 2–4, 8, 42, 171
Medcalf, Rory 52
Medvetz, Thomas 84, 98, 150
Mendizibal, Enrique 9
Menegazzi, Silvia 6
Microfluidic ChipShop GmbH 74
Milton, John 119
Ministry of Foreign Affairs in Poland (MFA) 155, 158, 160–2
Mission of the People's Republic of China to the European Union 70
Mitchell, George 41
Morocco 11–12, 172
Murk meter 47
Murphy, Jim 53
Murray, Charles 24

National Bureau of Economic Research 101
National Institute of Economic and Social Research (NIESR) 121
National Integrity System (NIS) 40
NATO 156, 167, 172
Natolin European Centre 157–8
Naughton, Barry 135
Nazi regime 107, 113
Nebrija, Antonio de 176
New Democratic Party 34
New Länder 106
New York Times 5, 8, 10, 11, 51, 55, 57, 87

NGOs 3, 7, 13, 25, 28, 39–40, 42–4, 46, 51, 55–7, 63, 66, 167
Nilsson, Måns 189
Nixon Center for Peace and Freedom 90; *see also* Center for the National Interest
Nobel Peace Prize 44
non-profit organizations 26, 56
North-South Institute 186–7
Norway 12, 46, 87
Norwegian government 12, 48, 50
Norwegian Ministry of Foreign Affairs 12
Nous Horitzons 170
Nuclear arms proliferation 7
Nueva Planta Decrees 168

Obama administration 90–1, 98
Observatory of Culture and Communication 181
OECD Anti-Bribery Convention 40
Öko Institute for Applied Ecology 104
Old Europe 116
Open Society Foundation 107, 156
Oppenheimer, Robert J. 88
Ordoliberal Institute 107
Oswald von Nell-Breuning Institute for Ethics in Society and Business 105
Otto Wolff von Amerongen Foundation 107

paradox of plenty 3–4
Paris Peace Conference of 1919–20 121–2
Party of Democratic Socialism 105
Peace Research Institute Frankfurt 104
Pelczynska-Nalecz, Katarzyna 162
Perot, Ross 90
Peterson Institute for International Economics 1, 10
Pew Research Center 10
Philosophic Radicals 120
Pitt, William 121
policy-making process 10, 14, 29–31, 65, 68, 83–4, 92, 94–5, 97, 162, 169, 182, 195, 197–8
Polish foreign policy 155–8, 161, 163
Polish Institute of International Affairs (PISM) 155–6, 158–61
Polish Robert Schuman Foundation 156
Political Action Committees (PACs) 30
Political and Economic Planning (PEP) 121
Political and Security Committee 65
Political Foundation for the Analysis of Societies and Political Education 105

Potsdam Institute for Climate Impact Research 106
Press Freedom Index 46
Pro Publica 53
Progress and Freedom Foundation 90
Prospect Magazine 9, 10, 191
public opinion 20, 25, 29–30, 45, 58, 73, 83, 89, 93, 97, 108, 122, 161, 163, 185, 190, 193, 196
public policy 29, 167, 169, 185, 187, 189–90, 192–8

Qatar 12, 87

Ramos, Howard 55
RAND Corporation 5, 9, 88, 94, 103, 115, 156, 187
Raskin, Marcus 89
Reagan administration 23, 197
Reagan, Ronald 23, 89, 197
Real Instituto Elcano 6, 160, 171–2, 177, 181–2
Reconquista 167
Reemtsma, Jan Philipp 112
Reform Party of Canada 34
Reiter, Janusz 160
Reporters Without Borders 46
Research Institute for Philosophy 105
Research Institute for Regional and Urban Development 103
Research Institute of the German Council on Foreign Relations 102
Research Institute of the Protestant Churches of Germany 102
Rhine-Westphalia Institute for Economic Research 101
Ricci, David 92
Rice, Condoleeza 91
Rich, Andrew 10
Robert Brookings Graduate School of Economics and Government 86
Rockefeller, John D. Sr. 86
Rockford Institute 89
Ron, James 55
Roodman, David 9–10
Rosa Luxemburg Foundation 105
Roth, Kenneth 54
Royal Institute of International Affairs (RIIA) 3, 37, 58, 120–1, 125, 128, 181; *see also* Chatham House
Royal United Services Institute (RUSI) 15, 120, 122–4, 127, 130
Rubio, Marco 1
RUSI Journal 127

Russell Sage Foundation 86
Russia's Institute of Law 47

Sage, Margaret Olivia 86
Sampson, Anthony 124
Sarajevo 41
Schleswig-Holstein Energy Foundation 107
Schleswig-Holstein Institute for Peace Research 105
Schneider, Hilmar 110
Science Council (Wissenschraftsrat) 106
Security and Defence Agenda (SDA) 73
Self, Robert 126
Shambaugh, David 134–5
Shanghai Institute of International Studies (SIIS) 16, 132, 140–51
Shaw, Geroge Bernard 121
Sikkink, Kathryn 38
Sikorski, Radoslaw 162
Silverstein, Ken 31
Simons, Greg 51
Single European Act 63
Slate 53
Slipyi, Josyf 45
Smith, James A. 92
Smithsonian National Museum of American History 20
Smocyznski, Wawrzyniec 154
Snyder, William 126
Sobieski Institute 157, 159, 162
Social media 8, 10, 30, 32, 38, 51–4, 95, 187, 193
Social Science Research Center Berlin 103
SocialFlow 54
Soros, George 41, 107, 155–6
Sousa, Luis de 39–40
Soviet Union 116, 128, 136, 155; *see also* USSR
Spanish Civil War 167
Spanish Constitution 168
Stefan Batory Foundation 156
Stiftung Wissenschaft und Politik 6
Stiftungsverband Regenbogen 105
Stockholm Environment Institute (SEI) 189
Stockholm International Peace Research Institute 5
Stone, Diane 7, 13, 37, 69–70, 119
Straw, Jack 128
Supersonic Transport (SST) 22
Survey of International Affairs 127
Survival 127, 129

Swedish Institute of International Affairs 160
Swieboda, Pawel 160
Swimelar, Safia 53
Szalamacha, Pawel 157

Talbott, Strobe 87
Teller, Edward 88
Thatcher, Margaret 124
The Bell Curve 24
The Economist 4
The Globe and Mail 191
The Observer 45, 127
The Times 123, 126
The Watch Committees 43
The World Today 127
Thunert, Martin 113–14
Towards a European Global Strategy: Securing European Influence in a Changing World 160
Toynbee, Arnold 127
Track-II Diplomacy 141, 143
Transatlantic Trade and Investment Partnership (TTIP) 73
Transnational advocacy network 38, 55
Transparency International 4–5, 13, 38–41; Corruption Perceptions Index (CPI) 5, 40, 46, 48
Treaty of Lisbon 14
Troy, Tevi 92
Twitter 9–10, 44, 52–4, 95–6, 194, 196

UAH Instituto-Franklin 172
UFZ Centre for Environmental Research 106
UK Department for International Development 46
UN Convention against Corruption 40
UN Global Compact 48
UN Security Council 50
UNI Enterprise Institute of the Association of Independent Entrepreneurs 105
Unió per la Mediterrània (Union for the Meditterannean) 175
United Arab Emirates 12
United We Stand 90
Universal Declaration of Human Rights 43
UNU Centre for Policy Research 119
Upworthy 53
Urban Institute 88
US Congress 197
US Congressional Research Service 136
US Department of State 52
US Foreign Policy 1, 2, 12, 13, 89

US Helsinki Watch Committee (HW) 43
US News & World Report 191
USSR 43, 156; *see also* Soviet Union

Veldhuis, Niels 188, 190

Wallace, William 125
Walter Raymond Foundation 102
Washington, DC 1–2, 6, 11–16, 20–1, 24, 31–2, 41, 83–4, 88–92, 95, 98, 175
Weapons of Mass Destruction (WMD) 129
Weaver, Kent 23
Webb, Beatrice 121
Webb, Sidney 121
Weyrich, Paul 21
What Are Think Tanks Good For? 119
Whitehall Papers 127
Williams, Brooke 31, 85, 87, 93
Wissenschaftlichkeit 111

Wissenschaftsgemeinschaft Gottfried Wilhelm Leibniz (WGL) 105–7, 110–11
Wolfensohn, James 40
Woodrow Wilson Center for International Scholars 1, 10
World Bank 39–41, 47–9, 51, 69
World War I 1, 85, 101, 121–3
World War II 37, 43, 87–8, 101–2, 107, 113–14, 155, 166
Wuppertal Institute for Climate, Environment and Energy 105

Yeoh, Dr. Michael 189
Yugoslavia 41
Zhao, Quansheng 135

Zhu, Xufeng 134–5
Zunker, Albrecht 115–16

Taylor & Francis eBooks

Helping you to choose the right eBooks for your Library

Add Routledge titles to your library's digital collection today. Taylor and Francis ebooks contains over 50,000 titles in the Humanities, Social Sciences, Behavioural Sciences, Built Environment and Law.

Choose from a range of subject packages or create your own!

Benefits for you
- Free MARC records
- COUNTER-compliant usage statistics
- Flexible purchase and pricing options
- All titles DRM-free.

Benefits for your user
- Off-site, anytime access via Athens or referring URL
- Print or copy pages or chapters
- Full content search
- Bookmark, highlight and annotate text
- Access to thousands of pages of quality research at the click of a button.

REQUEST YOUR FREE INSTITUTIONAL TRIAL TODAY

Free Trials Available
We offer free trials to qualifying academic, corporate and government customers.

eCollections – Choose from over 30 subject eCollections, including:

Archaeology	Language Learning
Architecture	Law
Asian Studies	Literature
Business & Management	Media & Communication
Classical Studies	Middle East Studies
Construction	Music
Creative & Media Arts	Philosophy
Criminology & Criminal Justice	Planning
Economics	Politics
Education	Psychology & Mental Health
Energy	Religion
Engineering	Security
English Language & Linguistics	Social Work
Environment & Sustainability	Sociology
Geography	Sport
Health Studies	Theatre & Performance
History	Tourism, Hospitality & Events

For more information, pricing enquiries or to order a free trial, please contact your local sales team:
www.tandfebooks.com/page/sales

 The home of Routledge books

www.tandfebooks.com